Curriculum and Teaching Dialogue

Volume 20, Numbers 1 and 2

Curriculum and Teaching Dialogue

Edited by

Chara Haeussler Bohan
Georgia State University

Associate Editor

Michelle Tenam-Zemach
Nova Southeastern University

Graduate Research Assistant

Cristy Sellers Smith
Georgia State University

INFORMATION AGE PUBLISHING, INC.
Charlotte, NC • www.infoagepub.com

Library of Congress Cataloging-in-Publication Data

CIP record for this book is available from the Library of Congress
http://www.loc.gov

ISBNs: 978-1-64113-381-4 (Paperback)

  978-1-64113-382-1 (Hardcover)

  978-1-64113-383-8 (ebook)

Copyright © 2018 Information Age Publishing Inc.

All rights reserved. No part of this publication may be reproduced, stored in a retrieval system, or transmitted, in any form or by any means, electronic, mechanical, photocopying, microfilming, recording or otherwise, without written permission from the publisher.

Printed in the United States of America

American Association for Teaching and Curriculum Leadership for 2017–2018

President
John Pecore, University of West Florida

Past President
Kevin Cloninger, Anthropedia Foundation

President Elect
Joseph Flynn, Northern Illinois University

Executive Council

Meg Jacobs	**Megan Kennedy**
Cornell College	*Westfield State University*
David Flinders	**Bradley Conrad**
Indiana University	*Capital University*
Paul Parkinson	**Dan Conn**
University of North Florida	*Minot State University*
Dana Haraway	**Trudi Gains**
James Madison University	*University of West Florida*
	Matthew Spurlin
	Denver University

Executive Secretary
Todd Hodgkinson, Drake University

2018 Program Chair
Aubrey Southall, Aurora University

Web Liason
John Pecore, University of West Florida

Editorial Review Board

Donna Adair Breault, PhD
Ashland University

David Callejo Pérez, PhD
Saginaw Valley State University

Robert Donmoyer, PhD
University of San Diego

David J. Flinders, PhD
Indiana University, Bloomington

Lyn C. Forester, EdD
Doane University

Sandra Guzman Foster, PhD
University of the Incarnate World

Alan W. Garrett, PhD
Eastern New Mexico University

Kate Kauper, PhD
Cornell College

Amy L. Masko, PhD
Grand Valley State University

Pardess Mitchell, EdD
William Rainey Harper College

Christy McConnell Moroye, PhD
University of Northern Colorado

Wesley Null, PhD
Baylor University

Bruce Uhrmacher, PhD
University of Denver

Dr. Bill White, EdD
James Madison University

Christine Woyshner, EdD
Temple University

CONTENTS

Acknowledgments xi

Presidential Address: Educating in a Time of Crisis: Why
  Well-Being Is Essential
  Kevin Cloninger xiii

AATC Keynote Address: Nature-Based Learning for Student
  Achievement and Ecological Citizenship
  Louise Chawla xxv

President's Message: Informing Education Within the Realities of
  the Diverse Perspectives of Schools
  John L. Pecore xli

VOLUME 20, NUMBER 1

Editor's Notes—Democracy, Education, Teaching, and
  Teacher Strikes
  Chara Haeussler Bohan xlvii

1. Learning and Teaching in a Visual World: Elementary
   Teacher Candidates Use of Visual Materials
   Kristy A. Brugar 1

2. Understanding the Research Engagement of Teachers in
   Three Urban High Schools
   Dante P. Petretti 15

3. Engaging Elementary Students Through Movement Integration in Mathematics and Reading: An Exploratory Study to Understand Teachers' Perceptions
   Stacia C. Miller and Suzanne F. Lindt 31

4. Practicing Social Justice Education Through Solidarity and Connection
   Kelli Woodrow 45

5. Audio Feedback on Student Writing: Could Voice Recording Foster the Tenets of Care Theory?
   Gregory Chalfin 61

6. A Morality of Inclusion: A Theoretical Argument for Culturally Consonant Character Education
   Chrystal S. Johnson and Harvey Hinton III 73

7. Assessment as Dialogue: Reframing Assessment
   Paul Parkison 89

VOLUME 20, NUMBER 2

Editor's Notes—The Claims of Children's Voices
   Michelle Tenam-Zemach 3

1. Do Teacher Credentials Matter? An Examination of Teacher Quality
   Daphney Leann Curry, Emily Reeves, Christina Janise McIntyre, and Matthew Capps 9

2. Teaching Mathematics Masterfully: Instructional Self-Regulation in Two PAEMST Finalists
   Melissa Peterson Schneider 19

3. "Keep It Real & Love 'Em Up": Student-Teacher Relationships in an Urban Middle School
   Amy L. Masko 35

4. A Study of Students' Social Identities and a "Historical Empathy Gap" in Middle and Secondary Social Studies Classes With the Instructional Unit "The Elizabeth Jennings Project"
   Katherine Perrotta 53

5. Advertising "Generosity" in Schools: Do You Want Fries With Your Curriculum?
   Joseph Zajdel and Daniel R. Conn 71

6. AAA+ Professional Development for Teacher Educators Who Prepare Culturally and Linguistically Responsive Teachers
   Carla Lynn Tanguay, Ruchi Bhatnagar, Kim Stevens Barker, and Joyce E. Many 87

7. Helping Early-Career Teachers to See the Aesthetic Dimension of Mathematics Within Standards-Based Curricula
   Aaron Samuel Zimmerman 105

OUTTAKES

Recruiting Queers: The Complexities of Finding Participants in an Often Invisible Population
  Lesley N. Siegel 125

Reaching New Possibilities on Lesson Study Collaboration
  Dittika Gupta, Mollie Appelgate, Lara Dick, Melissa Soto, and Shawn Broderick 129

A Culturally Candid Response: Tale of Two Professors' Reflections
  Melanie Fields and Laura Isbell 133

IRB Is Not Required: A Reflection on Oral History, Disability, and Playing by the Rules When the Rules Get in the Way
  Cristy Sellers Smith 137

Computational Problem-Posing With Urban Latinx Youth: Make Science Teaching Great Again
  Rouhollah Aghasaleh, Patrick Enderle, Anton Puvirajah, Andrew Boehnlein, Jennifer Rickard, Jacob Bornstein, and Renesha Hendrix 143

Fitting It All In: Time Challenges in Lesson Pacing
  Melissa Soto, Shawn Broderick, Lara Dick, Mollie Appelgate, and Dittika Gupta 149

BOOK REVIEWS

Teaching in a Globally-Connected World : Preparing Learners for the Future, edited by Ervin F. Sparapani and Pamela L. Ross McClain
Kim Stevens Barker 153

A. B.A.L.A.N.C.E: An Interactive Workbook for the "Kid" in All of Us by Reggie Gwinn
Katherine Perrotta 157

Across the Domains: Examining the Best Practices in Mentoring Public School Educators Throughout the Professional Journey by Andrea M. Kent and Andre M. Green
Aubrey Brammar Southall 161

White Fatigue by Joseph Flynn
Shelley Harris 165

Reel Education: Documentaries, Biopics, and Reality Television by Jaqueline Bach
Bradley Conrad 167

Critical Democratic Education and LGBTQ-Inclusive Curriculum: Opportunities and Constraints by Steven Camicia
Lauren Yarnell Bradshaw 171

About the Authors 175

ACKNOWLEDGMENTS

The editors want to extend a very special thanks to the following individuals for their service to *Curriculum and Teaching Dialogue:*

Rouhollah Aghasaleh, Adam Akerson, Susan Barnes, Blake R. Bickham, Donna Breault, Steven Camicia, Mary Beth Cancienne, Christina Cavallaro, Anita Charles, Liz Chase, Matthew Clay, Mary Clisbee, Daniel Conn, Bradley Conrad, Amy Corp, Caroline M. Crawford, Sabin Densmore, Robert Donmoyer, Ozlem Erden, Joseph Feinberg, Jim Ferrell, Joseph Flynn, Lyn Forester, Sandra Guzman Foster, Michelle Garcia-Olp, Alan Garrett, Rubén Garza, Mark Geary, Donna Goodwin, Derek Gottlieb, Aaron Griffen, Dittika Gupta, Dana Haraway, Chelsie A. Hess, Patty J. Horn, Crystal Howell, Carole Hruskocy, Benjamin Ingman, Reggie Gwinn Jr., Jeffrey Kaplan, Kate Kauper, Meridith Koester, Stephanie C. Konle, Tanji P. Reed Marshall, Amy Masko, Christine McConnell, Tara Meister, Iris Minor, Pardess Mitchell, Peggy Moch, Corey Nagle, Wesley Null, Paul Parkison, John Pecore, Lisa Perhamus, Katherine Perrotta, Naomi Petersen, Dante Petretti, Kristi A. Preisman, Jennifer Reeves, Herminia Janet Rivera, Amanda Rudolph, Melissa Peterson Schneider, Katie Sciurba, Kate Shively, Cristy Sellers Smith, Ervin Frederick Sparapani, Agnes Stryker, LaBotta Taylor, Bruce Uhrmacher, Sonja Varbelow, Elena Venegas, Vanessa Villate, Vaughn Watson, William White, Kathy Wigtil, Julie Williams, Jodie Wilson, Christine Woyshner, Jie Zhang.

The editors would like to share their recognitions and deep appreciation to the committee members of the Francis P. Hunkins Distinguished Article Award: Daniel Conn, Kate Kuper, Christy McConnell, and Matthew

Spurlin. Their commitment to *Curriculum Teaching and Dialogue* and AATC provides an example of why we should to continue our "Good" work in the fields of teaching and curriculum.

PRESIDENTIAL ADDRESS

EDUCATING IN A TIME OF CRISIS

Why Well-Being Is Essential

Kevin Cloninger

This year, I've invited the organization to consider a specific theme for our conference, namely ecology, sustainability, creativity, and well-being. I want us to reflect for a few days on what it means to live in harmony with a planet in crisis and explore the interrelationship between social and ecological justice, and personal, social, and ecological well-being. It's a timely theme given recent events. Before I start, let me briefly introduce myself. Unlike past presidents, I don't work in academia. In my role as executive director of the Anthropedia Foundation, I teach health care professionals, teachers, and others how to work on their health and well-being. We partner with districts, schools, clinics, and community organizations to help stem the rising tide of diseases linked to lifestyle and stress. This career path has afforded me certain perspectives on curriculum, and as such, I'd like to focus on the topic of educating in a time of crisis.

THE CRISES OF THE 21st CENTURY

The word *crisis*, interestingly, comes from the Greek word for "decision." Crises force us to make decisions because the only way to overcome them is to change our behavior; we cannot solve crises with typical approaches. A civilization that's faced with a crisis it cannot resolve generally experiences a period of obscurantism, a dark age characterized by an absence of fundamental aspects of human culture like science, art, the rule of law, and so on.

We can see crises developing in the United States of America. I've just come from St. Louis, where the Stockley verdict sent shockwaves through the community, reminding us all about the problems of racism and inequality that affect not just St. Louis but the country as a whole. Police officers equipped with military gear marched through my neighborhood firing rubber bullets and tear gas at friends and colleagues. Meanwhile, international tensions continue to rise, including renewed threats of a nuclear crisis with North Korea. The country and its neighbors have also been devastated by a series of massive hurricanes—products of our changing climate. At the same time, but with less attention paid by the media, India, Nepal, and Bangladesh have suffered devastating floods, affecting more than 16 million people and killing thousands. Did I mention the wildfires in the West and the two earthquakes in Mexico? If that were not enough, the worst mass shooting in the history of our country took place this week, one day after the International Day for Non-Violence, Gandhi's birthday. While it was the worst of its kind, it was by no means singular. The *New York Times* reported that there have been 521 mass shootings in the last 477 days. These are truly challenging times. Some have called the last couple months a "dress rehearsal for the apocalypse." Of course, these trends have been evident for quite some time, but they're becoming harder to ignore.

All that's to say that we're experiencing not one but at least five major crises:

1. **A social and humanitarian crisis:** War and hardship are rampant throughout the world with 65 million people forcibly displaced in 2015 alone. Seventy percent of women have experienced gender-based violence in some crisis settings. African Americans comprise only 13% of the U.S. population and 14% of the monthly drug users but are 37% of the people arrested for drug-related offenses in America (ActionAid, 2016; Alexander & Chilton, 2012).
2. **An ecological crisis:** Climate change is causing species extinction and rising oceans, while industrial agricultural practices threaten both humans and pollinators. An estimated 89 million people were affected by natural disasters in 2015 (Developmental Initiatives, 2016).

3. **A resource crisis:** We're exhausting the planet's nonrenewable natural resources and energy supply: oil, rare earth minerals, and fresh water. For example, according to the U.S. Geological Survey, we're likely to run out of zinc, silver, and gold in the 2030s (Desjardins, 2014).
4. **A financial and economic crisis:** We've never had greater levels of economic inequality than we do right now, and our current financial models almost led to the collapse of the entire system back in 2008. Despite the current stability in the stock market, other bubbles appear poised to burst.
5. **Finally, a health crisis:** Mental illness is on the rise, and rates of anxiety and depression are skyrocketing around the world (Vigo, Thornicroft, & Atun, 2016). Inability to manage stress is linked with the five leading causes of death: heart disease, stroke, respiratory illness, diabetes, and cancer.

Now more than ever we need to equip our children with the tools and knowledge they need to face these crises. Forget calls for "one iPad per child"—the technology children truly need has nothing to do with computers. They have to learn how to deal with stress, how to be self-sufficient, how to think like a scientist, how to preserve knowledge, and how to do many other things that children probably didn't need as much 50 years ago. While Silicon Valley sells its technology to consumers, those running the companies are building high-end bunker communities, hiring private militias, performing dental and eye surgeries, and working on how to grow their own food, all in preparation for the worst that climate change has to offer us. They have far less reason to be concerned than we do because they have the resources and time to get ready. Many of the 21st-century education ideas ring so hollow because they revolve around technology that could be erased in an instant.

As curriculum theorists and teacher educators, we need to develop new models of education, curriculum, and teaching that are able to face these threats and prepare our children for an unfamiliar future. Most of our current educational theory dates to the beginning of the Industrial Age. Models put forth by progressive thinkers in the last century attempted to adapt education to modern needs, and though we've struggled to implement these theories in current educational practices, they are already outdated to some extent because of the pace of change in modern society. Their fundamental quest to adapt our educational practices to the modern era was the right impulse, but they could never have anticipated the rapid advances in globalization, science and technology, and every other field. Ironically, we need to look back further in time to find civilizations that were facing as many crises as ours is today.

PARALLEL CRISES IN HISTORY: ANCIENT GREECE AND PLATO

Surprisingly, one of the best parallels to our times is Ancient Greece. The Cycladic, Minoan, and Greek civilizations were founded in one of most unstable volcanic arcs in the world. This area was especially active in ancient times, likely eradicated the Minoan civilization, and is one of the main candidates for the location of the mythic Atlantis. Athens during its Golden Age was the seat of knowledge inherited from the Egyptians, Babylonians, Minoans, and other ancient cultures. As the birthplace of democracy and our modern educational approaches, it had many of the same strengths and weaknesses of our current civilization.

Plato was born into an aristocratic family toward the end of the Greek Golden Age. There was great political instability after Pericles's death, and a healthy dose of demagoguery, corruption, and immorality, which led to the trial and condemnation of Plato's teacher, Socrates. In the aftermath of this infamous event, a 28-year-old Plato devoted his life to helping Athens emerge from its social and political crisis. In Plato's two dialogues, the *Republic* and *Laws*, we find a mature Plato describing the mechanisms that led society to ruin and making proposals for how to ensure a truly just society. We must remember that he is a philosopher of crisis, responding to the decline of his civilization and attempting to help future generations avoid the same traps.

In the *Republic*, Plato defines the dynamic of crises (Ohmann, 2013). He explains that societies lose their equilibrium as soon as the foundation of the society is no longer oriented around justice for all its citizens. He identifies several causes of imbalance, but the one that seems fatal to him is the quest for wealth. At one point, he says, men and women, through moral fragility, can choose money as the central value of the society. It is then the rich who rule society and money that gives power. Money becomes the hierarchical principle and the driving force of society. It is no longer the best, the fairest, and the most disinterested but the most fortunate who rule, and the aim of society becomes collective and individual wealth. Plato came up with a name for this social organization: oligarchy. It is this unrestrained search for wealth that inevitably leads to growing inequality in the distribution of wealth, which leads to conflicts at the heart of society. This leads to a desire for equality among the people and the search for a true democracy. Democracy, in Plato's estimation, has the unfortunate tendency to devolve into oligarchy every time wealth is worshiped as an end in itself.

Plato likens this shift from democracy to oligarchy to the Lotus-eaters from Homer's *Odyssey*. The lotus leads everyone to experience absolute pleasure, but it also makes them forget everything that's going on around them. In this perspective, people are led by the desire to do only what pleases them. Nothing ultimately matters except individual desire: Everyone has the right to do anything. Plato explains that this leads to an egocentric society, insensitive to the presence of others and unaware of reality.

Everything in this kind of society is commodified: relationships, work, war, human life; everything has a price. Due to this excessive commodification and so-called limitless "freedom," any restriction is considered an affront to liberty. Citizens are motivated by the desire to increase and perpetuate their individual freedom and wealth. Plato explains that such a society will lose the meaning of measure and foster excessive discrepancies between rich and poor, powerful and powerless. As an antidote, he prescribes a law of wealth differentials. Plato argues that anytime someone's wealth is greater than five times that of the less fortunate, he should restore that wealth to the community.

"What is the common good in such a society?" Plato asks. This notion of unlimited desire to acquire, instead of limiting ourselves to what we need, leads to an unnecessary accumulation of wealth. Society loses balance, and ultimately our natural resources can be overexploited and insufficient to maintain the community as a whole. Moreover, people are focused on satisfying their own desires, which leads to competition and ultimately to separation in the social body. There is a loss of the common good, of laws, the principles of cohesion and solidarity not only between men and women but also between humans and their world. Plato called this the broken "cosmic friendship." It ultimately devolves into the pseudo-unity of mob rule.

Sound familiar? These dynamics described by Plato sound strikingly modern. But that should come as no surprise, as we tend to repeat the same mistakes throughout history. Plato studied the famed Laws of Gortyn in Crete when he wrote his dialogue. He came to find out that their great Minoan civilization had been decimated due to natural disaster (in their case a volcanic eruption), as well as from war with the Mycenaeans. Some theories suggest that they may have run out of food and resources after the eruption and the tsunamis that followed, and when the Mycenaeans arrived, those who survived were starving and helpless.

HOW DO WE SOLVE THE CRISES?

Plato argues that it is useless to try to use laws to solve the crisis because they cannot change the souls of people (Ohmann, 2013). According to Plato, people must reevaluate the very foundations of society and have the courage to break with conformity and innovate. How can we as human beings adhere to a higher universal good that centers on justice and peace?

Solving the crises is, above all, human and moral. Individuals make up the society. If individuals change, so too does society, but society must also be organized based on a set of principles and values that ensure justice. Individual liberty leads to excesses that, if not articulated with a good that surpasses the individual and her interests, leads to injustice. In other words, when people become slaves to their desires, they can no longer act on what is most just, and so we must value temperance and moderation above the accumulation of wealth. The hierarchy of the city, Plato concludes, should be focused on caring for the soul, the mind, and the body, and only afterward on wealth.

He contends that the most important thing is the unity of the Republic. Money is not an end in and of itself (and there is no correspondence between one's wealth and moral value). For Plato, the individual's end is finding his or her role within the "vast arrangement" of the great cosmos. It is solidarity and friendship between fellow citizens and with nature and the world as a whole. Only then will we be able to order and regulate our place in society, work to ensure justice, and preserve the freedom, basic needs, and dignity of all people. Becoming aware of the underlying unity of all people is key to the development of the well-being of our society. In other words, the greatest good of the city should not be wealth but rather the happiness and well-being of its citizens. Those in power should be wise and good leaders who have moved beyond the desire to possess and dominate.

APPLYING THE LESSONS OF HISTORY

Plato's dialogues help us to understand these interrelationships between ecology, sustainability, creativity, and well-being. There are many lessons here that we can apply to our own educational endeavors. Plato's approach to the Greek crisis is worth considering as we seek to define our own version of an education in times of crisis.

Many of the problems described by Plato can be seen in today's schools. According to research conducted by the CDC, Kaiser Permanente, and the Center for Mental Health in Schools at UCLA, when we look at schools, 12 to 22% of students have a diagnosable mental disorder and more than 40% of students are in "bad educational shape" and are therefore unlikely to fulfill their promise. That is, their development has been stifled. One in three suffer from physical and emotional trauma, and many of them are self-medicating with drugs and alcohol. This leads, in turn, to a chronic problem of violence, bullying, and poor self-esteem. These problems are only compounded by the poverty that many children experience. All are consequences of a Platonic oligarchy.

Teachers as well struggle with their mental health. Rates of burnout are at an all-time high. Stress leaves them vulnerable to depression and anxiety, with 40 to 50% of new teachers leaving within the first 5 years. In two large school districts in the St. Louis area, 30 to 50% of teachers are taking antidepressants and anxiety medication. Similar rates can be seen across the country and throughout the world.

When we consider how to tackle these problems in schools and in society, these crises all have something in common: an inability to change our behavior and our ways of life. We're having trouble adapting (in an evolutionary sense) to the rapidity of change and the crises of the 21st century. Like Cro-Magnons who've turned up in a supermarket, we're unable to adjust to our surroundings. Our stress reactions functioned well when we were hunter-gatherers wandering around the savannah, but now we're having the same reactions when our boss chews us out or if we get in a fight with our partner. And it's making us sick. Now more than ever we need to reinforce ourselves and consider how to be well and creative. The very survival of our species is at stake. Well-being is not a luxury in the 21st century. In the face of a rapidly changing environment, we must reinforce ourselves and consequently our society. It is a fundamental human need that is being suppressed by a society that focuses on participation in the global economy over all else. A good job does not guarantee a good life.

The overemphasis on education as preparation to participate in the economy is not only making us miserable, but it's also shifting focus away from more vital preparation. We must think outside of the box, or in this case the cubicle. Recently I was delighted to hear that 22 schools in the state of Missouri put forward the idea of giving up state and federal funding so they could focus on the well-being of their students. These schools understand that we need to provide our students with the most valuable knowledge while teaching them how to manage the astonishing amount of information they receive each day. We need to help children develop, as Montaigne wrote, "a well-formed mind, instead of a well-filled one" (Montaigne, 2003), a mind that's focused on facing the challenges of our time. Peter Cookson Jr. (2009), writing about the parallels between us and the ancient Greeks, had this to say:

> My greatest fear about 21st century education is that Socrates' humility will be turned on its head. The noted philosopher once said, "I know nothing except the fact of my ignorance." My fear is that instead of knowing nothing except the fact of our own ignorance, we will know everything except the fact of our own ignorance...the great knowledge and communication tsunami of the 21st century may drown us in a sea of trivia instead of lifting us up on a rising tide of possibility and promise. (p. 8)

Solutions to problems like these require a multidisciplinary and multidimensional approach. Understanding the nature of climate change, biodiversity, and income inequality involves analyses at multiple levels: economic, political, social, cultural, scientific, and spiritual. These multiple levels of analysis also interact with each other. Economic shifts lead to shifts in culture and society and vice versa. We must adopt an approach that can deal with complex adaptive systems like these. Human beings are themselves complex adaptive systems that are interconnected with others. We're a reflection of the universe, and the universe is reflected within us.

CONCLUSIONS:
WHY WELL-BEING MATTERS NOW MORE THAN EVER

That's why it's difficult to understand how to approach well-being without understanding the being (Cloninger, 2004; Cloninger & Cloninger, 2011; Cloninger, Zohar, & Cloninger, 2010; Huppert, Baylis, & Keverne, 2007; Spinoza, 1948; Sussman & Cloninger, 2011). To properly foster well-being, to give people tools to cultivate well-being, we must address all aspects of the being: physical, mental, and spiritual. Understanding what we are and how we function enables us to live well, to reach well-being. These three aspects interact with each other and with their community, society, culture, planet, and universe. To educate a being, then, requires addressing the whole person and providing students with tools to exercise all three aspects. This then ensures that all students see how all this learning relates to their capacity to live better and to confront the crises of our times. It relates directly to their everyday experience. We cannot respond to a student asking about the relevance of a subject with "You don't want to work at McDonalds, do you?" It's essential that they see the intimate relationship between what they're learning and what and how they're living. For example, the study of physical health, coordination, dance, bodily awareness, nutrition, and hygiene may help students understand the proper functioning of the body. Similarly, study of all forms, literacy, subject-matter study, disciplinary knowledge, art and culture, and metacognition (thinking about thinking) can help students understand the proper functioning of their thoughts. What's more frequently overlooked are the spiritual components of well-being, especially in schools. We can help individuals increase their spiritual sensitivity by contemplating the significance of life, art and artistic creation, mythology, the nature of the self, intuition, and the moral dimensions of reality. It's not about presenting a religious doctrine but rather asking students to thoughtfully consider the aspects of reality that transcend the self.

We can take some analogies from medicine and mental health. Technology and drug development are viewed as the best ways to cure mental illness. Most people suffering from depression turn to antidepressants and other drugs to try to become happy. However, taking medication will do little to affect real change in an individual unless the individual takes steps to change the attitudes and behaviors that led them to depression in the first place (Cloninger, 2004; Cloninger & Cloninger, 2011; Cloninger, Svrakic, & Przybeck, 1993). Moreover, existential voids where people lack a sense of hope or self-transcendence may be unable to make progress in cognitive change, rendering medication useless. Similarly, educational approaches that focus exclusively on material advancement, like strict biomedical approaches, may be necessary but are not sufficient to promote long-lasting satisfaction and harmony in students. We need a different kind of education that deals with the whole person and their interconnections with their society and environment.

Compared with individual schools, or nonprofits like the one I run, universities and school districts are large, often cumbersome, bureaucracies. Like all large systems, people are often skeptical that changes can be made. Without a doubt, change takes time, but even if only a small number of the predictions related to climate change, clean water, and biodiversity are correct, we don't have any time to lose. We must actively reorient our strategy to help future generations develop the well-being and adaptability necessary to see their way through the storms to come. Whenever you despair and think that change isn't possible, remember the words of French ecologist Yann Arthus-Bertrand (Fourney, 2016): "It's too late to be pessimistic."

We've turned education into a commodity and assigned it a monetary value. It is being sold as a product to a consumer, eroding its higher purpose and demeaning the whole endeavor. But human well-being is priceless. The quest for greater knowledge, greater self-understanding, and greater justice are fundamental human needs. The hope for a good job can never replace our search for the good life, which is one of our fundamental aspirations. Perhaps this is why so many students feel that schools don't care about them (Noddings, 1993). It's the pure, mathematical precision of the commodification of education that makes it so monstrous. As Lamartine (1834) observed, "Numbers are the marvelous and passive instruments of tyranny." How, then, can we defy the aggressive forces of obscurantism in our culture, obscurantism that prevents people from realizing their full potential? This is not merely an academic question; it requires an active shift in lifestyle and awareness. To grow in well-being, we have no choice but to act. As Gandhi and Martin Luther King Jr. encouraged us, we must be the change we wish to see in the world. We must change our own lives before we can show future generations how to do the same. If we have any chance of helping our students, we must do much more than be practically minded and help them secure a job; we must inspire them to walk the path toward greater well-being in order to face the crises of our century. The real question is, do universities, schools, teachers, and students have the will, flexibility, and awareness needed to implement these changes? I hope so, but whatever the case, it is certainly too late to be pessimistic.

NOTES

1. As we know much of what is most important has already been said, I began searching for theories throughout history that could help us understand how to confront these crises. Looking back in our immediate past, we can see that the sixties' generation saw a need for a fundamental realignment of our values and priorities, but this movement that inevitably devolved into the hippie movement unfortunately offered few concrete propositions for how to achieve such goals, and the forces of obscurantism found ways of undermining and extinguishing the flame of change that illuminated that period. Moving back through history, there was the enlightenment and renaissance in Europe that offered some perspectives, but their times were not periods of crisis. On the contrary, it was the peace and prosperity of those ages that allowed for the rapid expansion in human knowledge.
2. Studies have verified the obvious conclusion that depressed teachers have a strong negative impact on the classroom learning environment (McLean and Connor, 2015). The effect on the classroom learning environment was proportional to the strength of the depression in the teacher. The effect on student learning was more pronounced in students who struggled in the subject matter being taught.

REFERENCES

ActionAid. (2016). *On the frontline: Catalyzing women's leadership in humanitarian action*. Retrieved from http://www.actionaid.org/sites/files/actionaid/on_the_frontline_catalysing_womens_leadership_in_humanitarian_action.pdf

Alexander, M., & Chilton, K. (2012). *The new Jim Crow: Mass incarceration in the age of colorblindness*. New York, NY: New Press.

Cloninger, C. R. (2004). *Feeling good: The science of well-being*. New York, NY: Oxford University Press.

Cloninger, C. R., & Cloninger, K. M. (2011). Person-centered therapeutics. *International Journal of Person Centered Medicine*, *1*(1), 43–52. doi:10.5750/ijpcm.v1i1.21

Cloninger, C. R., Svrakic, D. M., & Przybeck, T. R. (1993). A psychobiological model of temperament and character. *Archives of General Psychiatry*, *50*(12), 975–990.

Cloninger, C. R., Zohar, A. H., & Cloninger, K. M. (2010). Promotion of well-being in person-centered mental health care. *FOCUS*, *8*(2), 165–179. doi:10.1176/foc.8.2.foc165

Cookson Jr., P. (2009). What would Socrates say? *Educational Leadership*, *67*(1), 8–14.

Desjardins, J. (2014, September 04). A forecast of when we'll run out of each metal. Retrieved October 1, 2017, from http://www.visualcapitalist.com/forecast-when-well-run-out-of-each-metal/

Development Initiatives. (2016). *Global humanitarian assistance report 2016*. Retrieved from http://www.globalhumanitarianassistance.org/wp-content/uploads/2016/07/GHA-report-2016-full-report.pdf

Fourney, A. (2016, March 18). Yann Arthus-Bertrand au Luxembourg: Il est trop tard pour être pessimiste! Retrieved October 4, 2017, from https://www.wort.lu/fr/lifestyle/yann-arthus-bertrand-au-luxembourg-il-est-trop-tard-pour-etre-pessimiste-56eade761bea9dff8fa74a10

Huppert, F. A., Baylis, N., & Keverne, B. (2007). *The science of well-being*. Oxford, UK: Oxford University Press.

McLean, L., & Connor, C. M. (2015). Depressive symptoms in third-grade teachers: Relations to classroom quality and student achievement. *Child Development*, *86*(3), 945–954. doi:10.1111/cdev.12344

Lamartine, A. D. (1834). *Des destinées de la poésie*. Paris: Gosselin.

Montaigne, M. (2003). *The complete essays of Michel de Montaigne* (pp. 163–200). New York, NY: Penguin.

Noddings, N. (1993). *The challenge to care in schools: An alternative approach to education*. New York, NY: Teachers College Press.

Ohmann, I. (2013, December 1). Platon et la crise mondiale. *Revue Acropolis*. Retrieved from http://www.revue-acropolis.fr

Spinoza, B. (1948). *The Ethics*. New York, NY: E. P. Dutton.

Sussman, R. W., & Cloninger, C. R. (2011). *Origins of altruism and cooperation*. New York, NY: Springer Science+Business Media.

Vigo, D., Thornicroft, G., & Atun, R. (2016). Estimating the true global burden of mental illness. *Lancet Psychiatry*, *3*(2), 171–178. doi:10.1016/s2215-0366(15)00505-2

AATC KEYNOTE ADDRESS

NATURE-BASED LEARNING FOR STUDENT ACHIEVEMENT AND ECOLOGICAL CITIZENSHIP

Louise Chawla
University of Colorado Boulder

A CHANGING CLIMATE FOR EDUCATION

Teachers today work in a changing climate. In one sense, this is literally true. According to *Climate Change 2014: Synthesis Report Summary for Policymakers* by the Intergovernmental Panel on Climate Change (IPCC), "The atmosphere and ocean have warmed, the amounts of sea and ice have diminished, and sea level has risen" (IPPC, 2014, SPM 1.1). The report states: "Changes in many extreme weather and climate events have been observed since 1950" (SPM 1.4). It also notes that this is a social justice issue: "Risks are unevenly distributed, and are generally greater for disadvantaged people and communities in countries at all levels of development" (SPM 2.3). It concludes: "without additional mitigation efforts beyond those in place today, and even with adaptation, warming by the end of the 21st century will lead to high to very high risk of severe, wide-spread and irreversible impacts globally (high confidence)" (SPM 3.2).

The IPCC has high confidence that the changes underway can be attributed to human activities: "Human influence on our climate system is clear" (SPM 1). Because humans are responsible, it means that we also have the possibility of reversing course from actions that are destructive to our climate and biosphere to actions that can begin to heal the harm done and establish better relationships of harmony with the natural world. If we do so, we may find ourselves simultaneously addressing other positive goals and achieving co-benefits. In the words of the IPCC: "Effective adaptation and mitigation ... depend on policies and cooperation at all scales and can be enhanced through integrated responses that link adaptation and mitigation to other societal objectives" (SPM 4).

These conditions raise a grave question for education. How are educational policies and practices responding to global environmental change? Teaching about the environment has been the domain of environmental education, a special subject of study. The core subjects remain reading; writing; math; the sciences of biology, chemistry and physics; and social studies. In most schools teachers are not required to introduce students to the physics of a warming atmosphere, the chemistry of ocean acidification, the changing geography of states and nations as sea levels rise, or the passage of environmental legislation in response to citizen activism. These silos between subjects may have been excused when evidence of global warming and predictions about its effects were the specialized knowledge of a few scientists. Now that this knowledge is public and climate change is already reshaping our world, it demands attention.

Yes, in the United States climate change is a politically charged topic. In some communities, teachers can risk losing their jobs if they integrate education about climate change into their curriculum. But given a federal administration that denies the science of climate change, many cities and states have taken leadership to create green economies that rely on renewable energy, energy efficiency, and green infrastructure, and to protect and restore habitats for biodiversity as a strategy to build resilience. In some regions of the country, there is activism around climate justice. All of these initiatives provide opportunities for teaching about climate change in ways that inspire action rather than despair. For portals into teaching resources, see the websites of NASA (n.d.) and the Climate Literacy and Energy Awareness Network (n.d.).

This talk presents the emerging field of nature-based learning, given evidence that teaching in nature can advance many educational objectives as well as promote green school surroundings, which mitigates climate change. Educational benefits include greater student well-being, reduced inattention and impulsivity, more time on task during lessons, and higher academic achievement. There is also evidence that students from low-income and ethnic families may particularly benefit from access to nature at their schools, so that nature-based learning can help close the achievement gap between students from more and less economically advantaged backgrounds. The conclusion of this talk focuses on one aspect of nature-based learning: the development of informed and motivated ecological citizenship. It suggests steps that schools can take to enable students to form bonds of connection with the natural world and believe that they can work together with others to preserve a livable and biodiverse planet.

BENEFITS OF NATURE-BASED LEARNING FOR STUDENT WELL-BEING AND ACHIEVEMENT

"Nature-based learning" (NBL) is a recently defined term. In 2015, the National Science Foundation in the United States awarded a grant to the Children and Nature Network, the North American Association for Environmental Education, and affiliated research partners at the University of Minnesota and the University of Illinois Urbana-Champaign to create a Collaborative Research Network on the Science of Nature-based Learning. NBL is an educational approach that uses the natural environment as the context for learning. It investigates learning about nature through direct engagement with the natural world, learning outdoors in nature as a setting for all curriculum areas, and the impact of natural surroundings on learning in general. It includes informal learning as children and adolescents play and explore in natural areas, non-formal learning through programs at places like nature centers and parks, and formal education when a teacher takes students to an outdoor classroom or on a field trip to a natural area. It includes nature as a background to learning, such as the effect of plants in classrooms, green views outside school windows, and elements of nature on school grounds and in the surrounding neighborhood.

What is common across these different facets of NBL is that nature is accessible to children. At a minimum, they can see it, and in other cases they can experience it through all senses. Technology may advance these experiences, such as when a young person uses an iPhone app to identify a bird or tree during a hike, but digital nature in a film or website, by itself, constitutes learning about nature, not NBL.

In the last few years, a growing number of studies indicate that learning in nature is not only an advantage for subjects like biology and environmental education, but it can improve general conditions for student success in all subject areas. Benefits for self-regulation and social and emotional learning are already apparent in early childhood, in preschools and child care centers (Martensson, et al., 2009; Monti, Farné, Crudeli, Agostini, & Minelli, 2017; Ulset, Vitaro, Brendgen, Bekkhus, & Borge, 2017), but the sections that follow focus on studies in primary and secondary schools. In these grades, NBL is also associated with objective measures of academic success like standardized test scores and grade point averages. Rather than seeking to be comprehensive, the sections that follow highlight literature reviews and carefully controlled correlational designs, experimental designs, and multi-method case studies. All of the studies referenced in this paper controlled for potential confounding factors such as family income, parents' level of education, race, ethnicity, or school size, or conducted experiments with students who represented a single population.

School Grounds as Sites for Student Well-Being and Environmental Learning

Observations of students on kindergarten and elementary school grounds show that natural areas encourage more play in small groups, more gender balanced play groups with both boys and girls, and more mixed-age play (Bell & Dyment, 2008; Lucas & Dyment, 2010). Play quality is also more creative and varied, with more pretend play, constructive play and exploratory play, and more elaborated and extended play episodes: in contrast to short bursts of play and competitive, rule-bound games on large lawns and asphalt (Bell & Dyment, 2008; Luchs & Fikus, 2013; Moore & Wong, 1997; Samborski, 2010). The more open-ended, self-organized play in natural areas involves more social negotiation and cooperation.

In a Canadian study, 6 to 9-year olds evaluated their school grounds at two schools that were largely similar except for contrasting outdoor sites—one biodiverse and the other barren (Samborski, 2010). Students found more affordances for symbolic and constructive play on the biodiverse site, as well as more spaces where friends could gather for quiet reflection and conversation. These results are consistent with studies of elementary school and high school students in the United States, where students formed small supportive social groups in natural areas and described nature as peaceful, calm, and a refuge from stresses inside the school building and at home (Chawla, Keena, Pevec, & Stanley, 2014).

Measures of students' physiological responses and self-reported moods in nature provide further evidence that access to nature can enhance student well-being. In a Scottish study, young adolescents with no record of behavior problems, along with others diagnosed with attention deficit hyperactivity disorder or at-risk for exclusion or withdrawal from school, filled out surveys of their mood before and after a day in a forest school versus a school day indoors (Roe & Aspinall, 2011). After a day in the forest, each group reported a greater sense of energy and happiness and less stress and anger. When German students participated in learning activities in a forest one full day each week, they had healthier daily levels of cortisol across the school year—a measure of healthier levels of stress—compared to a control class without outdoor teaching (Dettweiler, Becker, Auestad, Simon & Kirsch, 2017). When students were assessed before and after the greening of an Austrian middle school, compared to two control schools without greening, students reported significantly greater well-being after greening and their blood pressure decreased only at the intervention school (Kelz, Evans, & Röderer, 2015). Nature has an effect even inside classrooms. When six small trees were placed at the back of a junior high school classroom in Taiwan, the treatment class immediately reported significantly greater feelings of preference and comfort for their class and believed that their class made them feel friendlier, compared to a control class in an otherwise identical room (Han, 2009). Students in the classroom with plants also had significantly fewer records of absences and punishments.

In addition to social, emotional and health benefits, green school grounds provide rich opportunities for environmental exploration and learning. In the Canadian comparison of students' responses to biodiverse and barren school grounds, for example, 6 to 9-year olds at the biodiverse school represented 79 different plant species when they were asked to draw their school ground, versus 2 species drawn by students at the school with barren grounds (Samborski, 2010). Tranter and Malone (2004) demonstrated, however, that even when elementary school children have trees and vegetation around their school, they are not observed exploring their environment unless teachers encourage them to manipulate and study their surroundings and allow them to get dirty in the process. A school's philosophy needs to encourage interactions with nature. When it does, activities in nature can be integrated into all curriculum areas (Moore & Wong, 1997) and school grounds can be designed to include resources for all parts of the curriculum (Danks, 2010).

Benefits of Green School Surroundings for Cognitive Functioning

Several studies indicate that children have better impulse control and more focused attention when they have more nature around their homes and neighborhoods or play outdoors in nature, after controlling for factors such as family income (Chawla, 2015). Studies conducted in schools show similar results. In a true experiment, high school students in classrooms with windows that overlooked a green space, versus a view of a wall or no windows, performed better on tests of attention and recovered more quickly after being stressed (Li & Sullivan, 2016). In another experiment, 6 to 11-year olds' performance was compared when they were given tasks that required close attention in a room with the window covered versus at a table in a naturalized area of a school (Torquatti, Schutte, & Kiat, 2017). Students working outdoors only performed significantly better than indoor students on a spatial working memory task, but measures of their brains' neuroelectrical activity showed that they achieved the same results on other tasks with less cognitive effort.

In addition to more efficient cognitive processing in nature, another mechanism of nature's influence may be less polluted air, as trees trap particulate matter. Primary school students in Barcelona with more greenness at home, around their school, and on their travel route to school had greater 12-month gains in working memory and reductions in inattentiveness; and this advantage was partly mediated by reduced exposure to air pollution (Dadvand et al., 2015). When absenteeism rates in Massachusetts public schools were compared, based on levels of vegetation around schools and levels of fine particulate matter in the air, more vegetation was associated with lower rates of chronic absenteeism, and more air-borne particulate matter with higher rates (MacNaughton, Eitland, Kloog, Schwartz, & Allen, 2017).

One reason why teachers may hesitate to take their students outdoors in natural areas is that some teachers fear that students will return to the classroom too keyed up to concentrate on subsequent lessons. To test whether this is the case, Kuo, Browning, and Penner (2018) asked two teachers in similar third-grade classrooms that served predominantly disadvantaged students to give a series of matched lessons over a 10-week period, with half of the lessons given in a grassy area outside school adjacent to trees, and the other identical lessons given inside the classroom. Following these treatments, students and teachers were observed during a subsequent lesson. Based on teacher ratings, counts of the number of times that teachers had to stop instruction to redirect students' attention to the task at hand, and blind ratings of photographs of the students at work, classroom engagement was significantly better after the lesson in nature. In almost half of the cases, it was better by a margin of one to two standard deviations or more.

Benefits of Green School Surroundings for Academic Achievement

Given students' better social, emotional and cognitive functioning when they have vegetated school surroundings, it is not surprising that studies are finding advantages for academic achievement as well. When public schools in the District of Columbia were compared on the basis of the number of trees, shrubs and grass cover around schools, students had a significantly greater percentage of proficient or advanced scores in standardized tests of reading and mathematics in schools with more tree cover

(Kweon, Ellis, Lee, & Jacobs, 2017). Similarly, third graders in Massachusetts public schools with more trees and other vegetation around their schools performed significantly better on standardized tests of English and mathematics (Wu et al., 2014). In public high schools in Michigan with more natural features such as trees and shrubs close to classroom and cafeteria windows, students had significantly higher standardized test scores and graduation rates, and greater percentages of students planned to attend college (Matsuoka, 2010). In this study and the study by Kweon et al. (2017), featureless landscapes like large lawns, athletic fields and parking lots were negatively associated with student performance.

NBL is often a component of place-based education, which connects learning to student's communities (Anderson, 2017; Smith & Sobel, 2010). A form of project-based learning, it can involve students in studying the built environment, such as traffic safety around their school; but frequently it focuses on local natural features such as a wetlands or watershed. It has been described as using the environment as an integrating context for learning across the curriculum (Lieberman & Hoody, 1998).

When Lieberman and Hoody (1998) evaluated the application of this approach in 40 schools across the United States, 98% of the teachers and administrators whom they interviewed noted greater student engagement and enthusiasm for school activities after they introduced this approach; ninety-seven percent said students did better at problem solving, and 89% said students stayed on task better. In 14 of the 40 schools, student achievement was compared in classes with an environment-focused approach versus conventional classrooms, measured by student grade point averages and scores on standardized tests. In 92% of the comparisons, students in environment-focused classrooms outperformed students in conventional classrooms, with advantages in reading, writing, mathematics, science, and social studies. Results were similar when standardized test scores were compared for a period of 5 years in four matched pairs of schools in California, with one school in each set practicing environment-focused teaching and the other conventional classroom instruction (State Education and Environment Roundtable, 2005). Students in environment-focused schools did better on 100% of the reading assessments and 93% of the math assessments.

There is evidence that teaching through the environment can close the achievement gap between students from more and less advantaged backgrounds. Over 3 years, student performance in three Louisiana elementary schools was compared with state averages when their schools adopted a teaching approach that focused on the study of local natural resources (Emekauwa, 2004). The schools were 80% African American, with 85% of the students receiving free or reduced lunches. At the beginning of the first year, students in these schools scored 10.7% lower in math and

15.6% lower in social studies. By the end of the third year, these gaps were reduced to 0.2% and 7.5%. In their book *Place- and Community-Based Education in Schools*, Smith and Sobel (2010) review a number of comparisons with similar results.

Schoolyard gardening is a particular form of place-based education. When Williams and Dixon (2013) reviewed studies published between 1990 and 2010 on the impact of garden-based learning on students' academic performance, 33 out of 40 studies showed better outcomes in science, math or language arts when students participated in garden programs versus conventional classroom instruction. In a recent experiment, 25 schools in four states in the United States were assigned to garden interventions and 24 schools to a control group (Wells et al., 2015). All schools were located in low-income areas where at least 50% of the students received free or reduced lunches. Students in second, fourth, and fifth grades were tested for science knowledge at four points over a year and a half. Students in the garden program showed greater gains in science knowledge, and this effect was stronger the more that garden-based teaching was implemented.

EDUCATION FOR ENVIRONMENTAL ACTION

The preceding sections demonstrate that NBL has many benefits for students. At any time, research suggests, it would be advantageous to green school grounds, take students on field trips to nearby natural areas, and integrate outdoor activities in nature into all areas of the school curriculum. But as the opening of this paper noted, this is not just "any time." Educators today work at a time when the climate of planet Earth is changing under the impact of human activity, with severe consequences. Students are inheriting a world where basic systems of the biosphere are being dismantled. Therefore, it is important for schools to not only make the natural world accessible to students, for students' benefits, but to also prepare students to live on this planet in more wise and caring ways than generations before them.

Research that investigates experiences associated with a person's development of caring action for the environment has been termed the study of "significant life experiences" (Chawla & Derr, 2012, p. 531). Initiated in the 1980s, this field of study has relied primarily on interviews and surveys: some open-ended, asking people to describe experiences in childhood that influenced their current environmental values and behaviors; and some close-ended, examining correlations between early experiences that people recall and the environmental behaviors that they report. Some studies have been exploratory, to understand a single group of people, such as conservationists, environmental educators, or youth in environmental clubs.

Other studies involve comparisons between more and less environmentally concerned and active people.

The formative experiences that emerge most frequently across studies are immersion in nature through free play and exploration in childhood and adolescence; observing appreciative and caring environmental behaviors in influential people, who are usually family members but can be other adult mentors or peers; and at some point, usually in adolescence or early adulthood, learning how to take action for the environment as an individual and a member of an organization (Chawla & Derr, 2012; D'Amore & Chawla, in press; Wells & Lekies, 2012). Other significant experiences include witnessing the destruction of a valued natural place, witnessing how environmental degradation impacts people—especially disadvantaged people, books about nature, and an influential teacher, school or course. In studies that include data about educational experiences, at least 20% of most samples say that they had significant environmental experiences in school, though this is usually in later years, such as an inspiring teacher in high school or classes in a university. The formative influence that appears most consistently across studies is free play and exploration in nature (Chawla & Derr, 2012; D'Amore & Chawla, in press; Wells & Lekies, 2012).

Another area of research is the evaluation of school programs that seek to instill a conservation ethic and caring environmental behaviors in students. These studies have been conducted in the field of environmental education but features of successful programs can be applied to any area of the curriculum. Across subject areas, teachers can help students understand their connection with nature and reliance on intact ecosystems.

Most evaluations of programs that aim to promote pro-environmental behaviors have the limitations that student behaviors are self-reported or reported by teachers, rather than observed, and they involve short-term outcomes, such as immediate comparisons of student behaviors before and after a program or assessed 2 to 3 months after a program ends (Chawla & Derr, 2012). Nevertheless, research across a wide range of programs and all grade levels indicates that students are more likely to practice pro-environmental behaviors when they have the following experiences (Chawla & Derr, 2012).

Effective programs *actively involve students in learning processes*, rather than treating them as passive recipients of instruction. This means inquiry-based learning, when students gather information about the environment themselves, driven by their own questions. It also means that they have opportunities to learn environmental action skills. A series of evaluations of the Issue Investigation and Action Training approach, which includes these features, show that students are more likely to report pro-environmental behaviors after they have investigated a local environmental issue and learned how people have taken steps to address it, versus students in a conventional classroom (Chawla & Derr, 2012; Hungerford, Litherland, Peyton, Ramsey, & Volk, 2003). This is true even when students do not proceed to take these action steps themselves. Most successful programs, however, go beyond learning *about* action to learning *through* action, as students set goals and then implement their ideas, such as setting up a recycling program in their school or restoring natural habitat (Sobel, 2008).

Effective programs also *connect learning to the real worlds of students' homes, communities and regions*. Students learn about the place where they live. They can see and touch what they are studying, and meet people who are directly affected, who may include themselves and their families. To take action, they will usually need to partner with adults, such as experts in conservation practices or decision makers in their schools or communities. In this process they learn how decisions are made and see that they can influence decisions.

Effective programs also have *long duration*. Research shows that this can be achieved in different ways. Students may investigate an environmental topic and plan action steps across the course of a semester or a multi-week segment of a class; or this way of learning may be embedded across classes if their school practices place-based education. For field trips, longer field trips are more impactful, such as a week at a nature center, or students have opportunities to take a series of field trips of different lengths (Zint, Kraemer, Northway, & Lim, 2002).

Research on students' reactions to climate change suggests that programs that support action for the environment help prepare students for the changing world that they inhabit. Climate change is a problem at a global scale, with such threatening effects, now and for the future, that students can easily feel overwhelmed and helpless. Working with students in Sweden, Ojala (2016) observed that teachers cannot just communicate about climate change factually; they must also help students manage the emotions that this knowledge arouses. Many students manage difficult emotions by denying that climate change is a serious threat or deciding that it doesn't affect them personally. These students are also less likely to believe that they can do anything to influence environmental problems or take any actions with this aim. Students who believe that they can influence climate change are more likely to perform pro-environmental behaviors, but given the scale of the problem, they are more likely to feel confidence in the future if they do not feel that they act alone. In the words of Ojala, students develop "constructive hope" (p. 215) when they believe that they can influence the environment positively and trust that adults in power are acting responsibly too. One of the best ways to build this hope is to engage students in collective action for the environment along with other members of their school and community.

BRINGING NATURE-BASED LEARNING AND CLIMATE ACTION TOGETHER

The needs of students and the natural world are not separate. This is true in a future sense—in the sense that schools need to graduate students who understand ecology and climate science and who feel motivated to protect the biosphere. It is also true in the here and now, in the sense that students do better when elements of nature are protected and restored around their schools. According to the Intergovernmental Panel on Climate Change (Edenhofer et al., 2014), effective action to address climate change must be multifaceted, and one of the critical directions for action is developing human capital and social capital. This means that individuals need knowledge and skills to make informed choices about the environment, and they also need opportunities to work with others to address problems that cannot be solved by individual actions alone. Another critical direction for action, the IPCC observes, is the greening of human settlements like cities and suburbs—which includes greening schools. Trees sequester carbon, a greenhouse gas, taking it out of the atmosphere and storing it for their life cycle. The Panel notes that trees and other vegetation provide co-benefits in addition to storing carbon (Seto et al., 2014). They reduce air pollution by trapping particulates, provide habitat for biodiversity, and moderate temperatures.

The Panel does not mention other benefits specific to school greening but buffering noise and creating a quieter environment for learning can be added. Additional benefits are restorative green views outside classroom windows; school gardens; outdoor areas for nature play; outdoor classrooms for peaceful settings for learning; opportunities to integrate the study of nature into all subject areas; and opportunities for service learning when students participate in greening projects in their communities. When students work with school administrators, teachers, parent volunteers and local experts in horticulture and habitat restoration, this creates conditions for "constructive hope" (Ojala, 2016, p. 215). Two of the directions for action that the IPCC recommends—the development of human capital and social capital, and the greening of cities and towns—come together when schools become hubs for greening school grounds and service learning projects for ecological restoration.

NBL invites taking at least some classes in each subject area outdoors. It also invites project-based learning that uses the environment as an integrating context for team teaching and interdisciplinary education, and service learning to naturalize school grounds and community open spaces. While teachers may take the step of leading classes outdoors, the more ambitious steps require clusters of teachers who want to work together across disciplines and school administrators who support their efforts. This paper is offered as a resource for advocating for these approaches.

One important conclusion from this paper's review may present a paradox for teaching and curriculum planning. Research on sources of people's motivation to protect the natural world indicates that the most important formative experience is routine free play and exploration in nature in childhood (D'Amore & Chawla, in press; Wells & Lekies, 2012). In past generations, teachers could assume that students roamed local green spaces outside of school, but studies of children's time use show a dramatic shift in the last generation as children's lives have largely moved indoors (Louv, 2008). Children in low-income families are most likely to live in barren neighborhoods with little access to nature (Jesdale, Morello-Frosch, & Cushing, 2013) and in unsafe neighborhoods that compel them to stay indoors. This means that recess on green school grounds should not be seen as just a break from school work. For many children, it is the only opportunity that they have to build bonds of connection with the natural world through autonomous play and discovery. It needs to be seen as an essential part of the curriculum of learning stewardship for the planet. If free time on green school grounds is valued in this way, then it provides an ever-fresh source of teachable moments, when teachers invite students to share their interests and discoveries and investigate them further through all subject areas of the curriculum.

REFERENCES

Anderson, S. (2017). *Bringing school to life*. Lanham, NJ: Rowman & Littlefield.

Bell, A. C., & Dyment, J. E. (2008). Grounds for health: The intersection of green-school grounds and health-promoting schools. *Environmental Education Research*, *14*(1), 77–90.

Chawla, L. (2015). Benefits of nature contact for children. *Journal of Planning Literature*, *30*(4), 433–452.

Chawla L., & Derr, V. (2012). The development of conservation behaviors in childhood and youth. In S. Clayton (Ed.), *The Oxford handbook of environmental and conservation psychology* (pp. 527–555). Oxford, England: Oxford University Press.

Chawla, L., Keena, K., Pevec, I., & Stanley, E. (2014). Green schoolyards as havens from stress and resources for resilience in childhood and adolescence. *Health & Place*, *28*, 1–13.

Climate Literacy and Energy Awareness Network (CLEAN). (n.d.). Collection of climate and energy educational resources. Retrieved from https://cleanet.org/index/html

Dadvand, P., Nieuwenhuijsen, M., Esnaola, M., Forns, J., Basagaña, X., Alvarez, P., ... Sunyer, J., (2015). Green spaces and cognitive development in primary schoolchildren. *Proceedings of the National Academy of Sciences of the United States of America*, *112*(26), 7937–7942.

D'Amore, C., & Chawla, L. (in press). Significant life experiences that connect children with nature. In A. Cutter-Mackenzie, K. Malone, & E. Barratt Hacking (Eds.), *International research handbook on childhood nature*. Melbourne, Australia: Springer.

Danks, S. G. (2010). *Asphalt to ecosystems*. Oakland, CA: New Village Press.

Dettweiler, U., Becker, C., Auestad, B., Simon, P., & Kirsch, P. (2017). Stress in school. *International Journal of Environmental Research and Public Health*, *14*, 475.

Edenhofer, O., Pichs-Madruga, R., Sokona, Y., Farahani, E., Kadner, S., … Zwickel, T. (Eds.) (2014). *Climate change 2014: Mitigation of climate change*. Cambridge, England: Cambridge University Press.

Emekauwa, E. (2004). *They remember what they touch: The impact of place-based learning in East Feliciana Parish*. Washington, DC: Rural School and Community Trust.

Han, K. T. (2009). Influence of limitedly visible leafy indoor plants on the psychology, behavior, and health of students at a junior high school in Taiwan. *Environment and Behavior*, *41*(5), 658–692.

Hungerford, H., Litherland, R., Peyton, R., Ramsey, J., & Volk, T. (2003). *Investigating and evaluating environmental issues and action skill development program*. Champaign, IL: Stipes.

Intergovernmental Panel on Climate Change. (2014). *Climate change 2014: Synthesis report summary for policymakers*. Geneva, Switzerland: Author. Retrieved from www.ipcc.ch/pdf/assessment-report/ar5/syr/AR5_SYR_FINAL_SPM.pdf

Jesdale, B. M., Morello-Frosch, R., & Cushing, L. (2013). The racial/ethnic distribution of heat risk-related land cover in relation to residential segregation. *Environmental Health Perspective*, *121*(7), 811–817.

Kelz, C., Evans, G. W., & Röderer, K. (2015). The restorative effects of redesigning the schoolyard. *Environment and Behavior*, *47*(2), 119–139.

Kuo, M., Browning, M., & Penner, M. L. (2018). Do lessons in nature boost subsequent classroom engagement? Refueling students in flight. *Frontiers in Psychology*, *8*, Article 2253.

Kweon, B.-S., Ellis, C., Lee, J., & Jacobs, K. (2017). The link between school environments and student academic performance. *Urban Forestry and Urban Greening*, *23*, 35-43.

Li, D., & Sullivan, W. (2016). Impact of views to school landscapes on recovery from stress and mental fatigue. *Landscape and Urban Planning*, *148*, 149-158.

Lieberman, G., & Hoody, L. (1998). *Closing the achievement gap*. San Diego, CA: State Education and Environment Roundtable.

Louv, R. (2008). *Last child in the woods* (2nd ed). Chapel Hill, NC: Algonquin Press.

Luchs, A., & Fikus, M. (2013). A comparative study of active play on differently designed playgrounds. *Journal of Adventure Education and Outdoor Learning*, *13*(3), 206–222.

Lukas, A. J., & Dyment, J. E. (2010). Where do children choose to play on the school ground? The influence of green design. *Education 3-13: International Journal of Primary, Elementary and Early Years Education*, *38*(2), 177–189.

MacNaughton, P., Eitland, E., Kloog, I., Schwartz, J., & Allen, J. (2017). Impact of particulate matter exposure and surrounding "greenness" on chronic absenteeism in Massachusetts public schools. *International Journal of Environmental Research and Public Health, 14*(2), 207.

Martensson, F., Boldemann, C., Söderström, M., Blennow, M., Englund, J.-E., & Grahn, P. (2009). Outdoor environmental assessment of attention promoting settings for preschool children. *Health & Place, 15*(4), 1149–1157.

Matsuoka, R. (2010). Student performance and high school landscapes. *Landscape and Urban Planning, 97,* 273–282.

Monti, F., Farné, R., Crudeli, F. Agostini, F., Minelli, M., & Ceciliani, A. (2017). The role of outdoor education in child development in Italian nursery schools. *Early Child Development and Care.* https://doi.org/10.1080/03004430.2017.1345896.

Moore, R. C., & Wong, H. H. (1997). *Natural learning.* Berkeley, CA: MIG Communications.

NASA. (n.d.). *Global climate change: Vital signs of the planet.* Retrieved from https://climate.nasa.gov/resources/education.

Ojala, M. (2016). Preparing children for the emotional challenges of climate change. In K. Winograd (Ed.), *Education in times of environmental crises* (pp. 211–218). New York, NY: Routledge.

Roe, J., & Aspinall, P. (2011). The restorative outcomes of forest school and conventional school in young people with good and poor behaviour. *Urban Forestry and Urban Greening, 10*(3), 205–212.

Samborski, S. (2010). Biodiverse or barren school grounds. *Children, Youth and Environments, 20*(2), 67–115.

Seto, K. C., Dhakal, S., Bigio, A., Blanco, H., Delgado, G. C. et al. (2014). Human settlements, infrastructure and spatial planning. In O. Edenhofer, R Pichs-Madruga, Y. Sokona, E. Farahani, S. Kadner, … T. Zwickel (Eds.), (2014). *Climate change 2014: Mitigation of climate change* (pp. 923–1000). Cambridge, England: Cambridge University Press.

Smith, G., & Sobel, D. (2010). *Place- and community-based education in schools.* New York, NY: Routledge.

Sobel, D. (2008). *Childhood and nature.* Portland, ME: Stenhouse.

State Education and Environment Roundtable. (2005). *California student assessment project, phase two: The effects of environment-based education on student achievement.* Poway, CA: Author.

Torquatti, J., Schutte, A., & Kiat, J. (2017). Attentional demands of executive function tasks in indoor and outdoor settings. *Children, Youth and Environments, 27*(2), 70–92.

Tranter, P., & Malone, K. (2004). Geographies of environmental learning. *Children's Geographies, 2*(1), 131–155.

Ulset, V., Vitaro, F., Brendgen, M., Bekkhus, M., & Borge, A. (2017). Time spent outdoors during preschool: Links with children's cognitive and behavioral development. *Journal of Environmental Psychology, 52,* 69–80.

Wells, N., Myers, B., Todd, L., Barale, K., Gaolach, B., Ferenz, G., … Falk, E. (2015). The effects of school gardens on children's science knowledge. *International Journal of Science Education, 37*(17), 2858–2878.

Wells, N., & Lekies, K. (2012). Children and nature: Following the trail to environmental attitudes and behaviors. In J. L. Dickinson & R. Bonney (Eds.), *Citizen science* (pp. 201–213). Ithaca, NY: Comstock.

Williams, D., & Dixon, P. (2013). Impact of garden-based learning on academic outcomes in schools. *Review of Educational Research*, *83*(2), 211–235.

Wu, C.-D., McNeely, E., Cedeño-Laurent, J., Pan, W.-C., Adamkiewicz, G., Dominici, F., … Spengler, J. (2014). Linking student performance in Massachusetts elementary schools with the "greenness" of school surroundings using remote sensing. *PLOS One*, *9*(10), e108548.

Zint, M., Kraemer, A., Northway, H., & Lim, M. (2002). Evaluation of the Chesapeake Bay Foundation's conservation education programs. *Conservation Biology*, *16*(3), 641–649.

PRESIDENT'S MESSAGE

INFORMING EDUCATION WITHIN THE REALITIES OF THE DIVERSE PERSPECTIVES OF SCHOOLS

John L. Pecore

This year the American Association for Teaching and Curriculum (AATC) celebrates a quarter of a century as an association dedicated "to promote the scholarly study of teaching and curriculum." The founders of AATC felt a strong need for a national learned society to serve the field of teaching and curriculum and its intersections with theory and practice. Thus, AATC is dedicated to fostering intellectual conversations among its members and producing scholarship that explores the relationship between theory, practice, and policy in teaching and curriculum. This issue of the association's journal, *Curriculum and Teaching Dialogue* **(CTD),** marks the 20th year of publication. The journal's purpose has been to extend scholarly investigations of teaching and curriculum and to further AATC's culture of dialogue. Founded under William E. Segall's AATC presidency, Susan Brown served as the editor for **the first 6 years** (1999–2004). Subsequent journal editors, who each deserve much gratitude for their tireless efforts, include Barbara Slater Stern (2005–2011), David Flinders (2010–2016),

P. Bruce Uhrmacher (2012–2014), and Christy Moroye (2015–2017). With volume 20, we welcome Chara Haeussler Bohan as the new CTD editor.

AATC has thrived in large part due to a dedicated membership willing to give of their time serving the association on committees, reviewing conference proposals, volunteering during conferences, and reviewing manuscripts for CTD. From graduate students and early-career faculty to midcareer and seasoned faculty, many benefit from the strong connections and culture of dialogue available through AATC. As an association centered on dialogue, AATC appreciates educators with differing educational perspectives, which leads to engaging conversations and debate.

AATC is an organization welcoming various perspectives of curriculum and teaching. Prominent education experts (i.e., Elliot Eisner, William Schubert, Herbert Kliebard) have conceptualized four main perspectives that help to shape AATC's dialogue. The first, *academic/intellectual*, prioritizes academic content to be taught. Second, *technology/social efficiency*, is vocationally oriented and emphasizes the acquisition of skills. The third, *experiential/child centered*, is constructivist oriented focusing on the natural development of personal and experiential meanings constructed by students and teachers. Fourth, *social reconstruction*, emphasizes critical thinking about personal, political and professional issues that shape and effect student lives toward taking action for a more just society (Shiro, 2013). Research indicates educators are likely to have more than one dominant perspective and will likely change their perspective throughout their lifetime. Therefore, diverse educational perspectives are important for both growth and change. AATC provides a space for these perspectives to enter into dialogue, generating both depth of understanding and innovative practical ideas. Take for example, the *Bridging Differences* dialogue between Deborah Meier and Diane Ravitch (2006), who concluded "Our differences helped us consider ways to rethink our ideas and find places where those holding different views might compromise, and perhaps learn to live under one umbrella" (p. 37).

At AATC's core the organization is grounded in the realities of schools while working to shape the educational perspective of teachers. To this end, the 2017–2018 school year marks the time in which states are required to have reaffirmed, modified, or improved their vision of educator effectiveness under the Every Student Succeeds Act, which amended the reauthorization of the Elementary and Secondary Education Act. This has meant the adoption by most states of classroom observation rubrics intended to provide a general description of good teaching. AATC has an important role to play in developing more robust descriptions of good teaching applicable to the context of the four previously mentioned perspectives. As an organization, members engage with both pre- and in-service teachers, for whom curriculum is designed and taught, to make practical ideas of effective teaching.

Additionally, the organization offers a forum for dialogue within diverse educational perspectives through conference presentations and published work. Thus, the work of AATC as a community of scholars and teachers helps to inform curriculum and teaching within the realities of the educational perspectives of schools.

REFERENCES

Meier, D., & Ravitch, D. (2006). Bridging differences. *Education Week*, *25*(38), 36–37.
Schiro, M. S. (2013). *Curriculum theory: Conflicting visions and enduring concerns* (2nd ed.). Los Angeles, CA: SAGE.

VOLUME 20, NUMBER 1

EDITOR'S NOTES

DEMOCRACY, EDUCATION, TEACHING, AND TEACHER STRIKES

Chara Haeussler Bohan

In honor of the 25 years since the founding of the American Association for Teaching and Curriculum (AATC), I have elected to focus this editorial on the history of democracy and education with a spotlight on the recent teacher strikes of 2018. An important component of AATC's mission, is to focus on the scholarly study of teaching. The majority of the chapters in both Issue number 1 and 2, emphasize the work of teachers and teaching. This research emphasizes the effort of a variety of teachers: K–12 in-service teachers, teacher educators, preservice teachers, and community leaders engaged in matters of teaching explicit or hidden curriculum. None of these chapters in Volume 20 of *Curriculum and Teaching Dialogue* specifically address teaching as an overtly political act; however, the chapter by Zajdel and Conn on the McDonald's McTeacher's night makes a robust statement about advertising "generosity" in American schools. Nevertheless, current events involving teacher protests remind readers that, as Sonia Neito (2000) expressed, "teaching is inherently political work" (p. 3). Thus, I offer readers an alternative lens through which to view the chapters in this volume. Consider how these authors also provide readers with a political view of teaching.

In the United States, democracy serves as the foundation of political government. Democracy's roots date back to ancient Greece. As a contemporary form of government, Enlightenment thinkers are credited with what Gordon Wood (1999) calls "people being judges in their own cause" (p. 309). Both Thomas Jefferson and Benjamin Franklin recognized that democracy requires an educated populace. Thus, both men established educational institutions in their respective home states of Virginia and Pennsylvania. However, democratic government does not ensure parallel classroom practices. Education is not necessarily democratic. The incubation of democratic classrooms began with the 19th century expansion of education in the United States. Philosophers such as John Dewey and practitioners such as A. S. Neill helped democratic classrooms mature.

Certain conditions must be established in order for democratic practices to thrive in the classroom. Walter Parker (2003) reminds readers that democracy is a social construct that must be cared for and nurtured; educators are its primary stewards. Other philosophers of democratic education offer different perspectives. Gert Biesta (2007) believes that tasking schools with the responsibility for democracy burdens them with unrealistic demands. Nonetheless, teachers who value democratic practices in classrooms need to understand common characteristics—what works and does not work when implementing democratic pedagogies. Active student decision making, where deliberation in a caring, respectful community, is of prime importance. Teachers and students must also value diversity. Many of the philosophers of democratic classrooms indicate that schools are a microcosm of society, and humans must learn to deliberate, especially when they encounter others whose points of view are dissimilar. In the current contemporary political climate, teachers and students establishing democratic practices in classrooms is of vital significance.

Not only is it important to establish democratic traditions in schools, but democracy must be nurtured in the larger society. The teachers in the states where strikes and protests have developed demanded increases in financial support for education, in both spending on infrastructure and students, as well as teacher pay. As of the end of May 2018, the "Red State Teacher Revolt" included West Virginia, Oklahoma, Kentucky, Arizona, North Carolina, and not-so-red Colorado (Fay, 2018). In addition to focusing on the substance of what teachers insisted upon from their state legislatures (all six states ranked near the bottom of per pupil spending and teacher pay), these teachers were serving as role models of democracy in action. By practicing dissent, the teachers were cultivating democracy and reminding the larger society of the power of collective action.

Several research chapters in Issue number 1 focus on the work of teachers. In fact, four of the seven examine the practices of teachers in real schools and universities in the context of local communities. The four studies where teacher practices in schools and universities are investigated include authors Brugar, Petretti, Miller and Lindt, and Woodrow. The other three chapters present theoretical arguments about teaching, but in each of the three the theoretical construct is grounded in real world experiences of the researchers who have considerable experience working with teachers. In her chapter on preservice teachers' use of visuals, Kristy Brugar highlights how burgeoning elementary school teachers select visual material in a world saturated with images. Brugar illuminates teacher candidates' conceptions and misconceptions about the use of visuals. As a reader, one might wonder how these preservice teacher selections may have been impacted knowingly or unknowingly by politics. In Dante Petretti's chapter, he assesses the research engagement of three teachers in urban high schools. He describes the necessary personal and political conditions that are critical for the teachers in his study to maintain research engagement despite myriad challenges. Clearly, local context and working conditions, forces strongly impacted by politics, effect teachers' abilities to conduct research. In Stacia Miller and Suzanne Lindt's study of movement in reading and math classes, the researchers engage in a real world examination of teacher perspectives on the use of traditional and nontraditional methods of teaching reading and mathematics. Again, the political climate of a school influences how traditional and nontraditional teaching methods are practiced. Finally, Kelli Woodrow, in an ethnographic study, examines the actual practices of two educators in a Catholic elementary school that had a stated mission of fostering social justice. Certainly, the teachers, school leaders, parents, and students in the school operated within a unique political context. The political conditions for social justice education (SJE) to thrive at this Catholic elementary school became vital to the success of the mission and the teachers' work.

Three chapters in Issue number 1 are theoretical in nature. Authors Gregory Chalfin, Crytal Johnson and Harvey Hinton, and Paul Parkinson describe improved possibilities for teachers and schools. Chalfin examines the possibilities of teachers fostering Nel Noddings's care theory through the use of audio feedback on student writing assignments. He argues that such feedback is important to improving student writing skills, but despite technological innovations that can facilitate this pedagogy, it remains a teaching practice that resides on the margins. Perhaps, the political conditions, where funding for schools has been cut over many years, are not ripe for supporting teachers to be able to engage in such labor intensive work. In the next theoretical chapter, Johnson and Hinton define culturally consonant character education where the aim is to develop positive outcomes among youth of color. Johnson and Hinton's work is based upon professional development activities and their approach to character education enhances relationships among diverse students. Finally, Parkinson presents an argument about reframing assessment measures, where assessment is viewed as dialogue between teachers and students, rather than standardized tests to be provided and passed.

As a new editor, I hope that the readers will enjoy all the research chapters, both experiential and theoretical, in Volume 20 of *Curriculum and Teaching Dialogue*. As well, both Michelle Tenam-Zemach and I believe that the outtakes are fun explorations in research activities that do not always transpire as planned. Finally, the authors of all the book reviews in this volume have provided careful examinations of books by fellow AATC members, so hopefully readers will take the time to read what AATC's author members are writing. If pressed for time, read the book reviews. Finally, I want to thank AATC for the privilege of trusting Michelle Tenam-Zemach and me with the responsibility of editing *Curriculum and Teaching Dialogue*. We are honored to serve the AATC community to facilitate this important intellectual contribution.

REFERENCES

Biesta, G. (2007). Education and the democratic person: Towards a political conception of democratic education. *Teacher College Record, 109*(3), 740–69.

Fay, L. (2018, May 14). With North Carolina teachers rallying this week, a look back at a season of strikes: What teachers asked for and what they received. *The 74*. Retrieved from https://www.the74million.org/with-north-carolina-teachers-rallying-this-week-a-look-back-at-a-season-of-strikes-what-teachers-asked-for-and-what-they-received/

Nieto, S. (2006). Teaching as political work: Learning from courageous and caring teachers. *The Longfellow Lecture*. Child Development Institute, Sarah Lawrence College. https://files.eric.ed.gov/fulltext/ED497692.pdf

Parker, W. (2003). *Teaching democracy: Unity and diversity in public life*. Multicultural Education Series. New York, NY: Teachers College Press.

Wood, G. (1999). The origins of American democracy, or how the people became judges in their own causes. The Sixty-Ninth Cleveland-Marshall Fund Lecture. *Cleveland State Law Review, 47*(3), 309–322.

CHAPTER 1

LEARNING AND TEACHING IN A VISUAL WORLD

Elementary Teacher Candidates' Use of Visual Materials

Kristy A. Brugar

ABSTRACT

People are inundated with visual information. In this study, I address the question: *When preservice elementary teacher candidates include visuals and graphics into social studies lessons, in what ways do they integrate these materials?* As part of a social studies methods course, participants created lesson plans. These plans included visuals and were analyzed, and instructional practices were identified. This study helps to better understand teacher candidates' conceptions and possible misconceptions of these ubiquitous resources that will impact elementary student learning.

From *The College, Career, and Civic Life (C3) Framework* ([C3 Framework] National Council for the Social Studies, 2013) and the Common Core State Standards ([CCSS] Council of Chief State School Officers & National Governors Association Center for Best Practices, 2010) to state curricular documents (e.g., California, New York, Texas), many standards include language about visuals and graphic representations. Further, classrooms are visual, dynamic places. The use of educational materials like maps, multimedia presentations, and virtual experiences demands students be visually literate. With the prevalence of visual materials (Werner, 2002), it is essential that colleges of education and teachers prepare students to "navigate, evaluate, and communicate effectively with visual information" (Pettersson & Avgerinou, 2016, p. 83).

Various visual materials (e.g., diagrams, maps, paintings, photographs, timelines) provide information as well as outlets for students to communicate their understandings. Yet for many teacher candidates, visual literacy has not been part of their educational experiences. In addition, their preparation in social studies may be limited (Hawkman, Castro, Bennett, & Barrow, 2015; Passe, 2006; Slekar, 1998) due, in part, to marginalization of elementary social studies (e.g., Heafner & Fitchett, 2012). Thus, instructional approaches tend to be more static than dynamic due to teachers' limited experiences and content knowledge. However, elementary social studies is filled with opportunities to engage students with visuals in order to access abstract and complex concepts across the social sciences from civics (e.g., authority, conflicts, rights) and economics (e.g., needs, opportunity costs, wants) to geography (e.g., community, landforms, transportation) and history (e.g., consequences, sequencing, time). The purpose of this study is to examine elementary teacher candidates' planning for and reported uses of visual materials and associated instructional strategies/practices as part of social studies instruction in order to better understand their conceptions and the possible misconceptions of these pervasive resources that will impact elementary student learning.

LITERATURE REVIEW

This study is situated at the intersection of social studies instruction, visual literacy, and teacher education. I use *visuals, visual materials,* and *graphics* interchangeably to describe nontext presentation of content (Norman, 2012). These nontext presentations or visuals include flowcharts, graphs, illustrations/drawings, maps, and tables as well as captioned photographs (Avgerinou & Pettersson, 2011). Visual experiences are opportunities for students to link prior knowledge and experiences to new and/or complex ideas (Bisland, 2010). There are a few studies that involve teachers' uses of visuals (e.g., Acheson, 2003; Barry, 2002; Nix, 2015). However, there is limited information about our understanding of visual literacy in the social studies (Brugar & Roberts, 2017; Nix, 2015; Roberts & Brugar, 2017), which is further complicated when thinking about teacher candidates.

Social Studies

A central goal of social studies education is to educate the next generation of citizens. Elementary social studies instruction utilizes literacy skills (e.g., listen, observe, read, speak, write) in order to better understand content (Boyle-Baise, Hsu, Johnson, Serriere, & Stewart, 2008; Brophy, Alleman, & Knighton, 2010; Duke & Bennett-Armistead, 2003). To be an educated citizen in an increasingly visual world, basic literacy skills and the ability to navigate and use the visual images are necessities. The National Council for the Social Studies (2017) advocates,

> To support effective teaching and learning, social studies enriched classrooms require a wide array of materials for young children to explore and manipulate. Equity requires that all programs have these resources, including visual images of diverse people and materials representing multiple perspectives. (para. 24)

Effective social studies instruction includes written as well as visual texts (Martinez, 2009; Staley, 2006). However, the information on graphical comprehension in social studies is limited (Brugar & Roberts, 2017; Nix, 2015; Roberts & Brugar, 2017), which is somewhat surprising with the prevalent use of visuals in social studies in classroom instruction (Brugar, 2018), text, and trade books (Fingeret, 2012).

In a content analysis of children's science and social studies textbooks, Fingeret (2012) found 30% of graphics in children's text and trade books reiterate information in the running, written text. Also, 60% of visual materials provide further information and meaning that is not present in the written text. Students must be able to read both the visual and running texts to fully access the content. There is some research on the complexities of visuals and text working together toward students' abilities to interpret and/or produce meaning (aspects of visual literacy).

LeCompte and Bauml (2012) found potential for students to explore complex concepts related to social studies through visual materials. Students' knowledge of the complex concepts and content often associated with social studies may be developed and fostered with visual literacy skills. For social studies students, the use of visual literacy skills means they must be able to contextualize and question various forms of visual sources. Students are often tasked to find meaning in graphical material and to describe the relationship between text and illustrations. In order to best utilize visual materials, teachers should use visuals within daily instructional practices in various ways.

Visual Literacy

For this study, I draw on various definitions of visual literacy, most notably Yenawine's (1997) description:

> the ability to find meaning in imagery. It involves a set of skills ranging from simple identification (naming what one sees) to complex interpretation on contextual, metaphoric and philosophical levels. Many aspects of cognition are called upon, such as personal association, questioning, speculating, analyzing, fact-finding, and categorizing. (p. 846)

In reference to visuals in text, Levin, Anglin, and Carney (1987) identified five common functions of visuals: (1) decorative, (2) representational, (3) organizational, (4) interpretational, and (5) transformational. More recently, Avgerinou and Pettersson (2011) described five aspects associated with visual literacy, including perception, language, thinking, learning, and communication. Understanding visual literacy is significant for those teaching K–12 social studies, which depends heavily on the use of varied texts, including visuals (e.g., captioned images, graphs, maps, timelines). Therefore, teachers must consider the ways in which they can use those visuals in educative ways to promote social studies content and visual literacy skills.

Comprehension is inclusive of a student's ability to read, interpret, and integrate the running text and related visuals (e.g., captioned images, maps, tables, timelines) as sources of meaning. Student comprehension of visual and running texts may further students' understandings of complicated information (Schnotz & Bannert, 2003). Thus, there is a need for teachers to mediate the intricacies of reading texts (e.g., using of text features, accessing content-specific information) including complex visuals (Carney & Levin, 2002; Simons & Elster, 1990; Werner, 2002).

Teacher Education

Teacher candidates have limited knowledge and experiences with elementary social studies (Hawkman et al., 2015). Further, Bolick, Adams, and Willox (2010) found that teacher candidates who did not observe social studies instruction in field placements struggled to define and design social studies experiences for their students when space was provided. Further, few teachers have experiences with visual literacy as part of their K–12 experiences or teacher preparation (Brugar & Roberts, 2017). Roberts, Norman, and Cocco (2015) advocated for explicit instruction of graphical devices. Cochran-Smith, Feiman-Nemser, and McIntyre (2008) described the need and importance of field experiences to connect the theory, often associated with methods courses, to practice.

Critically important is the acknowledgment and understanding of teacher candidates' understandings and perceptions of these materials. The pedagogical choices teachers and teacher candidates make in terms of what to include/exclude from their classroom instruction represent their pedagogical content knowledge (Shulman, 1986) and impact students' understanding of content.

However, a gap remains in understanding visual literacy in the social studies, particular to teacher candidates. It is critical to acknowledge and understand teacher candidates' understandings and perceptions as they make pedagogical choices about what to include/exclude from regular classroom instruction with their students. Often, elementary teacher candidates have limited knowledge and experiences with elementary social studies (Fitchett & Heafner, 2010; Passe, 2006). With this in mind, the research question for this study is: *When preservice elementary teacher candidates include visuals and graphics into social studies lessons, in what ways do they integrate these materials?*

METHODS

Data Sources and Analysis

This study utilizes exploratory qualitative methods for which data sources are teacher candidate lesson plans. First, the teacher candidates' lesson plans (2 lessons per participant, $n = 76$) were created as part of an elementary social studies methods course the semester prior to student teaching—there was a field component to this course. As a result, teacher candidates were creating lessons with specific curriculum and students in mind. Teacher candidates were encouraged, but not required, to teach both lessons in the field.

Cavanagh (1997) describes content analysis as a flexible way in which a researcher can analyze text data. In order to analyze these lesson plans, I conducted a summative content analysis (Hsieh & Shannon, 2005) that "goes beyond mere word counts to include latent content analysis. Latent content analysis refers to the process of interpretation" (Hsieh & Shannon, 2005, p. 1282). The interpretation is guided by prior research or theory, in this case Levie (1987) and Levin et al. (1987). In this case, the prior research on visuals and text was foundational in establishing the initial categories. Categories are defined as "a group of words with similar meaning or connotations" (Weber, 1990, p. 37). The use of categories is a recursive process in which a researcher revisits and amends codes as needed (Weber, 1990).

In order to analyze these data, I followed a three-step interpretivist approach (Miles, Huberman, & Saldaña, 2013). To begin, I read through all the data (i.e., lesson plans) and identified themes/patterns (e.g., teacher directs student attention to visual). These themes became codes. I determined six codes that represented increasingly more student-centered and sophisticated ways of using visuals with elementary-age students. These codes ranged from "no evidence of visuals" to "students create visuals to demonstrate new meaning." Next, I reread the lesson plans and identified instances that reflected the codes. Then, I organized the coded text into categories. Last, I revised the frameworks to encompass the three newly created categories (e.g., acknowledge, instruct, demonstrate), thus allowing me to make comparisons, identify quotes, and note patterns (Miles, Huberman, & Saldaña, 2013).

Next, a graduate student in social studies education and I (the researcher) read 13.16% ($n = 10$) of the sample lesson plans together to establish norms within these categories. Then, we read a group of 10 lesson plans independently (13.16% of the sample) in order to establish a preliminary inter-rater reliability (IRR) on the presence of visual materials in lessons. We established our inter-rater reliability to be 88.33%. In order to gain greater confidence and reliability, we independently read and coded another set of 10 common lesson plans: Our coding agreement on this set was 95%. As a result, we divided the remaining lessons equally for evaluation. We met and discussed questions or concerns that arose during this phase of evaluation. One notable point of discussion was around teacher candidates' use of film/video. If the teacher candidate used visual elements of the film to further social studies instruction, we identified it as a lesson in which visuals were used. For example, a teacher candidate showed a short film of the Pacific Northwest and asked her students to compare the environment they saw in the video to the environment students' see/experience every day. In contrast, another teacher candidate showed a video about the American Revolution and asked her students to record "10 facts they heard." Finally, the six categories were collapsed to three categories (e.g., acknowledge, instruct, demonstrate) to best convey the findings in the next section.

FINDINGS

When preservice elementary teacher candidates include visuals and graphics into social studies lessons, in what ways do they integrate these materials?

Lesson Plans

Before delving into these findings, it is important to note two points of clarification: (1) These teacher candidates were not instructed/required to include visuals in their lesson plans, and (2) the identified lessons represent the highest category evident in the lesson. Many lessons have evidence of various categories within the single lesson. The notion of "the highest level" aligns with Bloom's taxonomy (1956) and higher-order thinking skills. Those lessons identified as "no visuals" will not be described in these findings. Seventeen lessons, or 22.37% of the sample, were identified in this way. Of these lessons, many included dynamic, research-based instructional practices (e.g., using primary sources, problem-based learning); and one identified a state standard associated with visuals, but there was no evidence within the written plan. Thus, 59 lessons (77.63%) included acknowledgment, in some form, of visual material (i.e., interpretational and transformation, Levin et al., 1987) (See Table 1.1). Next, I describe each of these categories and examples of lessons and activities that exemplified the category.

Table 1.1.
Instances of Using Visuals in Social Studies Lessons (*n* = 76)

	No Use	Acknowledge	Instruct	Demonstrate
Lesson 1	8	2	1	27
Lesson 2	9	1	3	25
Total	17	3	4	52

Acknowledge. There were three lessons in which the teacher candidates simply acknowledged a visual or visuals as part of their lessons. In this category, I included a lesson in which the visual was present in the lesson as an embellishment or as decorative (Levin et al., 1987) as opposed to being used for overt instructional purposes. In one example, the teacher candidate simply included a map in the resource list of her lesson. Beyond the map being included in the written lesson plan, there was no further information provided about the ways in which this map may have enhanced instruction.

In many instances, the teacher candidates included a decorative use for visuals in addition to other categories. More often than simply including visuals in their lesson plans, these teacher candidates included opportunities for students to decorate their assignments with illustrations (Levie, 1987). For example, one teacher candidate wrote, "When children are finished, they can draw a picture on their paper." The lesson does not indicate if the picture should be content specific; it appears to be more of a classroom management technique to keep students occupied.

In addition in this category, teacher candidates often make a simple and sometimes verbal reference to a visual within the lesson. Most generally, "When we look at this painting we see the Founding Fathers signing the Declaration of Independence." There were two lessons in which two different teacher candidates included visuals but not as part of the current instruction. One teacher candidate presented a poster at the end of the lesson that she described as "a model for tomorrow's lesson." Similarly, the second teacher stated in her lesson, "I will show them the poster I created, and it will have everything we talked about so they can look at it when they are writing their poems."

In addition, maps were often references in these elementary social studies lessons. A teacher candidate working with fourth-graders designed a lesson about cultural contributions of various groups. The content standard she identified for the lesson was: "Content Standard 1.2D: Describe the diverse but unified nature of the American people by identifying the distinctive contributions to American culture of Native Americans, African Americans, major European groups, major Spanish-speaking groups, and Asian Americans" (Oklahoma State Department of Education, 2013, p. 18). She stated, "We will explore the French Quarter in New Orleans on street view of Google Maps, and students will make observations about what they see." It is unclear if there was more direct or further instruction during the lesson on how to "observe" or read a map, which is a common pitfall among practicing teachers (Brugar, 2018).

Among these data, teacher candidates referenced visuals as part of their instruction in many other lessons. These teacher candidates referenced anchor charts that were displayed around the classroom (and were most often created by their cooperating teachers).

Instruct. The instruct category describes lessons in which the teacher explicitly instructs about a content or process with a visual (Carney & Levin, 2002; Simons & Elster, 1990). There were four lessons in which teacher candidates instructed with a visual. For example, the teacher candidate presented a graphic organizer to students and instructed students about what the Venn diagram was and modeled how to use it. There was one lesson in which the teacher candidate instructed her students on ways to engage with visuals. She began this third-grade lesson about the early history of our state with:

> I will show all the students in a group at the carpet the picture that is provided below (Catlin, G., 1845) and ask them questions such as "What do you see? What is happening in the picture? How do you know?" to get them

thinking and engaged in the lesson. I want to show them this without telling them what it is to get them wondering about it and curious about what we will be discussing.

In this warm-up activity, she guided her students to use visual thinking strategies (Yenawine, 2013) in which students made observations, possibly engaging prior knowledge; presented hypotheses; and developed inquiry-based questions.

Demonstrate. The majority of lessons included opportunities for students to demonstrate their knowledge and understanding using visuals. Demonstrating knowledge and understanding varies greatly from lesson to lesson. In this category, I have included both content reproduced by students as well as opportunities for students to construct meaning using images. Among these lesson plans were 52 in which the teacher candidate created opportunities for students to reproduce information using visuals within the lesson to demonstrate meaning or understanding. In one lesson, a teacher described students organizing information into a table after discussing it as a class. "Go back over the table we made as a class" (Marti, Garcia-Mila, Gabucio, & Konstantinidou, 2011). She proceeded to say, "I will also restate what explorers go with what accomplishment so I am certain my students have the right information in their charts." In this case, the students were simply repeating/copying the information presented in class. The teacher candidate's priority was the accuracy of content within the table, but she modeled the appropriate use of this graphic device and study tool.

Throughout the examples in this category, these teacher candidates utilized a variety of graphic organizers with their students (Coleman, 2010) from cluster maps to timelines and Venn diagrams. These organizers provided students an opportunity to organize information and present what they had learned. Bridging the space between reproduction and creation were K-W-L charts. Across grade levels and social studies content, students were asked to document "what you know" (K) to create questions/points of inquiry about "what you would like to know about X topic" (W) and to describe "what you have learned about the topic" (L). Elementary students are able to use this three-column table to present what they know or have learned as well as create new questions or understandings about the topic being presented (Marti, Garcia-Mila, Gabucio, & Konstantinidou, 2011).

Within this category, there were 22 lessons (28.95%) with evidence of teacher candidates creating opportunities for students to use visuals within the lesson in a way that helped them construct or convey new understandings. For example, a teacher candidate working in a fifth-grade classroom designed a lesson in which her stated objective was:

> The students will be able to create a foldable [three-dimensional graphic organizers] to aid in defining social studies vocabulary including the words swamp, hurricane, minerals, delta, bayou, petroleum, plantation, segregation, fall line, agriculture, flood plain, and foothills, which are specific to the Southeast region.

These students had the opportunity to demonstrate their understandings through a combination of words and pictures (Schnotz & Bannert, 2003). Another teacher candidate working with fifth-graders asked her students to listen to a reading of *The Scrambled States of America* (Keller, 1998). After the read aloud: "The students will be asked to write and illustrate a comic strip that has two states talking about the experiences they had when he or she switched places." In this lesson, her students were able to communicate their understandings about state geography as well as provide hypotheses in images and written text (Cochran, DeRuiter, & King, 1993).

Misconceptions. Teachers should be knowledgeable about the content they are teaching. However, it was evident in these lessons that there were misconceptions or misunderstandings when these teacher candidates were teaching with various visuals. For example, a preservice teacher working with first-graders designed a lesson about identifying continents. In the written lesson plan, she consistently referred to maps as diagrams. A map is "a graphic representation of selected characteristics of a place, usually drawn to scale on a flat surface" (National Geographic Society, 2005), whereas a diagram is a graphic that describes a process (e.g., how a bill becomes a law). This inaccurate interchangeable use of terms has the potential to confuse students and/or present the possibility for misuse and misinterpretation of these different devices in the future. Teacher educators must recognize misconceptions and critically interrogate misconceptions with teacher candidates to help them better understand content and grow pedagogically.

Limitations

One notable limitation in this study is recruitment. The teacher candidates who participated in this study were all enrolled in the same elementary teacher preparation program at a large university. They had fairly common educational experiences. Although they were not in a formal cohort program, during the final four semesters of their program, they were taking the same classes with the same group of people. This study occurred during the third semester.

IMPLICATIONS AND CONCLUSION

There are implications of this study for educational researchers, teacher educators, and practitioners. This study contributes to understanding of (1) the visual materials elementary teacher candidates select and use and (2) the goals/purposes of elementary teacher candidates' use of visual materials for student learning in social studies.

First, in an effort to identify visual/graphical social studies materials that might be used, it is possible to develop an understanding among teacher candidates/teachers and teacher educators of available visual materials. Being aware of the visuals available, teacher educators can guide teacher candidates and in-service teachers (as part of professional development) in meaningful ways to promote inquiry using these resources (NCSS, 2013).

Second, a clearer picture of the goals/purposes for teacher candidates' use of visual materials contributes to our understanding of student learning. Teachers purposefully select materials that will best connect with their students and the content being explored, which influences students' retention of information and attitudes about content and learning (Brophy, Alleman, & Knighton, 2010). Often, visual materials are found in informational text. Engaging students in the use of all aspects of informational text may further literacy and enhance the development of social studies concepts and content beginning at the elementary level (Brugar & Roberts, 2017).

When teachers use visual materials, the potential for greater access for children is significant. As a result, meaningful social studies instruction utilizing visual materials is worth exploring for the purpose of increasing student access to and understanding of social studies (and other) materials. The use of visuals to increase student's understanding of social studies is a possible avenue for future research.

REFERENCES

Acheson, G. (2003). *Teaching the tool of the trade: An exploration of teachers' beliefs, knowledge, and practices about maps* (Doctoral dissertation). Retrieved from ProQuest Dissertations and Theses database, UMI:3117476.

Avgerinou, M., & Pettersson, R. (2011). Toward a cohesive theory of visual literacy. *Journal of Visual Literacy, 30*(2), 1–19. doi:10.1080/23796529.2011.11674687

Barry, A. (2002). Reading strategies teachers say they use. *Journal of Adolescent & Adult Literacy, 46*(2), 132–141.

Bisland, B. M. (2010). Another way of knowing: Visualizing the ancient silk routes. *The Social Studies, 101*(2), 80–86.

Bloom, B. S. (1956). *Taxonomy of educational objectives: Cognitive domain* (Vol. 1). New York, NY: McKay.

Bolick, C. M., Adams, R., & Willox, L. (2010). The marginalization of elementary social studies in teacher education. *Social Studies Research and Practice, 5*(2), 1–22.

Boyle-Baise, M., Hsu, M., Johnson, S., Serriere S. C., & Stewart, D. (2008). Putting reading first: Teaching social studies in elementary classrooms. *Theory and Research in Social Education, 36*(3), 233–255.

Brophy, J., Alleman, J., & Knighton, B. (2010). *Inside the social studies classroom.* New York, NY: Routledge.

Brugar, K. A. (2018). "We don't have students color maps anymore ..." A survey of social studies teachers' use of visual materials. *Journal of Visual Literacy, 36*(3–4), 142–163. Retrieved from https://doi.org/10.1080/1051144X.2017.1397380

Brugar, K. A., & Roberts, K. L. (2017). Seeing is believing: Promoting visual literacy in elementary social studies. *Journal of Teacher Education, 68*(3), 262–279. doi:10.1177/0022487117696280

Catlin, G. (1845). *Hunting scenes and amusements of the Rocky Mountains and prairies of America* [Painting], New York. Retrieved from https://digitalcollections.nypl.org/collections/catlins-north-american-indian-portfolio-hunting-scenes-and-amusements#/?tab=about

Carney, R. N., & Levin, J. R. (2002). Pictorial illustrations *still* improve students' learning from text. *Educational Psychology Review, 14*(1), 5–26.

Cavanagh, S. (1997). Content analysis: Concepts, methods and applications. *Nurse Researcher, 4*(3), 5–16.

Council of Chief State School Officers & the National Governors Association Center for Best Practices. (2010). *Common core standards English language arts & literacy in history/social studies, science, and technical subjects.* Retrieved from www.corestandards.org/assets/CCSSI_ELA Standards.pdf

Cochran, K. F., DeRuiter, J. A., & King, R. A. (1993). Pedagogical content knowledge: An integrative model for teacher preparation. *Journal of Teacher Education, 44*(4), 263–271.

Cochran-Smith, M., Feiman-Nemser, S., &McIntyre, J. D. (2008). *Handbook of research on teacher education: Enduring questions in changing contexts.* New York, NY: Routledge.

Coleman, J. (2010). Elementary teachers' instructional practices involving graphical representations. *Journal of Visual Literacy, 29*(2), 198–222.

Duke, N. K., & Bennett-Armistead, V. S. (2003). *Reading & writing informational texts in the primary grades: Research-based practices.* New York, NY: Scholastic.

Fingeret, L. (2012). *Graphics in children's informational texts: A content analysis* (Order No. 3524408). Retrieved from ProQuest Dissertations & Theses Global. (1039317370). Retrieved from https://search-proquest-com.ezproxy.lib.ou.edu/docview/1039317370?accountid=12964

Fitchett, P. G., & Heafner, T. L. (2010). A national perspective on the effects of high-stakes testing and standardization on elementary social studies marginalization. *Theory and Research in Social Education, 38*(1), 114–130.

Hawkman, A. M., Castro, A. J., Bennett, L. B., & Barrow, L. H. (2015). Where is the content? Elementary social studies in preservice field experiences. *Journal of Social Studies Research, 39*(4), 197–206.

Heafner, T. L., & Fitchett, P. G. (2012). Tipping the scales: National trends of declining social studies instructional time in elementary schools. *Journal of Social Studies Research, 36*(2), 190–215.

Hsieh, H., & Shannon, S. E. (2005). Three approaches to qualitative content analysis. *Qualitative Health Research, 15*(9), 1277–1288.

Keller, L. (1998). *The scrambled states of America*. New York, NY: Henry Holt.

LeCompte, K. N., & Bauml, M. (2012). Artful rights: Using images to teach the First Amendment. *Social Studies Research and Practice, 7*(2), 102–112.

Levie, W. (1987). Research on pictures: A guide to the literature. In D. M. Willows & H. A. Houghton (Eds.), *The psychology of illustration* (pp. 1–50). New York, NY: Springer-Verlag.

Levin, J. R., Anglin, G. J., & Carney, R. N. (1987). On empirically validating functions of pictures in prose. In D. M. Willows & H. A. Houghton (Eds.), *The psychology of illustration: Basic research* (Vol. I., pp. 51–85). New York, NY: Springer Verlag.

Marti, E., Garcia-Mila, M., Gabucio, F., & Konstantinidou, K. (2011). The construction of a double-entry table: A study of primary and secondary school students' difficulties. *European Journal of Psychology of Education, 26*(2), 215–234. doi:10.1007/sl0212-010-0046-1

Martinez, K. (2009). Image research and use in the humanities: An idiosyncratic bibliographic essay. *Art Documentation: Bulletin of the Art Libraries Society of North America, 28*(1), 9–15.

Miles, M. B., Huberman, A. M., & Saldaña, J. (2013). *Qualitative data analysis: A methods sourcebook* (3rd ed.). Thousand Oaks, CA: SAGE.

National Council for the Social Studies. (2013). *The college, career, and civic life (C3) framework for social studies state standards: Guidance for enhancing the rigor of K–12 civics, economics, geography, and history*. Silver Spring, MD: Author.

National Council for the Social Studies. (2017). *Powerful, purposeful pedagogy in elementary school social studies*. Retrieved from www.socialstudies.org/positions/powerfulandpurposeful

National Geographic Society (2005). *Mapmaking guide (6–8)*. Washington, DC: Author.

Nix, J. (2015). *Looking at the past: Eighth grade social studies teachers and historical visual text* (Doctoral dissertation, Georgia State University). Retrieved from https://scholarworks.gsu.edu/mse_diss/23/

Norman, R. R. (2012). Reading the graphics: What is the relationship between graphical reading processes and student comprehension? *Reading and Writing, 25*(3), 739–774. doi:10.1007/s11145-011-9298-7

Oklahoma State Department of Education. (2013). *Oklahoma academic standards for the social studies*. Oklahoma City, OK: Author.

Passe, J. (2006). New challenges in elementary social studies. *The Social Studies 97*(5), 189–192.

Pettersson, R., & Avgerinou, M. D. (2016). The teacher as information designer: Blending with confidence. In M. D. Avgerinou & S. P. Gialamas (Eds.), *Revolutionizing K–12 blended learning through the i2Flex classroom model* (pp. 69–87). Hershey, PA: Information Science Reference.

Roberts, K. L., & Brugar, K. A. (2017). The view from here: Development of visual literacy in the social studies. *Reading Psychology, 38*(8), 733–777.

Roberts, K. L., Norman, R. R., & Cocco, J. (2015). Relationship between graphical device comprehension and overall text comprehension for third-grade children. *Reading Psychology, 36*(5), 389–420. doi:http://dx.doi.org/10.1080/02702711.2013.865693

Schnotz, W., & Bannert, M. (2003). Construction and interference in learning from multiple representation. *Learning and Instruction, 13*(2), 141–156.

Shulman, L. S. (1986). Those who understand: Knowledge growth in teaching. *Educational Researcher, 15*(2), 4–14.

Simons, H. D., & Elster, C. (1990). Picture dependence in first-grade basal texts. *Journal of Educational Research, 84*(2), 86–92.

Slekar, T. D. (1998). Epistemological entanglements: Pre-service elementary school teachers' "apprenticeship of observation" and the teaching of history. *Theory and Research in Social Education, 26*(4), 485–508.

Staley, D. J. (2006). Images of *The Rise of the West:* Cognitive art and historical representation. *Journal of the Historical Society, 6*(3), 383–406.

Weber, R. P. (1990). *Basic content analysis.* Beverly Hills, CA: SAGE.

Werner, W. (2002). Reading visual texts. *Theory and Research in Social Education, 30*(3), 401–428.

Yenawine, P. (1997). Thoughts on visual literacy. Essay. In J. Flood, S. B. Heath, & D. Lapp (Eds.), *Handbook of research on teaching literacy through the communicative and visual arts* (pp. 845–846). New York, NY: Macmillan Library Reference.

Yenawine, P. (2013). *Visual thinking strategies: Using art to deepen learning across school disciplines.* Cambridge, MA: Harvard University Press.

CHAPTER 2

UNDERSTANDING THE RESEARCH ENGAGEMENT OF TEACHERS IN THREE URBAN HIGH SCHOOLS

Dante P. Petretti

ABSTRACT

Research-engaged teachers (RET) are those who participate in three research activities: reading research, conducting research, and data collection, analysis, and use. In this study, I describe the perceptions and attitudes of this often-overlooked teacher population by highlighting the intrinsic and extrinsic motivations to become and remain research engaged, teachers current level of participation in these research activities, and the ways that the RETs manage the facilitators and barriers to these activities that they encounter in their work.

In the current standards-based education climate, with mounting pressures for school and classroom-level accountability, some believe that teaching should be an evidenced-based profession, much like the medical field (Bird, 2001; Hargreaves, 1996), and as such, teachers should be "trained" to use research-based best practices to achieve a variety of aims. Often, the most important aim for members of the public is an improvement in standardized test scores. Cochran-Smith and Lytle (1999) place much of the onus for this problem on the influence of "outsiders." They note that this myopic view on standardized test scores has led to:

> research-based whole school improvement models becom[ing] increasingly widespread, the concept of best practices guild[ing] discussions about student achievement and … the authoritative role of outsiders in school improvement become[ing] the rule. (p. 22)

Often, the professional development offered to teachers working in these school environments reflects the outdated epistemology of practice of technical rationality, which reduces solutions to the problems faced by practitioners to simple questions of means and ends (Schön, 1983). Because of their tendency toward bureaucracy, some large, urban districts rely on professional development that encourages predictable outcomes (Kennedy, 1997; Weiner, 2000). Zeichner (1999) states that,

> [educational research] is often simply presented as given or used as the justification for the imposition of some prescriptive program for teachers to follow … [it] ignores what teachers already know and can do and relies primarily on the distribution of prepackaged and allegedly research-based solutions to school problems often in the form of skill training. (p. 161)

The reliance on this type of professional development to support specific training of skills for teachers could potentially contribute to a climate of stagnation and may make teachers feel less professional and effective (Kraft & Papay, 2014; Weiner, 1993).

However, there is an alternative and competing epistemology that promotes the belief that professional development should "engage teachers more fully both with (through reading) and in (by doing) educational research" (Borg, 2009). Accordingly, professional development has been metamorphosing to accommodate this shift with more and more teachers participating in inquiry-based professional development activities such as teacher research (Cochran-Smith & Lytle, 1999; Cochran-Smith & Lytle, 2001; Cochran-Smith & Lytle, 2009; Zeichner, 2003) and working in data teams analyzing state, district, and classroom data (Ikemoto & Marsh, 2007; Mandinach & Jackson, 2012; Marsh, Pane, & Hamilton, 2006). The benefits of professional development that involves teachers participating in research activities such as these are profoundly different from more traditional forms because, although the process is itself focused on evidence-based practice, teacher research does not ignore the context in which it takes place. Rather, it specifically addresses the context and makes it part of the overall process.

These activities and modes of teacher inquiry run counter to the traditional ideas of an evidenced-based view of teaching and educational research. Hargreaves (2001) suggests that the term *evidenced-based* is misleading because decisions in the classroom are never based solely on evidence and research but also "take into account a range of unique contextual factors." He believes that, instead, teaching should be considered as an evidenced-informed profession. Implicit in Hargreaves's choice of terminology is the belief that research should be one tool for teachers to use as they manage their work in their own particular contexts. Furthermore, it challenges the notion of the supremacy of traditional education research and researchers as the sole proprietors of knowledge in the field of education.

RATIONALE

The study described here was partly a response to the call made to researchers by Kennedy (1999), Weiner (1993), and Borg (2009) to address the phenomenon known as the research-practice gap that exists between education research and the classroom teacher. According to Kennedy, a common problem with researchers' thinking on the subject of the research-practice gap is that teachers are a homogeneous group that will react to and use research in the same way. Kennedy urges future research to examine that contention. Weiner suggests that in order to understand "how urban school policies and the conditions they nurture, influence teaching and learning … [r]esearchers need to reject the historic focus of most scholarship on individual characteristics of students and teachers divorced from the social conditions of urban schools" (p. 84). Lastly, Borg suggests that "localized studies of research engagement can deepen understandings of how research is perceived in particular contexts and help promote more informed consideration of feasible forms of teacher research engagement in those contexts" (p. 377).

In this chapter, I describe aspects of a larger study in which I examined the research-practice gap, and more specifically teacher research engagement, from a point of view that has generally been ignored in the research on this topic—that of the research-engaged, urban classroom teachers themselves. I accomplished this by exploring the motivations, perceptions, attitudes, and behavior of nine research-engaged teachers, three from each of three high schools in one large urban district in New Jersey.

CONCEPTUAL FRAMEWORK

The conceptual framework for the study that serves as the basis for this article is rooted in a developing grounded theory about the existing population of research-engaged teachers that have been previously overlooked by the research community. Until now, the discussion of the research-practice gap has been approached from a deficit-based perspective, which views research, researchers, and practitioners as needing to be "fixed." One example of this paradigm is Kennedy's (1997) work, in which she analyzed her own research and the research of others on the subject of the research-practice gap. Kennedy identified four possible explanations as to why research has failed to impact teaching. These are the lack of persuasiveness of research, the lack of relevance of research, the lack of accessibility to research, and educational systems that are incapable of change.

Based on the findings, Kennedy concluded that if researchers were able to make their work more persuasive, relevant, and accessible, teachers would be likely to use that research to inform their practice. In her 2012 presidential address to the American Educational Research Association (AERA), Arnetha F. Ball made similar recommendations to researchers so that their work could make more of an impact on education. While these calls for relevance, persuasiveness, and accessibility of education research are important, they highlight only one aspect of the problem of the research-practice gap. One can find little to contradict Ball's (2012) and Kennedy's (1997) calls for research to be more relevant, persuasive, and accessible. However, even if and when all of the conditions that these esteemed researchers lay out are met, the ultimate decision on whether or not to look to research as a resource, either by reading the work of others or by conducting it themselves, lies with the teachers.

In their work, Kennedy (1997) and Ball (2012) do not consider the role that teacher attitudes, perceptions, and motivations play in encouraging teachers to become research engaged. While their recommendations may help to improve education research to bridge the research-practice gap, these measures will not resolve this issue. Recommendations such as these will not explain how and why teachers are motivated to pick up a journal article or a book. They will not describe the process that brings teachers to engage in research themselves nor will they describe how motivated teachers navigate their workplaces and work situations to use research while others in similar situations do not or cannot. They do not address the issue of whether or not teachers are "ready" to be research engaged and willing to consider using research to help address problems or inform their practice. The most persuasive, relevant, and accessible journal article cannot make a teacher open a research journal and read it. Other factors conspire to make such behavior viable or acceptable and beg the question, what aspects of the teachers' background, education, personal experience, teaching assignment, work context, and so on motivate or dissuade them from seeking the solutions to their problems by engaging in research activities as part of their everyday work?

Using data on nine research-engaged teachers, this study was undertaken to answer the following research questions:

1. What are the attitudes, perceptions, and motivations that influence the beliefs of research-engaged teachers about research and its potential to inform and improve their practice?
2. What are some of the barriers and facilitators to research engagement?

METHODS

Selection of Participants

Participants for this study were selected using purposeful sampling because according to Bogdan and Biklen (1998), the selected participants "are believed to facilitate the expansion of the developing theory" (p. 65). Teachers from three high schools in Parkside were asked to take the survey on teacher research engagement, modeled after the survey used by Borg (2009). Using the descriptors of "Never," "Rarely," "Sometimes," and "Often," teachers reported their level of activity in three research-related tasks: reading research; doing research; and collecting, analyzing, and using data. The potential number of teachers to complete this survey was 161; 58, 53, and 50 from each of the three schools. The results of the survey were analyzed and scored, thereby creating a final T.R.E. score for each of the participants. The T.R.E. score was used as one of the selection criteria for the final group of study participants. Purposeful sampling was also employed to ensure that the final nine participants were as diverse as possible in terms of education, age, years of experience, and content area.

Initial Interviews

For this study, there were three phases of data collection. The first occurred shortly after all participants had been identified and consisted of an in-depth, open-ended, semistructured interview with each participant that lasted approximately 45 minutes. These interviews focused on each participant's background including but not limited to education, student teaching experience, school culture, and previous professional development. The initial interview provided the participants the opportunity to fully explain their opinions of and motivations for their engagement with the three research activities.

Journal Submissions and/or Short Interviews

For the second phase of the data collection, the participants were given the choice of providing two written journal submissions or two short, unstructured interviews. There were two submission points during the 3-month data collection period. The participants who selected the written submission forwarded their typed journal entries directly to me. The participants who selected the short interviews met personally with me, and our discussions were recorded for accuracy and later transcribed verbatim. These short interviews were teacher driven and unstructured to allow for the "add[ition] of other questions … to probe unexpected issues that emerge" (Lodico, Spaulding, & Voegtle, 2010, p. 124). This method affected the conversation length, which generally lasted approximately 15 minutes. The short interviews focused on specific facilitators or barriers to being research engaged that the participant encountered during his or her workday.

Focus Group

The final phase of data collection was a focus group of the nine participants. This focus group lasted approximately 40 minutes and was an open-ended, semistructured discussion among the participants. The interactions and group dynamics of the focus group "enable(d) participants to build on each other's comments, producing ideas or details that would not occur in individual interviews" (Lodico et al., 2010, p. 123). While the discussion was open-ended, the participants tended to focus on the similarities and differences of their experiences in terms of school settings, school culture, administrative support, professional development opportunities, and access to data. The focus group met at a comfortable location away from the school and was recorded and videotaped for accuracy.

DATA ANALYSIS

All initial interviews, journal entries and short interviews, and focus group discussions were recorded to ensure data accuracy. These recordings were then transcribed, verbatim, by a transcription service. The transcripts were reviewed and entered into the Nvivo software. I maintained all data from all study participants within the Nvivo program. Next, based on an initial, cursory review of the data, I created an initial set of code category folders called "nodes" in the Nvivo software. Specifically, these nodes described points in the teachers' reflections on their research engagement and the factors that either hindered or facilitated the use of a variety of research practices. Examples of these points were administrative support, peer support, time issues, school cultural issues, procedural issues, and professional development opportunities.

During the data analysis, additional nodes were added based on the particular descriptions and responses of the participants. For example, the node "union and contractual issues" was not initially anticipated as a necessary node and, therefore, needed to be added after the data analysis began. The coding of the data from all sources continued with the researcher highlighting each reference made by the participants and placing that reference into its corresponding node until all relevant data was coded and filed.

I used the coded data stored in Nvivo, including the results of initial interviews, short interviews, and journal entries to provide a holistic, descriptive analysis of the perceptions, backgrounds, and motivations of the participants and the ways in which they managed the facilitators and barriers to remaining research engaged over a period of time.

I employed an emergent design at the onset of the study described here because, as Creswell (2009) states, the researcher has "to learn about the problem or issue from participants and address the research to obtain [and present] that information" (p. 176). After an analysis of the data, it became evident that to address research question one, it was necessary to create profiles for each participant to best capture her or his background, perceptions, and motivations for being research engaged. To address research question two on the facilitators and barriers to research engagement, each example mentioned by the participants was explored using data from all three data sources as support. All participants are referred to in this article using pseudonyms.

FINDINGS

The data gathered in this study yielded some interesting findings that spoke to the RETs' attitudes, perceptions, and motivations that contributed to their research engagement and the ways in which they managed the barriers and facilitators of that engagement. The most pertinent results were centered around the following four major themes; life experiences, administrative support, relevance of research, and power. Additional information summarizing each participant is available in Table 2.1.

Table 2.1.
Study Participants With Demographic Data

Participant	School	Gender	Age	Educ	Content	Alt Cert?	Yrs Exp
Lucy	Abbott	F	50–59	MA	SCIENCE	N	8
Gloria	Abbott	F	40–49	BA+	ENGLISH	N	5
Monica	Abbott	F	60+	BA	ENGLISH	Y	45
Nicole	Brookside	F	30–39	BA+	SPED	N	5
Joseph	Brookside	M	30–39	BA+	SCIENCE	Y	<1
Jerry	Brookside	M	30–39	MA	BUSINESS	Y	5
Elaine	Chester	F	22–29	MA	SCIENCE	Y	< 1
Erin	Chester	F	50–59	MA+	ENGLISH	N	3
Robert	Chester	M	40–49	MA+	SPED	N	14

Life Experiences and Research Engagement

Six of the RETs in this study discussed a connection between earlier research engagement and their current research engagement. All six had some personal or work-related experience with research, had people in their personal lives who had earned doctorates, or had conducted research themselves. While this result cannot be generalizable to other settings or even other RETs, it is noteworthy.

When asked about influences possibly contributing to their research engagement, the participants attributed their attitudes to their lifelong exposure to research behaviors. Monica worked at a library and was a research librarian. Robert, Elaine, Erin, and Lucy had relatives who earned PhDs or MDs. Erin's ex-husband owned and operated a media research company, and she worked with him in that business. She also had a parent who was an academic journal editor. Jerry believed that his propensity for science was the basis for his research engagement and his work as a research scientist in public health. Monica and Lucy both talked about how their experience as mothers contributed to their development as research-engaged teachers. Although difficult to make a direct correlation between these life experiences and research engagement, the participants themselves believed that they played some role in their development into research-engaged teachers.

The three participants who did not report these early experiences with research described themselves as self-motivated learners who always looked to more knowledgeable "others" to help solve problems encountered in both their professional and personal lives. Many times, the teacher turned to a book, an article, or some other research to find the answers to their questions.

In the interviews with the research-engaged teachers, none of the participants cited professors in their graduate, undergraduate, or alternate-route teacher preparation programs as having influenced their research engagement other than providing the assignment to conduct research as part of course requirements. This fact corresponds with the participants having almost no knowledge of teacher research as a form of professional development, but it may also suggest that the propensity for research engagement starts at some earlier time in the teacher's life.

Administrative Support and Research Engagement

All of the participants described varying amounts of administrative support. The three participants from Abbott High described poor to limited support from administrators. The three participants from Brookside High described limited to mixed levels of administrative support. All six participants believed that these levels of administrative support were a barrier to staying research engaged. Conversely, participants from Chester High spoke positively about the support they received from their administrators, specifically their principal. Two of the Chester participants, Erin and Elaine, were new teachers who found the New Teacher Support Group held biweekly by Chester's principal to be positive and helpful. Elaine said:

> [The principal] has [a] novice teacher support thing that we go to every other week, once a month, it kind of depends on everyone's schedule and it's been extremely helpful because that is from the perspective of this school and everything else is from the perspective of education in general. So the fact that I can meet with other teachers who are starting out in this school is very helpful because they have a lot of the same problems that I have.

Erin also commented that "[the principal] started a novice teacher meeting, which has been really helpful."

Both Erin and Elaine noted that Chester High's principal incorporated research practices into the new teacher support group and sent the members articles to be discussed at the meeting. Elaine reported that on at least two occasions, the principal e-mailed the group participants, asking them to read a journal article in preparation for the next meeting. In addition, the principal shared articles with the entire staff, and although she did not insist that the teachers read them, she did encourage it. Elaine said:

> She has e-mailed us some articles that she'll just say, "Oh, I found this interesting." She won't make you read it, but she'll send it to you. I usually read them because if she finds them interesting, I usually find them interesting, too.

Erin also discussed this practice of her principal. She said:

> I think that [the principal] is trying. She sends us articles and stuff, and she started a novice teacher meeting, which has been really helpful. So I would say [the principal] and Suzie (another teacher) at my school are the two people that I feel I have a "meeting [of] the minds" with them.

Another example of the principal's support was acknowledging and rewarding research engagement and modeling research engagement. Elaine described a particular instance in which a teacher at Chester High sent an e-mail about a research project on which she had been working. She said, "One teacher told [the principal] something that she had done, and [the principal] e-mailed it to everybody and said, 'This is really nice; look at this.' So yeah, I guess they do—they get rewarded." Robert, the third participant from Chester High, described the principal as someone who "keeps attuned to the data" and is "a reader [who] likes to read all that [research]." All three of the participants from Chester reported that the administrative support they received was a facilitator for their research engagement.

Relevance of Education Research and the Research-Engaged Teacher

Despite the assertion that relevance in education research is very important to practitioners (Kennedy, 1997; Weiner, 2000; Zeuli, 1994), 1 participant reported a lack of relevance in some of the research he had read. Specifically, he commented about having a negative, knee-jerk reaction to research that he felt did not represent what he knew to be true of the urban classroom environment.

Despite this participant's comment, however, relevance of research to their work situations was mentioned to be important by four of the participants. Furthermore, none of the other eight participants reported dismissing any research on the basis of a lack of perceived relevance to urban schools. In fact, some participants suggested that research-engaged teachers in these urban settings demonstrated an ability and willingness to adapt or modify the findings and recommendations of research to better fit their work contexts. For example, Erin made some contradictory comments about research that applied to her particular work context as unimportant.

Yet, in a short interview, she described applicability of research as being important.

When Erin was asked about this apparent contradiction between interviews, she explained that her understanding of "applicability" led her to believe the research had to reflect her specific work context, that is, teaching English in an urban area, and so on. She went on to say that her comments about relevance and applicability referred to whether or not the research provided information that she could use in her work in a general sense, even if it meant she would have to adapt it to suit her needs and her students' needs.

Research, Power, and Urban Schools

The study participants cited many of the same barriers to research engagement as participants in other studies have (Borg, 2009; Cochran-Smith & Lytle, 1993; Mandinach & Gummer, 2013). These barriers included time pressures, lack of access to research, and unconducive school cultures. However, the intensity of these problems seemed to be magnified in this study's three urban schools. For example, Gloria was particularly vexed by problems common in many urban schools like a lack of supplies and resources and the time necessary to make up for them. She said:

> [I am always] making copies because we have no vocabulary books. We don't have enough texts. We [are] constantly making things, creating our own documentation, [asking], "Where are the questions that go with Othello?" We don't have anything that goes with Othello, yet it's [in the curriculum]. Then I have to go create everything from scratch. I just think like those little setbacks, not having a grammar book, not having a vocabulary book. Everything needs to be copied and created, so it's just time consuming and it takes away time for you to be research-engaged.

Similarly, Joseph felt that a lack of consistent technology resources led him to have to waste time that he devoted to research and resource gathering online. He said:

> Well, I may look this up and you get the work, and the computer connection is down for the day. Then, it's time where you may not have enough time to say, well, I want to try this or I want to look at this, but then something else may come up.

Monica summed up this sentiment succinctly by saying, "There's a total limit of time, there's a total limit of resources, and there's a total limit of energy."

Lucy found that some of the challenges of an urban setting also had an effect on the amount of time she could devote to research activities. She described these challenges by saying:

> Doing all the paperwork for if a student cuts the class, you know, filling out the reports for that, sending it down to the, bringing it down to the correct office, calling homes, sometimes you don't get an answer, you have to do repetitive phone calls. So there is, you know, there is just a lot of responsibility put on the teacher to make sure the student is successful, which is fine, which is fine, but it doesn't leave us enough time to be research engaged.

While time constraints are an issue for many teachers, the urban teacher participants in this study noted the lack of resources in their schools as worsening this problem. They were, in essence, spending their time developing materials, making copies, and locating physical resources because their schools were unable to provide them. The participants also cited the lack of working computers, Internet access, and necessary space as having a direct impact on their ability to remain research engaged.

A majority of the study participants referred to the lack of meaningful professional development in their schools. For many years, the subject district relied on professional development focusing on adherence to prescribed methods of instruction. Accordingly, much of the professional development opportunities tended to be "information sessions" regarding school procedures and rules rather than meaningful professional development. The new state teacher evaluation system further confounded this situation as the district was forced to allocate valuable professional development time to provide "training" for teachers in the new system, including lengthy presentations regarding the rubric used for the district's required observations and evaluations.

Finally, the participants stressed the lack of opportunities for collaboration among teachers in their respective schools. Despite the fact that each school had built "common planning time" into its schedule, something that many schools have difficulty managing, some of the participants reported that this time was often used by administrators to discuss mandates, rules, and school business. This finding echoes Weiner's (1993) assertion that urban schools often do not provide opportunities for teachers to develop professionally.

Unfortunately, the influence of the urban setting is much greater than just the increased or magnified barriers that teachers face in their efforts to remain research engaged. During their interviews, four participants all made specific comments regarding power. One described research engagement as power in that it provided her with tools that made her better able to make decisions for herself and for her students. Two expressed frustration with the fact that district administration would not be open to the opinions of teachers in the decision-making process. In the discussions related to a newsletter that focused on synthesizing current education research for practitioners, two participants discussed the frustration with the district's decision to purchase access to the publication yet only distribute it to administrators rather than the entire faculty. One participant called the process "structural hypocrisy" in that it relegated resources, in this case access to research, to only a few administrators.

This situation reflects Weiner's (1993) interpretation of Lipsky's (1980) work of the urban teacher as a "street-level bureaucrat" in that they have virtually no control or power over the pace, resources, or outcomes of their work. The street-level bureaucrat is merely given enough information for the particular segment of work for which their administrators deem them responsible. Although Weiner discusses this feeling of powerlessness in terms of the general work of teachers, the participants' comments connect this idea specifically to their attempts at remaining research engaged in an urban setting.

IMPLICATIONS AND CONCLUSION

The research-engaged teachers in this study were conscientious, dedicated individuals who used research to help them make instructional decisions during the course of their daily work. They were generally open to reform efforts and were amenable to the possibility of contributing solutions to the problems encountered in their schools. For these reasons, schools of education as well as school and district-level administrators may wish to consider ways of fostering research engagement in preservice and in-service teacher education.

The data also suggest that some of the ways to foster teacher research engagement include employing the use of data/research coaches to serve as role models and facilitators of research engagement in both preservice and in-service teacher education. Another recommendation for school districts that value these practices is offering rewards or incentives to teachers who are research engaged. Finally, districts may wish to consider professional development for administrators who focus on identifying, nurturing, and supporting job-embedded research engagement with their teachers. Efforts such as these can help administrators in urban schools to identify research-engaged teachers, encourage their involvement in improving their schools, and challenge them professionally to be the teachers that they want and need to be.

REFERENCES

Ball, A. F. (2012). To know is not enough: Knowledge, power, and the zone of generativity. *Educational Researcher, 41*(8), 283–293.

Bird, E. (2001). Teaching as an evidence-based profession. In F. Banks & A. S. Mayes (Eds.), *Early professional development for teachers* (pp. 273–296). London, England: David Fulton.

Bogdan, R. C., & Biklen, S. K. (1998). *Qualitative research in education: An introduction to theory and methods* (3rd ed.). Needham Heights, MA: Allyn & Bacon.

Borg, S. (2009). English language teachers' conceptions of research. *Applied Linguistics, 30*(3), 358–388.

Cochran-Smith, M., & Lytle, S. L. (1993). *Inside/outside: Teacher research and knowledge*. New York, NY: Teachers College Press.

Cochran-Smith, M., & Lytle, S. L. (1999). The teacher research movement: A decade later. *Educational Researcher, 28*(7), 15–25.

Cochran-Smith, M., & Lytle, S. L. (2001). Beyond certainty: Taking an inquiry stance on practice. In A. Lieberman & L. Miller (Eds.), *Teachers caught in the action: Professional development that matters* (pp. 45–58). New York, NY: Teachers College Press.

Cochran-Smith, M., & Lytle, S. L. (2009). *Inquiry as stance*. New York, NY: Teachers College Press.

Creswell, J. W. (2012). *Qualitative inquiry and research design: Choosing among five approaches*: Thousand, Oaks, CA: SAGE.

Hargreaves, A. (1996). Transforming knowledge: Blurring the boundaries between research, policy, and practice. *Educational Evaluation and Policy Analysis, 18*(2), 105–122.

Hargreaves, A. (2001). Emotional geographies of teaching. *Teachers College Record, 103*(6), 1056–1080.

Ikemoto, G. S., & Marsh, J. A. (2007). Cutting through the "data-driven" mantra: Different conceptions of data-driven decision making. *Yearbook of the National Society for the Study of Education, 106*(1), 105–131.

Kennedy, M. M. (1997). The connection between research and practice. *Educational Researcher, 26*(7), 4–12.

Kennedy, M. M. (1999). A test of some common contentions about educational research. *American Educational Research Journal, 36*(3), 511–541.

Kraft, M. A., & Papay, J. P. (2014). Can professional environments in schools promote teacher development? Explaining heterogeneity in returns to teaching experience. *Educational Evaluation and Policy Analysis, 36*(4), 476–500.

Lipsky, M. (1980). *Street-level bureaucracy: Dilemmas of the individual in public services*. New York, NY: Russell Sage.

Lodico, M. G., Spaulding, D. T., & Voegtle, K. H. (2010). *Methods in educational research: From theory to practice* (Vol. 28). New York, NY: John Wiley & Sons.

Mandinach, E. B., & Gummer, E. S. (2013). A systemic view of implementing data literacy in educator preparation. *Educational Researcher, 42*(1), 30–37.

Mandinach, E. B., & Jackson, S. S. (2012). *Transforming teaching and learning through data-driven decision making*. Thousand Oaks, CA: Corwin.

Marsh, J. A., Pane, J. F., & Hamilton, L. S. (2006). *Making sense of data-driven decision making in education.* RAND. Retrieved December 17, 2012, from http://www. rand. org/content/dam/rand/pubs/occasional_papers/2006/RAND_OP170. pdf

Schön, D. A. (1983). *The reflective practitioner: How professionals think in action.* New York: NY: Basic Books.

Weiner, L. (1993). *Preparing teachers for urban schools: Lessons from thirty years of school reform.* New York, NY: Teachers College Press.

Weiner, L. (2000). Research in the 90s: Implications for urban teacher preparation. *Review of Educational Research, 70*(3), 369–406.

Zeichner, K. (1999). The new scholarship in teacher education. *Educational Researcher, 28*(9), 4–15. doi:10.3102/0013189x028009004

Zeichner, K. M. (2003). Teacher research as professional development P–12 educators in the USA. *Educational Action Research, 11*(2), 301–326.

Zeuli, J. S. (1994). How do teachers understand research when they read it? *Teaching and Teacher Education, 10*(1), 39–55.

CHAPTER 3

ENGAGING ELEMENTARY STUDENTS THROUGH MOVEMENT INTEGRATION IN MATHEMATICS AND READING

An Exploratory Study to Understand Teachers' Perceptions

Stacia C. Miller and Suzanne F. Lindt

ABSTRACT

Movement integration is an interdisciplinary method of teaching that may lead to greater student learning outcomes and long-term knowledge acquisition. The perspectives of classroom teachers and preservice teachers toward the use of integrated movement lessons in the elementary classroom and the impact on student content retention were explored in this study. Results highlight the relationship between integrated and traditional formats, suggesting that movement integration may be a beneficial strategy as the teachers perceived students to be interested, engaged, and learning.

As teachers aim to deliver more content to students each year, they seek innovative teaching activities to help students remain attentive to the lessons and increase their retention of content knowledge. Activities that engage students' interest may lead to greater student learning outcomes and long-term knowledge acquisition (LeFevre et al., 2013); and Norris, Shelton, Dunsmuir, Duke-Williams, and Stamatakis (2015) explain that a growing body of evidence indicates that physical activity in the classroom can benefit both health and academic performance for children. The academic benefits of content-related physically active lessons in the K–12 classroom is an underexplored area, eliciting an opportunity to improve the learning environment and the accrual of physical activity.

Movement integration has traditionally been defined as any type of physical activity infused into normal classroom time, including academic lessons that incorporate physical activity, short physical activity breaks, and physical activity during transition periods (Webster, Russ, Vazou, Goh, & Erwin, 2015). Previous research establishes that teachers perceive many barriers to integrating movement (Fletcher, Mandigo, & Kosnik, 2013; Howie, Newman-Norlund, & Pate, 2014; Vazou & Skrade, 2014), but emerging evidence offers that classroom teachers may be partial to movement integration activities if the lessons are connected to the academic content (McMullen, Kulinna, & Cothran, 2014). Providing students with interesting lessons may lead to greater sustained attention, which may help students to commit concepts to their long-term memories (Hidi, 1990). This study focused on physically active academic lessons, which integrate physical activity into academic content, contributing to a child's physical activity during the school day.

The primary aim of this exploratory study was to examine teachers' and preservice teachers' perceptions on the effectiveness of using integrated movement lessons in the classroom. Furthermore, the effect of the intervention on students' concept retention was assessed as an explanatory variable. The research questions for this study were:

1. How do preservice elementary teachers and classroom teachers perceive students' interest, engagement, and learning when using integrated movement activities and when using traditional classroom activities?
2. Do integrated movement activities in the elementary classroom increase students' concept retention more than a traditional lesson?

THEORETICAL FRAMEWORK

Despite the evidence that integrated movement classroom lessons contribute to increases in physical activity, boosts in students' on-task behaviors, and greater student interest and engagement, classroom teachers may not be willing to sacrifice classroom time for physical activity because of their belief that movement detracts from academics (Howie et al., 2014; Vazou & Skrade, 2014). However, academic lessons that combine physical activity with academic content may not only increase physical activity but also engage students in learning (Norris et al., 2015). Recent research suggests that movement activities in the classroom can positively influence children's learning in math (Adams-Blair & Oliver, 2011; Martin & Murtagh, 2015) and retention in spelling (Bartholomew & Jowers, 2011). Most importantly, findings from recent research from the Centers for Disease Control and Prevention (CDC) suggest that integrating movement into the classroom does not diminish student learning or compromise learning outcomes (CDC, 2010). As much of the current research has utilized standardized testing to assess academic achievement and performance related to physical activity in the classroom (Donnelly et al., 2009; Norris et al., 2015), additional research should consider the potential for integrated movement lessons to impact student learning, engagement, and interest in the classroom setting.

Most of the existing research on academic performance and student achievement promotes physical activity infused into the class time, and the physical activity may not be related to the content taught. Integrated movement, which considers the course content, may provide not only an opportunity for students to become more physically active but may also provide students with a greater learning opportunity. Physical activity interventions incorporating physical activity unrelated to the content may positively impact learning outcomes (Erwin, Fedewa, Beighle, & Ahn, 2012), but teachers may still be reluctant to incorporate physical activity because they may perceive movement activities as taking away from class time. Research indicates that classroom teachers think more positively regarding movement activities if these activities are related to content (McMullen et al., 2014); therefore, it is important to determine how teachers perceive movement integrated activities. Research highlights that teachers' efficacy beliefs influence teaching behavior (Cantrell & Callaway, 2008) and positively relate to a teachers' willingness to integrate movement into the academic classroom (Cothran, Kulinna, & Garn, 2010; Parks, Solomon, & Lee, 2007). Bandura's (1997) theory on self-efficacy for learning, specifically vicarious experiences, was used to frame the current research.

METHODS

Participants

The study was implemented at a public elementary campus in North Texas, serving kindergarten to sixth-grade students. The school was selected for convenience. The campus demographics were 49.4% economically disadvantaged, 3.6% English language learners, and 12.1% special education. A mixed-methods embedded design (Creswell & Plano Clark, 2011) was used to address the research questions, and secondary results were used to enhance understanding of the observational data. Selected classes included second-grade mathematics and reading and third-grade mathematics and reading. Although all students in the four classrooms participated in the lessons and assessments, researchers only collected assessment data from those students who obtained parental consent and who provided assent for the research study. Data from 76 second- and third-grade elementary students (49.4% female, $n = 37$) were analyzed in the research study. The students were identified as White (71.4%, $n = 54$), Hispanic (16.9%, $n = 13$), African American (6.5%, $n = 5$), Asian (2.6%, $n = 2$), or Other (2.6%, $n = 2$).

A total of four elementary classroom teachers participated in the study because they volunteered their classes. All of the teachers were female, varying in age and in years of teaching experience. The four preservice teachers selected to implement the intervention were all female, undergraduate, teacher education students with extensive observational and teaching hours from their field experiences. Furthermore, each of preservice teachers had completed a required course, Movement Activities for Children, where they learned pedagogy for teaching in a physical environment and how to integrate movement into the classroom. Based on their success in the Movement Activities for Children course, their current GPA in teacher education courses, and their willingness to volunteer, the students were selected from a pool of students submitting applications to work on the project.

Procedures

The program was implemented for 2 weeks at the end of the school year to integrate physical activity into the regular mathematics and reading classroom. Before beginning the study, researchers, preservice teachers, and elementary classroom teachers gathered to outline intervention procedures, to design movement integration lessons aligned with the curriculum, and to align instructional and evaluative procedures.

Crossover design was used to identify any differences between participation in traditional lessons versus movement integrated lessons; the students acted as their own control. Therefore, two of the classes were the control group while the other classes received the intervention in the first week. Then, in Week 2, the classes flipped so that the other two classes received the intervention. The students attended reading and math daily, and during the intervention week each daily lesson had to incorporate movement with a focus on the academic content. During Week 1, Classrooms A and C received instruction in a movement integration format while Classrooms B and D received instruction in a standard classroom format. During Week 2, Classrooms B and D received instruction in a movement integration format while Classrooms A and C received instruction in a standard classroom format.

The undergraduate preservice teachers collaborated with the mentor teachers to select a topic for instruction as related to the curriculum in the selected grade level and course. For the movement integration lessons, the preservice teachers used the activities and objectives of the traditional lessons, shared by the mentor teachers, to search for and/or create suitable activities to align with the content that was covered. The goal was to develop movement activities with a focus on the academic content as a substitute for various components of the lessons (i.e., introduction, worksheets, assessment). For example, one of the mathematics classes was learning about lines, points, and planes. In the integrated movement lesson, the teacher taped patterns of lines to the floor in stations around the room, and students were asked to identify different points, lines, and planes by jumping, walking, and hopping the patterns. In the traditional lesson, students were given worksheets with patterns of lines and were asked to draw pictures of points, lines, and planes. In one of the English language arts classes, students were learning about emotions of different characters. In the movement lesson, the teacher had students act out emotions by playing the game of charades. In the traditional lesson, students' understanding of emotions was assessed through students' identification of faces with different emotions on a worksheet. All lesson plans were approved by the mentor teachers and were edited by the faculty researchers, both certified teachers at the K–12 level. The preservice teachers led all of the lessons, both control and intervention, in both weeks of the study, which reduced the chances of experimental contamination.

Measures

Qualitative data consisted of teacher observations and teacher education majors' reflections to answer the research question to explain how classroom teachers and undergraduate preservice teachers perceived students' interest and concept retention during each lesson. The researchers, students' regular classroom teachers, were unobtrusive, and all field notes were written during the observations (Brantlinger, Jimenez, Klingner, Pugach, & Richardson, 2005). During each lesson, classroom teachers noted students' on-task and off-task behaviors and made comments following their observations on a preconstructed observational form. In a prior meeting, researchers discussed the form with teachers, asking them to: (a) tally student off-task behaviors, which included but were not limited to daydreaming, head-on-desk sleeping, talking to students when not part of the assignment, disrupting others; (b) comment on recognizable differences in student on-task and off-task behaviors; (c) summarize the instructional environment following the lesson; and (d) discuss the engagement of the students following the lesson.

In addition, the preservice teachers completed video reflections following the teaching of lessons on the same day they were taught. As a guide in their daily reflections, researchers provided the preservice teachers with questions that asked them to consider students' engagement, learning, and on-task and off-task behaviors during the lessons. Content assessments and student interest scales were used to collect data on student interest and concept retention.

Concept retention, which varied by classroom, was assessed through lesson-specific pretests created by the preservice teachers each week. The classroom teachers shared their age-appropriate assessments to serve as templates, and the researchers provided guidance regarding the amount and types of questions. All concept retention tests had to be 10 questions, with each question worth 10 points, and a total assessment score of 100 points. Using pretests as the template, the researchers created the posttests given at the end of each week. Pretests were administered at the beginning of Week 1 and Week 2 before the teacher candidates taught the content. To determine whether learning outcomes were met, students in both classes took the content posttest over the material learned at the end of each week.

DATA ANALYSIS

Teacher Observations and Preservice Teacher Reflections

The classroom teachers' observations and preservice teachers' reflections were uploaded into NVivo 10 Software for qualitative analysis. Constant comparative analysis with member checking was used to glean classroom and preservice teachers' perspectives of students' interest and concept retention (Leech & Onwuegbuzie, 2011). First, a word frequency search was conducted using the transcribed observations and reflections. Several words and other iterations of words materialized from the frequency analysis (i.e., engage, engaged, learn, enjoyed). As related words emerged from the process, codes were developed (e.g., engaged-movement). The coding categories were compared across each of the observations and reflections to establish an overall depiction of the teachers' perspectives. Using the code categories, three themes emerged related to the research question and supported by teacher comments.

Concept Retention

To assess student concept retention change during the intervention, pretests and posttests were administered for content knowledge in both reading and mathematics classes. Each concept test was 10 questions and was scored on a 100-point scale. Results of the pretests and posttests were then scored for each student and entered into a database. Content score differences between the pretests and posttests were calculated for Week 1 and Week 2 for each subject and grade level to determine whether traditional lessons or movement integration lessons yielded higher assessment scores.

RESULTS

Teacher Observations and Preservice Teachers' Reflections

Results of the qualitative data analysis culminated in three main themes: (1) students' enjoyment of lessons, (2) students' engagement during the lessons, and (3) students' learning during lessons. Table 3.1 provides samples of participants' responses related to the themes.

Student enjoyment. Importantly, the most prominent theme of the analysis was teachers' recognition of the students' excitement and enjoyment during all lessons. The majority of responses ($n = 43$) referred to the high level of enjoyment and excitement during the movement lessons. Both the classroom teachers and preservice teachers perceived students' verbal and nonverbal actions as fun and enjoyment during the movement activities lessons. Only a few responses ($n = 7$) referred to the high level of enjoyment and excitement during the traditional lessons. One teacher wrote, "Even without the movement, the students enjoyed the lesson," while another stated, "Students really enjoyed the material."

Student engagement. Compellingly, all of the teachers remarked on students' on-task behaviors during the lessons, using words and phrases such as "participation, engaged, and paying attention." The teachers mentioned that the students were engaged, on-task, and participating during the movement lessons ($n = 25$) and during the traditional lessons ($n = 9$). One classroom teacher noted, "All kids participated in the game. Everyone actively involved," while a preservice teacher commented, "They were all so excited, on-task, working together; everybody was involved in solving equations." Most intriguing were the comments provided during

Table 3.1.
Participants' Responses Related to Students' Enjoyment, Engagement, and Learning During Movement Lessons

Participants' Responses/Role	Sample Response
Student Enjoyment	
Preservice teachers	"The students were very excited when they had created their shape and would say, 'Ms. Z, Ms. Z, come look at our shape,'" and "One of the boys came up to me afterward and said, 'Can I have another problem?' because he really didn't want to stop."
Classroom teacher	
	"Students loved the game where they did jumping jacks; they were excited and competitive."
Student Engagement	
Preservice teachers	"One of the Special-Ed students who is prone to crawling around the room was engaged in figuring out how to make different shapes with his elbow."
Classroom teacher	"Alan loved this lesson. Students were able to figure out the meanings of many common idioms. Ned was engaged more than normal. Sandy was highly engaged."
Student Learning	
Preservice teachers	"They did learn as well because we talked about it at the end about false advertisement, and they knew what it was. They were able to give examples."
Classroom teacher	"Students learned the skill quickly."
	"Singing with new words made them easy to learn."

Note: This table was created using Microsoft Word.

movement lessons about students who were typically more difficult to engage in the classroom during traditional lessons. A few of the teachers did make negative comments ($n = 10$) regarding the lack of engagement and participation during the traditional lessons, while very few negative comments were given regarding students' participation and engagement in movement activities. Teachers made statements such as "We did a worksheet for this lesson and I lost a lot of people" and "Some were bored. Very restless. Heads down."

Student learning. A final recurring theme identified by both classroom and preservice teachers was the acknowledgment of learning during the lessons. Both the classroom teachers and preservice teachers remarked about student learning during the movement lessons ($n = 20$). The teachers also recognized learning during the traditional lessons ($n = 10$) stating, "The non-movement class also learned the 9's trick for multiplication," and "They learned because we had the same kind of conversation about remembering idioms and the meaning."

Concept Retention

The results for concept retention were different for different conditions and grade levels. In mathematics, Class B and Class D had greater concept retention scores in the movement condition, while Class A and Class C had greater concept retention scores for students in the traditional condition (see Figure 3.1). In reading, Class B and Class C had greater concept gains in retention in the movement condition when compared to traditional teaching. For Class A and Class D, concept retention was better in the traditional teaching condition (see Figure 3.2).

DISCUSSION

In a time of great accountability, both students and teachers in the elementary grades may benefit from content-based lessons to help students improve and retain their content knowledge throughout the year (Browning, Edson, Kimani, & Aslan-Tutak, 2014). Continued research to develop lessons for content improvement is salient to the field of education. The purpose of this study was to explore teachers' and preservice teachers' perceptions on the effectiveness of using movement integrated lessons in the classroom. The observational and reflection data from the teachers provides evidence that the students were interested, engaged, and learning during the movement integrated lessons. Qualitative findings suggest that students were more interested in the movement activities, and this interest may have led to teachers' observed improvement in student engagement throughout the lessons (Martin & Murtagh, 2015). Consistent with results from previous studies (Bartholomew & Jowers, 2011; Mahar et al., 2006; Martin & Murtagh, 2015) increased interest from movement activities offers a significant result because previous research implies that interest is important to students' attention, motivation, and learning (Hidi & Renninger, 2011).

Study findings substantiate that if teachers perceive students are interested in lessons and learning from the movement integration, they may be willing to adopt more movement integrated lessons into the curriculum. Bandura (1997) explains that self-efficacy may increase as a result of vicarious experiences. The teachers found the movement integration lessons to be effective, which supports the notion that teachers may build self-efficacy

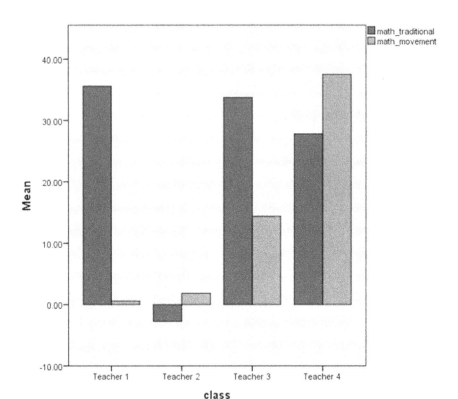

Figure 3.1. Mathematics content mean score increase by teacher.

for utilizing movement integration in the classroom, which could be related to their inclination to integrate movement (Cothran et al., 2010; Parks et al., 2007). Providing professional development opportunities supporting movement integration may be one support strategy to build self-efficacy.

Students' concept retention was also explored to determine the effectiveness of movement integrated lessons in the classroom. The results were mixed in that concept retention scores were both higher and lower when comparing the movement to the traditional lessons. These results suggest that further research is needed to determine whether movement may lead to grea

Implications for Research and Practice

One reason teachers may be reluctant to incorporate movement into the classroom is that they are apprehensive about taking away from the content

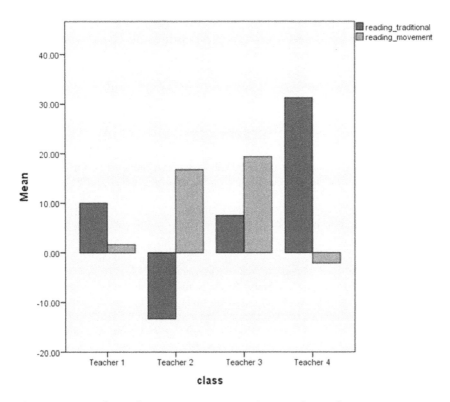

Figure 3.2. Mathematics content mean score increase by teacher.

(Morgan & Hansen, 2008). However, participating in movement activities may not negatively affect student learning as teachers often believe. The results of the current study build on previous studies, which indicate that active academic lessons may lead to improved academic achievement for some students (Donnelly et al., 2009; Erwin, Beighle, Morgan, & Noland, 2011; Martin & Murtagh, 2015). Furthermore, teachers held similar beliefs that students were interested, engaged, and learning during movement integration lessons. Following the intervention, the teachers indicated that they wanted copies of the lessons, suggesting that professional development and vicarious experiences may play an important role in shaping teachers' perceptions of movement integrated lessons.

Results from this research do offer that movement integrated lessons might provide students with greater engagement in the classroom and eliminate frequent off-task behaviors. The researchers acknowledge that movement activities may influence student learning differently relative to the content, placement of the activity in the lesson, timing of the assessment of learning, and other instructional variables. Teachers who seek to provide students with lessons that are interesting and engaging may consider integrating movement activities into the classroom, and these data provide support for further investigation of physically active lessons in the classroom and possible directions for future research studies.

REFERENCES

Adams-Blair, H., & Oliver, G. (2011). Daily classroom movement: Physical activity integration into the classroom. *International Journal of Health, Wellness & Society, 1*(3), 147–154.

Bandura, A. (1997). *Self-efficacy: The exercise of control*. New York, NY: W. H. Freeman. Bartholomew, J. B., & Jowers, E. M. (2011). Physically active academic lessons in elementary children. *Preventive Medicine, 52*(Suppl.), S51–S54.

Brantlinger, E., Jimenez, R., Klingner, J., Pugach, M., & Richardson, V. (2005). Qualitative studies in special education. *Exceptional Children, 71*(2), 195–207.

Browning, C., Edson, A. J., Kimani, P., & Aslan-Tutak, F. (2014). Mathematical content knowledge for teaching elementary mathematics: A focus on geometry and measurement. *Mathematics Enthusiast, 11*(2), 333–383.

Cantrell, S. C., & Callay, P. (2008). High and low implementers of content literacy instruction: Portraits of teacher efficacy. *Teaching and Teacher Education, 24*(7), 1739–1750.

Centers for Disease Control and Prevention. (2010). *The association between school based physical activity, including physical education, and academic performance*. Atlanta, GA: U.S. Department of Health and Human Services.

Cothran, D. J., Kulinna, P., & Garn, A. C. (2010). Classroom teachers and physical activity integration. *Teaching and Teacher Education, 26*(7), 1381–1388.

Creswell, J. W., & Plano Clark, V. L. (2011). *Designing and conducting mixed methods research* (2nd ed.). Thousand Oaks, CA: SAGE.

Donnelly, J. E., Greene, J. L. Gibson, C. A. Smith, B. K., Washburn, R. A., Sullivan, D. K., ... Williams, S. L. (2009). Physical activity across the curriculum (PAAC): A randomized controlled trial to promote physical activity and diminish overweight and obesity in elementary school children. *Preventive Medicine, 49*(4), 336–341.

Erwin, H. E., Beighle, A., Morgan, C. F., & Noland, M. (2011). Effect of a low-cost, teacher-directed classroom intervention on elementary students' physical activity. *Journal of School Health, 81*(8), 455–461. doi:10.1111/j.1746-1561.2011.00614.x

Erwin, H., Fedewa, A., Beighle, A., & Ahn, S. (2012). A quantitative review of physical activity, health, and learning outcomes associated with classroom-based physical activity interventions. *Journal of Applied School Psychology, 28*(1), 14–36. doi:10.1080/15377903.2012.643755

Fletcher, T., Mandigo, J., & Kosnik, C. (2013). Elementary classroom teachers and physical education: Change in teacher-related factors during pre-service teacher education. *Physical Education and Sport Pedagogy, 18*(2), 169–183.

Hidi, S. (1990). Interest and its contribution as a mental resource for learning. *Review of Educational Research, 60*(4), 529–552.

Hidi, S., & Renninger, K. A. (2011). The four-phase model of interest development. *Educational Psychologist, 41*(2), 111–127.

Howie, E. K., Newman-Norlund, R. D., & Pate, R. R. (2014). Smiles count but minutes matter: Responses to classroom exercise breaks. *American Journal of Health Behavior, 38*(5), 681–689. doi:10.5993/AJHB.38.5.5

Leech, N. L., & Onwuegbuzie, A. J. (2011). Beyond constant comparison qualitative data analysis: Using NVivo. *School Psychology Quarterly, 26*(1), 70–84. doi:10.1037/a0022711

LeFevre, J., Berrigan, L., Vendetti, C., Kamawar, D., Bisanz, J., Skwarchuk, S., & Smith-Chant, B. L. (2013). The role of executive attention in the acquisition of mathematical skills for children in grades 2 through 4. *Journal of Experimental Child Psychology, 114*(2), 243–261.

Mahar, M. T., Murphy, S. K., Rowe, D. A., Golden, J., Shields, A. T., & Raedeke, T. D. (2006). Effects of a classroom-based program on physical activity and on-task behavior. *Medicine & Science in Sports & Exercise, 38*(12), 2086–2094.

Martin, R., & Murtagh, E. M. (2015). Preliminary findings of active classrooms: An intervention to increase physical activity levels of primary school children during class time. *Teaching and Teacher Education, 52*, 113–127.

McMullen, J., Kulinna, P., & Cothran, D. (2014). Physical activity opportunities during the school day: Classroom teachers' perceptions of using activity breaks in the classroom. *Journal of Teaching in Physical Education, 33*(4), 511–27.

Morgan, P. J., & Hansen, V. (2008). Classroom teachers' perceptions of the impact of barriers to teaching physical education on the quality of physical education programs. *Research Quarterly for Exercise and Sport, 79*(4), 506–516.

Norris, E., Shelton, N., Dunsmuir, S., Duke-Williams, O., & Stamatakis, E. (2015). Physically active lessons as physical activity and education interventions: A systematic review of methods and results. *Preventive Medicine, 72*, 116–125. doi:0.1016/j.ypmed.2014.12.027

Parks, M., Solmon, M., & Lee, A. (2007). Understanding classroom teachers' perceptions of physical activity: A collective efficacy perspective. *Journal of Research in Childhood Education, 21*(3), 316–328.

Vazou, S., & Skrade, M. (2014). Teachers' reflections from integrating physical activity in the academic classroom. *Research Quarterly for Exercise and Sport, 85*(S1), A38–A39.

Webster, C. A., Russ, L., Vazou, S., Goh, T. L., & Erwin, H. (2015). Integrating movement in academic classrooms: Understanding, applying and advancing the knowledge base. *Obesity Reviews, 16*(8), 691–701. doi:10.1111/obr.12285

CHAPTER 4

PRACTICING SOCIAL JUSTICE EDUCATION THROUGH SOLIDARITY AND CONNECTION

Kelli Woodrow

ABSTRACT

In this ethnographic case study, the researcher examines the school-wide and everyday practices of two social justice educators situated within a school designed around social justice and equity. Findings suggest that fundamental to the social justice work permeating the school is an emphasis on solidarity and connection. Social justice educators may benefit from everyday school and classroom examples of practices and perspectives that promote social justice through a foundation in connection and solidarity.

As a graduate teacher educator in critical multicultural education, the courses I teach examine the moral, political, and ethical contexts of teaching and focus on issues pertaining to equity, access, and social justice. My students and I explore transformative perspectives and practices aimed at examining personal bias and prejudice as well as those perspectives and practices that challenge oppression and inequality. My courses are designed to link theory and practice through a combination of readings, lecture, K–12 classroom observations, and targeted reflection. While my graduate teacher education students wrestle with the controversial content, as their critical consciousness grows, they are generally eager to develop curriculum and practices that promote their emerging understandings of educational equity and opportunity for all students. The question that generally confounds my students, though, is "how"—how do teachers educate for social justice in today's sociopolitical context and educational landscape focused on testing and accountability; how does abstract social justice theory translate into everyday teaching in schools like theirs? The "how" that echoes Ladson-Billings (2015) exchanges with teacher education students where she notes that apparent resistance to social justice education (SJE) among some teacher education students is not necessarily an opposition to teaching for social justice but rather a reaction to being overwhelmed by the complex yet basic work of the job. Ladson-Billings recounts,

> ... the young man was not opposed to social justice. Rather, he was overwhelmed by the demands of a teacher education program that seemed to require him to teach students basic skills (e.g., reading, writing, and mathematics), prepare them for the information age (e.g., through science and technology), and ensure that they lived productive and enjoyable lives (e.g., through social studies, art, music, and physical education). When was he going to have time to "save the world." (p. xiv)

This young man, like my students, is seeking answers to the "how" that describes contemporary, everyday SJE practices and school structures grounded in actual teaching and learning. Unfortunately, the "how" is also elusive in both recent SJE literature and in many of the local classrooms where teacher education students observe K–12 practices.

Largely as a response to my students' questions of "how" to teach for social justice in contemporary classrooms, I conducted a semester-long qualitative research study in a private, dual-language, urban, and low-income school that operates with an SJE mission. I focused the investigation on the structural school-wide features of social justice education and the practices of two educators who are committed to social justice and whose everyday practices embody these ideals. I set out to offer my teacher education students—and others like them—a vision of what SJE looks like in real schools and classrooms like their own. In the process, I discovered that solidarity and connection—ideas absent in much of the current SJE literature—were fundamental to implementing the more common features of SJE at this school. In what follows, I describe the SJE work of the school and of the two teachers and connect and enlarge the SJE landscape through a discussion of findings about the role of connection and solidarity. I seek to make whole the circle where theory and practice inform one another.

CONCEPTUAL FRAMEWORK

The term and concept *social justice education* has gained a significant foothold in the field in the last two decades; a decade ago it was described as the "latest catchphrase" (North, 2008, p. 1182). North's document search of "social justice" in ERIC returned 475 sources, while a book search of "social justice education" in Amazon returned 3,500 titles. Today it is even more popular. In February 2018, the same search returned 12,314 sources (ERIC) and 6,239 book titles (Amazon). So, the "latest catchphrase" has not lost currency. Unfortunately, time seems to have brought little if any clarity of meaning across the many contexts in which the term is invoked (Boylan & Woolsey, 2015).

To better understand the different areas emphasized in this growing body of literature and to connect the SJE work of the school and the everyday SJE practices of the teachers in this study back to the theory, it is important to articulate a conceptual framework for social justice education. To do this, I draw on and build upon the important work of Connie North (2008), who contends that the notion of social justice education encompasses three interlocking ideas: recognition/redistribution, micro/macro, and knowledge/action.

The first of these three interlocking ideas, recognition and redistribution, refers to " 'cultural' groups claims for respect and dignity (recognition) and socioeconomic classes' demands for more equitable sharing of wealth and power (redistribution)" (North, 2008, p. 1185). The latter is similar to Boyles, Carusi, and Attick's (2009) exploration of the roots of social justice in classical philosophy where notions of justice were traced back to Plato's *Republic* and subject to Socrates questioning on "justice" and bear similarity to current formulations of social justice concerned with proportional and distributive justice.

The second of the three interlocking ideas North presents is concerned with the micro/macro level. North's macrolevel is the institutional and sociopolitical arena where policy and management are developed and implemented. North contrasts that with the micro level where face-to-face interactions occur. North argues that while the microlevel and macrolevel are often presented as a binary, in reality there is constant interplay between them—described by Nieto (2015) as the sociopolitical context containing levels of the personal, collective, institutional, and ideological. In this study, the interplay is evident through the everyday educational practices where the educators aim to foster action at increasingly higher levels of organization.

Finally, North presents a discussion of the treatment of knowledge and action in social justice education. She notes that knowledge (i.e., intellectual development) is the most commonly cited purpose of education;

however, some educational scholars advocate for broader aims that incorporate actions beyond learning about injustice to working with students to address social injustice (Ayers, Quinn, & Stovall, 2009). Furthermore, it is argued, action should address both the teaching and learning environment as well as the larger social structure (Gorski, 2018; Zeichner, 2009). Some advocates suggest that liberation is best achieved through a dialogue between local actors and institutions, explaining that a focus on both the individual and the structural is central to ending oppression.

> The concern of social justice as it is conceived here is ending that oppression. Additionally, an ongoing dialogue in which interlocutors, such as teachers, students, administrators, and parents, actively address social justice as apart from and corollary to distributive justice can serve as an emancipatory practice by identifying and eradicating the institutional and individual constructs which work to oppress members of the school community. (Boyles, Carusi,& Attick, 2009, p. 39)

These and other SJE advocates note that while a focus on the institutional and individual constructs is critical to an education aimed at ending oppression, individualized and isolated actions are not likely to bring about larger change. Rather, these social justice educators highlight the fact that only when similarly minded communities join together in coalitions might people overcome the dehumanization of oppression.

Bell (2016) describes the community-centered, connected nature of this work as social responsibility: "Social justice involves social actors who have a sense of their own agency as well as a sense of social responsibility toward and with others, their society, and the broader world in which we live" (p. 3). In this statement, Bell echoes earlier social justice advocate Paulo Freire (1970), who argues that education leading to liberation requires a view of connection and interconnection.

> Education as a practice of freedom—as opposed to education as the practice of domination—denies that man is abstract, isolated, independent, and unattached to the world; it also denies that the world exists as a reality apart from men. (p. 69)

Connection or solidarity has long been an organizing principal in struggles for equity and justice. Indeed, Martin Luther King Jr. (2013) in his famous "Letter from a Birmingham Jail," argued passionately for the project of solidarity in the face of injustice:

> Moreover, I am cognizant of the interrelatedness of all communities and states. I cannot sit idly by in Atlanta and not be concerned about what happens in Birmingham. Injustice anywhere is a threat to justice everywhere. We

are caught in an inescapable network of mutuality, tied in a single garment of destiny. Whatever affects one directly, affects all indirectly. Never again can we afford to live with the narrow, provincial "outside agitator" idea. (p. 254)

King expresses the notion that oppression is not a uniquely individual and isolated experience; it impacts all people through common destiny. King calls it a network of mutuality—I refer to this as "connection," and stemming from this connection, "solidarity," or the acknowledgment of others sharing similar feelings and experiences and potentially uniting in action.

While significant, North's conceptual framework neither focuses on the "connection" nor "solidarity." It is in this area that I intend to broaden the framework that North (2008) advances. In this study, I present a case study that highlights the common SJE practices that North (2008) discusses, while setting them in a larger project of developing solidarity and connectedness. While I use North's conceptual framework for social justice education, I am also incorporating the ideology of other social justice educators like those noted above to build an ever-evolving notion of social justice education.

METHODOLOGY

This ethnographic study was conducted over 4 months at Academy Bilingüe (a pseudonym for the actual school), a small, Catholic, urban, dual-language school serving low-income K–5 students in a Rocky Mountain city. The school was founded in 1999 to serve the needs of the working-class Latino population in the neighborhood and centers on a commitment to social justice and equality in the tradition of the Catholic faith (Our Mission, 2015). Academy Bilingüe enrolls 126 kindergarten through fifth-grade students; 90% are Latino, with an even split of learners from Spanish-dominant households and learners from English-dominant households. Ninety-five percent of the learners are on scholarship and 57% of the learners participate in the federal free and reduced lunch program. Learners enter the extended-day (8:00–4:00) program in kindergarten or first grade and exit the program at the end of fifth grade. All learners receive instruction in all subjects in both English and Spanish. This is accomplished through the use of thematic units organized around essential questions and big ideas, where the language of instruction alternates throughout the unit. Dual-language instruction is also supported by intensive second-language development blocks in the early grades (K–2) and a closed admission practice where students must begin the program in kindergarten or first grade.

Data Collection

I selected an ethnographic approach to data collection because of its ability to illuminate everyday practices and how they are produced within the community. The ethnographic data collection procedures I used included regular (two to three times a week) classroom observations over the course of 4 months and semi-structured interviews. While my early fieldnotes were relatively general—following general observation guidelines based upon the work of the theorists noted above—they grew to be more specific over time as a result of open coding. Fieldnotes were written *in situ* and expanded as soon as possible following the observation period, documenting areas that required deeper analysis (Sanjek, 1990). These expanded fieldnotes were the beginnings of theoretical memos (Glaser & Holton, 2004).

After several weeks in the classroom and having developed targeted questions, I recorded a 90-minute semi-structured interview (DeWalt & DeWalt, 2011) with each of the participating teachers, with the current principal, and with a founding member of the school. Finally, I used digital photographs to record room environment, seating information, published and handmade posters, charts, lists, instructions, and digital projections. The photographs were downloaded and saved with the fieldnotes for that day. They provided a visual record to accompany the written record.

Data Analysis

I analyzed data using the grounded theory approach (Glaser & Holton, 2004; Holton, 2007) and the qualitative analysis software *Dedoose*. I engaged in open coding throughout the data collection process, somewhat refining the focus of the observation guidelines and interview questions. I developed more detailed memos both in the expanded fieldnotes stage (as bracketed portions of the fieldnotes) and during open coding. Finally, to ensure the quality of the data, I used emerging selective coding (Glaser & Holton, 2004).

TEACHER PARTICIPANTS

The teachers in the study were selected using a theory-based operational construct sampling. This kind of participant selection is congruent with grounded theory and used when seeking to examine the manifestation of a construct or theory (Patton, 2015; Russell & Gregory, 2003). First, the school was selected based on its stated core values, "Justice, Respect,

Excellence, Community and Leadership"; its urban population reflective of the region; its high levels of academic achievement; and its service work in the community. To examine classroom practice, school administrators nominated two teachers based on the following criteria: (a) teaching multiple subjects in the general education classroom, (b) having worked in the school for several years, and (c) teaching with a focus on equity. I confirmed the nominations with follow-up observations. This particular selection criterion was important because it increased the likelihood of observing social justice teaching practices.

Audrey, Third-Grade Teacher

Audrey has spent her entire 8-year career teaching third grade at Academy Bilingüe. Growing up in a monolingual English household in the area, Audrey first learned Spanish in college, became fluent through an intensive Spanish immersion program in Guatemala, and refined her Spanish by volunteering in a community theater program in Honduras. A strong advocate for service learning, Audrey organizes the school-wide service learning program and engages her class in a monthly service learning program.

Luis, Fourth- and Fifth-Grade Teacher

Luis has been at Academy Bilingüe for 6 years, but this is only his second year as the teacher of record of the fourth/fifth-grade split. In the past, he functioned as the literacy paraprofessional. Luis grew up in South Central Los Angeles in a Spanish-dominant household and learned English in his public elementary school. He is a committed local activist, seeking to improve the out-of-school recreational sports opportunities for area youth.

FINDINGS

Although not explicitly referenced by the Academy Bilingüe teachers or administrators, an overarching theme of "connection" emerged from the data and undergirds the social justice work being done there. This orientation toward connection and solidarity is essential to Bell's (2016) definition of social justice, referenced earlier, involving individual agency and social responsibility toward increasingly broad levels of community. Solidarity or the notion of "mutuality" is evidenced in the physical classroom environment that emphasizes collaboration and community; behavior management centered on restorative justice intended to correct the damage or harm caused to the individual and the community; and curriculum designed with an emphasis on connecting the school, class, and students with increasingly larger circles culminating with the global community.

Physical environment. The physical environment often conveys a "hidden curriculum" that can reinforce the stated mission and goals of a school or offer an alternative message to those ideals. The powerful mural projects around both the interior and exterior of the school convey messages of hope and justice. Figure 4.1 depicts a mural of intellectual and social justice leaders together with Academy Bilingüe students, teachers, and community members and suggests that all people share the same canvas and tree of life. This mural is on display across the entire library wall and demonstrates how the school's physical environment reinforces the ideals of the school.

Figure 5.1. Love One Another mural.

Classroom space. A visit to Luis's or Audrey's classroom reveals an overt message of justice and more nuanced messages of connection and social responsibility. Both classrooms have a somewhat homey feel with live houseplants and classroom pets and overtly promote issues of social justice through wall coverings and bulletin boards. Much of the overt messaging is evident in locally produced material that is created in class and related to the curriculum. For example, Luis's walls and bulletin boards are covered in content related to the essential question guiding the unit of study and feature historical documents and images from the Library of Congress, Prints, and Photographs Division. For example, during the social studies unit focused on the question "How could we work for social and economic justice?" Luis presented the early history of the United States through examining the history of slavery and emancipation. Students created large timeline posters on butcher paper using the images to locate various events. These timeline posters crowd the back wall, while other justice-centered messages speak to students' rights in the classroom and the world. For example, Audrey's classroom features a students' rights bulletin board created by members of the classroom community and includes a poster adapted from "The United Nations Convention on the Rights of the Child" and a section on students' rights in the classroom that were developed collectively. There are also more traditional classroom wall coverings such as class schedules, world maps, writing process posters, number lines, and posters that name emotions. All of the written material appears in both English and Spanish.

In addition to these materials, overt messages of social justice, connection, and social responsibility are conveyed through the use of space and posted classroom duties. Both classrooms feature a variety of spaces designed for collaboration and dialogue; student work spaces are table groupings, small spaces set aside for peer conflict mediation and resolution and a large, open, carpet area near a whiteboard and projector. These ideas are further reinforced through postings of rotating duties, including table leaders, pencil sharpeners, rabbit hutch cleaners, and garbage collectors.

Behavior management and discipline. Restorative justice is a building-wide expectation for any kind of conflict. Academy Bilingüe teachers engaged in professional development focused on the principles and practices of restorative justice, therefore, the language of peer mediation and conflict resolution is shared across classrooms. Both teachers in this study have spaces devoted to peer conflict mediation, yet classroom management differs between the two classrooms. Audrey's classroom management appears more traditional, featuring some elements of reward and consequence. Luis conversely does not apply rewards and consequences. When asked about his management practices, he stated, "I do not believe in rewards and consequences. I want to encourage the students to make the right choices because it benefits them and their classroom community." Indeed, Luis rarely publicly addresses behavior issues; instead, when a student is disruptive, Luis often approaches the student and begins working alongside him or her. On occasions where off-task or disruptive behaviors are more widespread, Luis speaks to the class as a group and shares his feelings and thinking with the students.

The intended and enacted behavior management practices correlate loosely with notions of recognition that are equated with "respect and dignity" (North, 2008, p. 1185) and convey a perspective toward the student (s) as one of mutual interdependence and compassion. Jesuit priest and activist working with gang-affiliated youth in Los Angeles, Father Gregory Boyle (2011) describes compassion as "being anchored in some profound oneness with them" (p. 72). It is being one *with* others not one *for* others that Father Boyle references. Boyle adds, "Compassion is always, at its most authentic, about a shift from the cramped world of self-preoccupation into a more expansive place of fellowship, of true kinship" (p. 72) and the fruit of that compassion is a "palpable sense of solidarity among equals, a beloved community" (p. 80).

Curriculum. Academy Bilingüe only purchases prepackaged curriculum in math; the remaining content areas are connected to one another and taught through locally developed curriculum using a thematic approach organized around an essential question and subject-specific big ideas. This approach is illustrated through a closer look at how Luis worked through this process. Luis first identifies the essential question framing the unit in his fourth/fifth-grade classroom: "How could we work for social and economic justice?" Once the essential question has been identified, grade-level state content standards for each subject are then aligned with the essential question and are developed into the big idea adapted for the dual-language environment. So, in this case, Luis adapted several fifth-grade social studies standards to result in the following big idea: "The historical development of human rights and social justice in the United States and Mexico are fundamental to shaping our country, our community, and our lives." Finally, the teacher synthesizes all of this information to shape the learning targets: In Luis's unit, the related learning target became "I can describe how the Emancipation Proclamation and the Guerrero Decree impacted legal slavery."

Luis and Audrey apply social justice themes in social studies as well as in most of the other content areas through the content they select rather than through the standards. In other words, they foreground the essential question, then they think of (or find) content that proves a good segue into the big idea rather than teaching to the standard; they match the standards to their content rather than the reverse. For example, Luis applies the same essential question "How could we work for social and economic justice?" to literacy focused on narrative (historical fiction) and expository (nonfiction text, biographies) texts addressing reading strategies, point of view, and textual evidence. Luis chooses themed curricula first and only then ties it to standards. He meets state standards, but his first priority is to find the right content for his school and classroom context.

As suggested in the lesson examples, the material the teachers select is designed to build students' knowledge of injustice, struggle, and action—relating back to North's (2008) interlocking theme of justice and action. The curriculum is intended to develop learners' understandings of themselves and others in the world and their agency to affect positive social change. Elva, the founding member of the school and instructional architect, explains a little more about the philosophy of Academy Bilingüe's thematic units:

> So basically we create three units for each year, one for each quarter. So we organize the curriculum into essential questions. So, for example, rather

than teaching a traditional Native American unit that inculcates a lot of stereotypes, we create a unit about the indigenous people and their struggles for life, land, and liberty. We incorporate the Zapatistas into that unit, we incorporate the Wampanoag into that unit, who struggled for clean water and unpolluted land. We incorporate the Mayans into that unit, so we look at indigenous peoples, but we start with who are indigenous people today.... We have parents join us at different times during the unit, where parents also tell stories of times they had struggles for life, land, or liberty.

Careful thought of representation of the "other" is evident in the development of the Native American unit and addresses issues of recognition. Furthermore, this unit, organized around the question "Who are the indigenous people of the world?" and "How have they struggled for life, land, and liberty?" not only offers an opportunity to examine the connection different oppressed people experience, it also grounds that understanding in how it has been experienced by the student and his or her family, making visible the network of mutuality that King (2013) addresses. These thematic units include an orientation toward both the macro (the larger world issues) as well as the micro (students' individual and collective cultural experiences) (North, 2008), where students, parents, and teachers mutually navigate meaning via dialogue.

Community meeting. Though less overtly centered on social justice, school-wide community meetings offer the time and space to students and teachers to create community in the classroom through relationship building and shared understanding. Students returning from lunch/recess meet in a circle on the carpet, where their teacher poses a question such as "If you could have lunch with any four people from any time in history, who would you invite?" or "What are you doing in the moments you feel happiest?" During this time, the power dynamics are shifted to be more flat than in the other spaces of practice, and the teacher engages with students as facilitator/mentor. As is evident in this excerpt from a community meeting, Luis even uses social justice as a means to manage student behavior during these community meetings:

(Kids comment to one another enthusiastically—overlapping speech.)

Luis interrupts their lively conversations, "We are doing social justice. One way to practice is by listening when others are speaking. When you have the ball, it is the only time you can speak."

(The ball is passed, and students take turns sharing their thoughts.)

In this example, Luis offers purpose and relevance to the work by explaining the relationship between the community meeting activity and their broader goals of social justice. He makes students actors in social justice through respectful listening. This community meeting structure offers the opportunity to build positive social identities, to see a relationship between these identities and school, and to begin work as actors advancing toward social justice. It offers a "knowledge and action" opportunity on a micro-level while developing students' social responsibility within community.

Service learning. The community at Academy Bilingüe practices service learning as a way to connect and authentically discover the value of human relationships and mutuality. In kindergarten and first grade, service learning focuses on connecting with others in the school through cross-age "readers," students who are paired up to read to one another across classrooms. Beginning in third grade, service learning extends beyond the school for each class in different ways. On a monthly basis, Audrey, for example, engages her students with seniors at a local senior care facility; students in Luis's class host a number of community soccer events.

As a building-wide effort, once a year the school community works together in service. Service opportunities are posted several weeks in advance, and students sign up for his or her desired service opportunity. Audrey organizes the service day for the whole school, and in the interview, she shared that it has become such a popular tradition that many of the parents take days off of work to participate alongside their children. Elva noted that they work with the children to see service not as charity but as a reciprocal experience:

> When that charity issue was really important, was when we were going out into the community. That we benefit from the experience as well. And we did that *abuelitos* (grandparents) program where they would interact with the elderly at the community house.... After an activity, we always talked about how did you benefit from that experience? Not just that we're doing things for others, with a charity model, but when we help others in the community and interact with others in the community, what do we learn and gain from it.

Like the strategies around behavior management, the service learning experiences afford students the opportunity to grow their community, to practice compassion, to be one with others. The practice of service learning at Academia Bilingüe is part and parcel of social justice education in the mold of action and community, aligning with both notions of connection and action (North, 2008) as well as building students' agency to positively impact social conditions at increasingly higher levels of organization.

Connection through homework. Academy Bilingüe addresses student/family relationships both at the school through a variety of events and at home through homework. The relationship maintenance and development work that the school does intentionally connects the school and home and the student, parent, and teacher; it also establishes a family routine and identity that include school and schoolwork. Elva explained that there was common homework was shared across classrooms that called for parents' direct involvement in homework.

> We use [the class] syllabus to support that work: what they should be reading about at home, what they should be getting at the library, and to direct some of the current events work. So then that pairs with what teachers are doing at school.

This homework expectation not only encourages student and parent connection but also a broader understanding of their relationship and place in a global community—and validates family knowledge as integral to student learning and relevant to macrolevel issues (North, 2008). All students in the school have a common current events assignment that they work on in the classrooms during the week and do in collaboration with their families on the weekends.

DISCUSSION AND CONCLUSION

The work of solidarity and connection evidenced in Academy Bilingüe functions to contextualize, support, and encourage the larger social justice project. Freire (1970) explains the value of this approach in social justice education:

> Students, as they are increasingly posed with problems relating to themselves in the world and with the world, will feel increasingly challenged and obliged to respond to that challenge. Because they apprehend the challenge as interrelated to other problems within a total context, not as a theoretical question, the resulting comprehension tends to be increasingly critical and thus constantly less alienated. (p. 69)

While educators and social activists such as Paulo Freire, Dr. Martin Luther King Jr., and Father Gregory Boyle highlight the primacy of solidarity, there are few concrete examples of how solidarity manifests in local educational practice. Academy Bilingüe focuses on both solidarity and connection through a curriculum centered on social justice knowledge and action (North, 2008). These ideals are evident in the many school-wide structures such as the public art in the physical environment, school-wide behavior management, and curriculum design. The teachers play an integral role in implementing these ideals through their arrangement of the classroom spaces, classroom behavior management, and classroom instruction. The teachers' everyday practices embody the three interlocking elements of social justice education (North, 2008) enacted in tandem with more fundamental notions of solidarity and connection (Bell, 2016;

Freire, 1970; King, 2013) and may offer a grounded vision of SJE practice in actual schools and classrooms to those seeking examples of theory in action. Furthermore, teacher educators seeking to develop transformative teachers may find that teacher education candidates are better able to translate these frameworks to actual practice in social justice classrooms where the heterogeneity of the community oftentimes demands solidarity to generate collective action. Mutuality and compassion related to connection and solidarity may be the most fundamental of the ideals that social justice educators seek to foster.

Theorizing local situated practice by mapping theory to real teaching and learning closes the circle between social justice education theory and everyday practice. Though this study was small and conducted in a particular context, it offers a vision of enacted SJE that may guide others working in this area. To promote social justice education, particularly in teacher education, more studies of contemporary everyday practices of social justice educators, schools, students, and communities are necessary, particularly so when embedded in schools that may not share an SJE orientation.

ACKNOWLEDGMENTS

I am grateful to Academy Bilingüe students, teachers, and administrators for sharing with me their important work. I appreciate my students for challenging me to offer a balance of practice and theory. I am thankful to the editors and anonymous reviewers of CTD for carefully and thoughtfully critiquing my chapter.

REFERENCES

Ayers, W., Quinn, T. M., & Stovall, D. (2009). Preface. In W. Ayers, T. M. Quinn, & D. Stovall (Eds.), *Handbook of social justice in education* (pp. xii–xv). New York, NY: Routledge.

Bell, L. A. (2016). Theoretical foundations for social justice education. In M. Adams & L. A. Bell (Eds.), *Teaching for diversity and social justice* (pp. 3–26). New York, NY: Routledge.

Boylan, M., & Woolsey, I. (2015). Teacher education for social justice: Mapping identity spaces. *Teaching and Teacher Education*, *46*, 62–71.

Boyle, G. (2011). *Tattoos on the heart: The power of boundless compassion*. New York, NY: Simon and Schuster.

Boyles, D., Carusi, T., & Attick, D. (2009). Historical and critical interpretations of social justice. In W. Ayers, T. M. Quinn, & D. Stovall (Eds.), *Handbook of social justice in education* (pp. 30–42). New York, NY: Routledge.

DeWalt, K. M., & DeWalt, B. R. (2011). *Participant observation: A guide for field workers.* Lanham, MA: Rowman Altamira.
Freire, P. (1970). *Pedagogy of the oppressed.* New York, NY: Seabury Press.
Glaser, B. G., & Holton, J. (2004). Remodeling grounded theory. *Forum Qualitative Sozialforschung/Forum: Qualitative Social Research, 5*(2), Art. 4. Retrieved from http://nbn-resolving.de/urn:nbn:de:0114-fqs040245
Gorski, P. C. (2018). *Reaching and teaching students in poverty: Strategies for erasing the opportunity gap.* New York, NY: Teachers College Press.
Holton, J. A. (2007). The coding process and its challenges. In A. Bryant & K. Charmaz (Eds.), *The SAGE handbook of grounded theory* (pp. 265–289.) Los Angeles, CA: SAGE.
King, M. L., Jr. (2013). Letter from a Birmingham jail. In A. Kavanagh & J. Oberdiek (Eds.), *Arguing about law* (pp. 254–264). New York, NY: Routledge.
Ladson-Billings, G. (2015). Foreword. In K. Kumashiro (Ed.), *Against common sense: Teaching and learning toward social justice* (pp. xvii–xxviii). New York, NY: RoutledgeFalmer.
Nieto, S. (2015). *The light in their eyes: Creating multicultural learning communities.* New York, NY: Teachers College Press.
North, C. E. (2008). What is all this talk about "social justice"? Mapping the terrain of education's latest catchphrase. *Teachers College Record, 110*(6), 1182–1206.
Our Mission. (2015). [Brochure]. Denver, CO: Academy Bilingüe.
Patton, M. Q. (2015). *Qualitative research &evaluation methods: Integrating theory and practice.* Los Angeles: CA, SAGE.
Russell, C. K., & Gregory, D. M. (2003). Evaluation of qualitative research studies. *Evidence Based Nursing, 6*(2), 36–40.
Sanjek, R. (Ed.). (1990). *Fieldnotes: The makings of anthropology.* Ithaca, NY: Cornell University Press.
Zeichner, K. (2009). *Teacher education and the struggle for social justice.* New York, NY: Routledge.

CHAPTER 5

AUDIO FEEDBACK ON STUDENT WRITING

Could Voice Recording Foster the Tenets of Care Theory?

Gregory Chalfin

ABSTRACT

Audio commentary on student writing has yet to become a mainstream method of grading practices. However, in considering the impact of voice recording in fostering the tenets of Nel Noddings' care theory, the author finds great potential for the practice to realize Noddings' tenets of developing a practice of care: modeling, dialogue, practice, and confirmation. The development of this method could have significant implications for caring educational practice.

I never liked English much more than I liked any other subject. After all, they stood in the way of getting to soccer or basketball practice. Ninth-grade English was particularly harsh. I struggled to find relevance to any part of the course. However, my experience with English, with writing, all changed when I became a sophomore. Ms. Alice Knox had taught at my high school for decades, and when I entered her class, she had what seemed to me to be a strange request: Turn in your next paper with an audio cassette tape. Indeed, Ms. Knox would narrate comments of feedback to us after returning drafts of our papers.

Now, more than 15 years later, in developing my own practice as a teacher, I have realized that I have, with help from colleagues, developed an Internet-age version of Ms. Knox's cassette tape narrations using software called Jing to record audio comments over a screencast of the student's electronically submitted paper. Papers on *1984* can now include the narrative, detailed feedback capable of being rendered in 2017. This chapter will explore how audio feedback on student papers can have meaningful impact for students as they are assessed on their writing and develop the implications that this method of feedback has in fostering an ethic of care that aligns with the vision of educational theorist Nel Noddings.

LITERATURE REVIEW

The technological innovation of audio feedback on student writing is not a new one. Indeed, Ms. Knox employed cassette tapes long before I was her student in the early 2000s. As Cavanaugh and Song (2014) writes, "Analyses of the use of audio feedback were conducted as early as the 1970s when instructors experimented with giving audio comments to students using cassette tapes" (p. 123). Dixon (2015) adds, "From the 1980s onward, researchers suggested that teachers use a tape recorder for recording responses to written work as an alternative to the 'less instructive' comments written in the margin of a paper" (p. 96).

As digital media has become more commonly available, the use of audio feedback has evolved and has pervaded the educational landscape. The goals of the use of such technology, done in a variety of forms, were to provide more personalized and effective instruction to students on their writing and to help humanize a school process that, in its worst forms, can feel dehumanizing. As Dixon (2015) writes, "In the [United Kingdom] Higher Education sector, National Student Survey (NSS) results consistently show lower satisfaction scores for assessment and feedback than for other aspects of students' learning experiences" (p. 96). Technology often can be guilty of contributing to such depersonalization. A face-to-face conversation becomes a chain of e-mails. An in-person class moves online. Lecture notes move to Khan Academy. Screens become ever more central to a student's school experience. In this case, however, technology can aid a student's experience. The use of audio feedback to provide student feedback could help to improve a marginalized aspect of students' experiences.

In general, research has shown the use of audio feedback to be received positively by students and to contribute to a sense of pastoral care (Dixon, 2015) from their teachers, in comparison to traditional notions of written feedback on student writing. As Dixon (2015) noted, this juxtaposition of technology humanizing the writing process may seem ironic: "If we can recognize that the use of technology contributes to a dehumanizing process in Higher Education, there is an implicit irony that increased use—that of audio feedback—may help to alleviate this" (p. 101). Some of the current literature (Ice, Curtis, Phillips, & Wells 2007; Wolsey, 2008) indicated adoption of this technique in online courses where in-person, face-to-face conversations about a writing assignment are not possible. Other articles (Bauer, 2011; Gould & Day, 2013; Merry & Orsmond, 2008) suggested that adoption of audio feedback has also occurred in traditional classroom settings.

The literature reveals that the goals of teachers who use audio feedback can be categorized into a triad of themes: positive impact on student engagement and performance, greater comprehension of feedback, and an increased feeling of being cared for, resulting in greater motivation in the writing process.

The results of the literature bear out that these goals are often met. With respect to student engagement and performance, most students provided audio feedback report positive feelings about its impact on their work and on their engagement with the writing process. Indeed, Bauer (2011) writes of how her students felt "personally engaged in the process of receiving feedback with their frequent references to their feelings and level of confidence" (p. 65). Gould and Day (2013) build on this idea of positive impact on student engagement and performance through their quantitative study that revealed that between 80 and 90% of the respondents in their survey of nursing students at a British university felt that audio feedback "contributed to their learning" (p. 559) and enabled improvement in the quality of the final piece of work.

Additionally, audio commentary provides a remedy to some of the challenges of comprehension that come with traditional written feedback. Students do not have to contend with illegible handwriting (Merry & Orsmond, 2008, p. 7), nor do they have to "decode [the teacher's] handwritten remarks in the margins" (Wolsey, 2008, p. 321). Moreover, when students meet with teachers about illegible or incomprehensible written comments, they often forget what was said during a one-on-one meeting. Audio commentary allows students to review their teachers' comments multiple times by replaying the recording at their leisure. Bauer (2011) reports that her students replayed the comments offered often, thereby strengthening their comprehension of her feedback:

> Since students reflected on their experience days after listening to audio comments, their recollection of specific suggestions indicates that they listened carefully and repeatedly, thus maximizing the benefit of the feedback and increasing the likelihood that they have internalized advice and will be able to access it in future writing situations. (p. 66)

Finally, and most importantly for the purposes of this manuscript, teachers use audio comments to demonstrate care toward the ends of increased motivation among their students. Cavanaugh and Song (2014) found that "students in the study noted that the instructor's tone was quite favorable when receiving audio comments. They found [the tone of comments] in contrast to the tone communicated in written format" (p. 126). Bauer (2011) uses praise frequently in her audio comments, and "not only is this kind of information a pleasure to receive, it provides the writer with a template for following one successful performance with another in the future" (p. 65). Merry (Merry & Orsmond, 2008) discovered that the students in her study found the "feedback more personal or that it showed that the tutor [teacher] cared about the work" (p. 7). All of these aspects contribute to a stronger student-teacher relationship. These relationships are the foundation of care theory, a theoretical construct that has been developed over the past 30 years.

THEORETICAL FOUNDATIONS

Care theory was born out of the ideas of Carol Gilligan and Nel Noddings (McKenzie & Blenkinsop, 2006, p. 91). Born out of the work of her 1982 book, *In a Different Voice: Psychological Theory and Women's Development*, Gilligan (1982) posits that people "puzzle through moral dilemmas using two different value systems: what she called the 'ethic of justice' and the undervalued 'ethic of care' " (Graham, 2012). Building on ideas of feminist thought, Gilligan argued that while "men make decisions based on individual rights ... women are concerned with responsibilities to others" (Graham, 2012). Nel Noddings built on Gilligan's work in the educational realm, demonstrating how caring relationships could "dismantle the often rigid and oppressive student-teacher relationship models that view students as receptors of the teacher's knowledge and, in effect, construct barriers to [the teacher's] and [one's] students' education and learning" (Barrow, 2015, p. 47). In short, for Gilligan and Noddings, in contrast to an ethic of justice, moral dilemmas require participants who need "to talk to the participants, to see their eyes and facial expressions, to receive what they are feeling" (McKenzie & Blenkinsop, 2006, p. 93).

Given its relation to and focus on educational environments, Noddings's care theory is the focus of this discussion. Four main components comprise her ideas of how to best develop and inculcate a philosophy of care: modeling, dialogue, practice, and confirmation (Bergman, 2004, p. 154). All elements have a relationship with audio commentary to be explored.

By modeling, Noddings is alluding to the notion that care theory has to be shown to students through the actions of the adults in the community: "Thus we do not merely tell [our students] to care and give them texts to read on the subject; we demonstrate our caring in our relations with them" (Noddings, 1995, p. 190). Modeling strengthens the student-teacher relationship, demonstrating a care for the students' input to the process. In using audio commentary, teachers are demonstrating that the paper is more than something just to be written on, handed back, never to be seen again. They are modeling that they care about more than the words on the page. They care about the receipt of feedback by the student. This is imperative to Noddings's (2005) understanding of care, which is a relationship that involves "a connection or encounter between two human beings—a carer and a recipient of care, or cared-for" (p. 15). In caring relationships, both parties must be engaged with and receptive to the encounter. Audio commentary facilitates such a relationship between teacher and student.

Noddings builds on the notion of modeling with the tenets of dialogue, practice, and confirmation and these tenets demonstrate that teachers can serve as role models for students to learn principles of care (Bergman, 2004, p. 155). Here, we see that Noddings understands these tenets as fluid and overlapping, building off one another. They are inclusive, asserting that "in the caring relations of parenting and teaching, interests of children accompany basic needs and wants. Parents and teachers need to know the children in their care and know what is interesting to them" (Stone, 2006, p. 30). These tenets serve as guides toward a moral education, helping educators, who are continually developing themselves, "experience a satisfying completion when he sees his caring received with care, when he sees a student growing in care for others and her own ethical ideals" (Bergman, 2004, p. 156).

Over the past 30 years, care theory has developed to inform schools in important and significant ways. Noddings has described central goals for setting up schools in the spirit of honoring care theory. She makes suggestions that include having students stay together for multiple years, eliminating comparative grading practices, and having students study what it means to care (Stone, 2006, p. 26). Moreover, Noddings has offered curricular wisdom, asking teachers to consider caring centers that examine various aspects of the relational and natural world, including how we care for the environment, one's self, and others. Each of these comes back to Noddings's central goal for schools: "The main aim of education should be to produce competent, caring, loving, and lovable people" (Noddings, 2005, p. 174).

These suggestions seem straightforward, but as Barrow (2015) acknowledges, being a caring teacher in the modern age can bring about complexity, especially when boundaries between students and teachers become ambiguous. Where does the distinction from faculty to friend disappear? When, if ever, is such an erasure of the distinction appropriate? As Meyers (2009) writes: "Effective, caring faculty members balance their connection with students by setting limits as needed, by enforcing classroom policies in consistent and equitable ways, and by maintaining democratic and respectful authority in the college classroom" (p. 207).

Ultimately, care theory comes down to basic relational elements: "For Noddings, the potential cared-for must be brought into proximity with the one caring-for and must be receptive to and acknowledge that proffered care" (McKenzie & Blenkinsop, 2006, p. 97). Relationships in schools inform our discussion of how the aims of audio commentary on student writing fit with the tenets of care theory. Moreover, through the lens of Noddings's care theory, educators are able to reenvision how audio commentary might fulfill the intentions of care theory were it to be altered or implemented in a distinct fashion. Already, elements of this feedback revolution are beginning to occur in some educational settings, including online educational environments (Ice et al., 2007; Wolsey, 2008). Specific recommendations of the use of audio commentary that embodies the spirit of care theory follow in the next section.

RECOMMENDATIONS

Audio commentary already fits with many of the tenets of care theory. It provides an opportunity for teachers to provide a greater quantity of feedback and thus, an ability to provide greater individual attention. While the margins of pages limit teachers to writing only nominal comments at the edges, a teacher, through audio commentary, can act as though sitting next to a student, highlighting different passages and commenting in greater depth and detail in the moment the student is reviewing their paper. While it is true that teachers can, and often do, write longer narrative comments at the end of a paper, audio commentary allows students to receive in-depth feedback as they go through it instead of having a general comment at the end of the paper. As Bauer (2011) writes, "I was able to incorporate many elements of a successful writing conference such as making a personal connection and getting to know the writer" (p. 65).

Successful writing conferences are ones that meet the demanding requirements of an ethic of care. As Noddings (2005) writes, an ethic of care is one that involves what she describes as "motivational displacement" (p. 16). When this occurs, the one caring-for is completely engaged with the cared-for, and the cared-for exudes qualities of "reception, recognition, and response" (p. 16). To provide audio commentary, to speak about a paper, a teacher must be fully engaged with doing so, and a student must really listen to what is being said. For the teacher, shorthand comments do not suffice, and attention to elements like tone, pace, and emphasis are required. For students, receiving feedback requires sustained attention and a willingness to listen, a skill unto itself. Scanning comments in the margin is not enough. While teachers, myself included, would love to conference individually with every student about every paper, logistical demands of time rarely allow for such meaningful meetings to consistently take place without devoting significant portions of class time to do so. Instead, audio commentary can place the reader and writer in the same virtual room, allowing the teacher to navigate and negotiate tone and emphasis in a manner that other forms of feedback cannot.

Moreover, when done well, audio commentary fits with care theory in that it centrally fulfills Noddings's tenets of modeling and confirmation. Teachers model, defined as "purposefully exhibiting a specific behavior" (Shadiow, 2009, p. 198), their care by talking through both the positive areas of improvement and the areas to improve. Moreover, they encourage the writer through their words. The most effective audio comments always demonstrate positivity toward and belief in the student as writer. For example, in suggesting to a student a way to change their paper, I would be able to begin the statement by offering a comment about a piece of the paper that I like: "I really like the way you've provided specific detail here, but it might be helpful to re-structure this sentence so it uses an introductory clause to improve the fluency of this sentence." Through audio commentary, I can demonstrate to the writer how the writing sounds when read aloud, thereby helping the author hear places of awkwardness with grammar, diction, and sentence structure. Such an explanation potentially provides more context for students revising their work.

Moreover, this is important in thinking about feedback models applied in other settings. As one *Harvard Business Review* article entitled "The Ideal Praise-to-Criticism Ratio" notes, the highest-performing teams in business settings had the highest ratio of praise-to-critique, with nearly 6 comments of praise for every 1 criticism (Zenger & Folkman, 2013). Students, too, like to hear praise while receiving feedback. As Gould and Day (2013) report, "Most students in the study found audio feedback supportive" because the feedback was "'sensitive, positive, and improved my confidence'" (p. 561). When teachers are thoughtful and affirming in their feedback, the goals of care theory begin to align with the impacts of audio commentary.

Audio commentary, however, still has ways it could be reimagined to more closely align with the Noddings (2005) vision of producing individuals who prioritize care. Notably, Noddings's tenets of dialogue and practice could become more central to the application of audio commentary on student writing. In so doing, teachers could reenvision the ideas of audio commentary feedback to provide a chance for students to record their response to their teachers about what they gleaned from their teachers' audio comments. Additionally, students could ask questions of their teachers in the response, creating a more genuine dialogue. When a student and teacher enter into the endeavor of the writing process, neither knows where the paper will conclude. Conversation, continual questioning, grappling, and consideration of the other's perspective hones the writer's voice toward a more thoughtful, nuanced, and complex piece.

Moreover, teachers might consider how audio commentary could be used in peer-to-peer interactions, allowing students to comment on each other's writing. Peer review in this manner could enhance the sense of community within a classroom, helping bridge the gap between peers who typically do not interact with each other and allow them to model and practice care for their peers. As Ice et al. (2007) write, audio comments "reinforce[d] the sense of community" and "decreased social distance" (p. 18) for his students in asynchronous online courses.

Many technology platforms seem to have recognized the power of audio feedback on student assessments. Learning management systems such as Canvas, Schoology, and Moodle have the functionality to be able to provide such comments easily to students, and grading platforms such as Turnitin.com also have the ability to provide this kind of feedback. As grading moves toward these platforms, audio commentary has the potentiality to more easily become mainstream.

CONCLUSION

With the more easily available use of digital technology and learning management platforms, the diffusion of audio commentary on student writing continues to permeate the work of teachers. Although it is unclear exactly how widely the practice of audio, or video (a practice known as screencasting), commentary occurs nationally and how quickly the practice is being diffused among educational classrooms, more scholars wrote about the practice in the past 5 years. A search of the phrase "screencasting student papers" in the research database Education Source, an EBSCO host database, revealed one article published between the years of 1997 and 2007. There have been 26 articles published in the past 10 years (2007–2017).

With that said, audio commentary on student writing is still "a long way from becoming a mainstream method of grading" (Woodhouse, 2012). As a 2012 *Ann Arbor News* article about screencasting stated in quoting one student's experience at the University of Michigan, "Still in 2012, the standard feedback on papers at the University of Michigan is a red pen and maybe some notes in the margin, but usually just a paragraph or two at the end of the paper." Change in education moves slowly, and through the influence of their own school experience, many teachers replicate feedback norms ingrained over time.

Despite its slow adoption by the education community, great potential exists for the diffusion of this method because it can apply to any course and content. Using Koehler and Mishra's (2009) technology, pedagogy, and content knowledge framework (TPACK), audio commentary on student papers falls into the category of technological pedagogical knowledge (TPK). As the authors write, "Teachers need to reject functional fixedness and develop skills to look beyond most common uses for technologies, reconfiguring them for customized pedagogical purposes" (p. 66). Teachers who have employed audio commentary with their students have done just that. Video conferencing helps solve student absences, and Smartphones replace the need for grading implements (Bauer, 2011).

Given that, as Koehler and Mishra (2009) argue, "Most popular software programs are not designed for educational purposes" (p. 66). It will take innovation and creativity for teachers to implement audio commentary on student papers and to do so with the intentions of care theory in mind. However, given the positive feedback and implications of such an innovation, it is worth pursuing.

Whether audio commentary on student writing increases student achievement is unclear; the current literature does not directly address such a question, providing an important area for future research. However, as has been discussed, the research literature does suggest that students have greater engagement and comprehension from audio commentary than from written comments, which could positively impact student achievement. Moreover, this medium of audio commentary on student writing humanizes the process. As Dixon (2015) writes, "If we recognize that the use of technology contributes to a dehumanizing process in Higher Education, there is an implicit irony that increased use—that of audio feedback—may help to alleviate this" (p. 101). This, too, could aid in the development of students and student achievement.

Educators and researchers are just beginning to scratch the surface of the potential "pastoral" (Dixon, 2015) and motivational impacts that audio commentary on student writing might have. The development of this technological innovation in the spirit of Noddings's care theory could have substantial impacts for students of all grade levels and disciplines.

REFERENCES

Barrow, M. (2015). Caring in teaching: A complicated relationship. *Journal of Effective Teaching. 15*(2), 45–59.

Bauer, S. (2011). When I stopped writing on their papers: Accommodating the needs of student writers with audio comments. *English Journal, 101*(2), 64–67. Retrieved from http://0-search.proquest.com.source.unco.edu.unco.idm.oclc.org/docview/902575227?accountid=12832

Bergman, R. (2004). Caring for the ethical ideal: Nel Noddings on moral education. *Journal of Moral Education, 33*(2), 149–162. Retrieved from http://0-search.proquest.com.source.unco.edu.unco.idm.oclc.org/docview/232576634?accountid=12832

Cavanaugh, A., & Song, L. (2014). Audio feedback versus written feedback: Instructors' and students' perspectives. *Journal of Online Learning & Teaching, 10*(1), 122–138.

Dixon, S. (2015). The pastoral potential of audio feedback: A review of the literature. *Pastoral Care in Education, 33*(2), 96–104. Retrieved from http://0-search.proquest.com.source.unco.edu.unco.idm.oclc.org/docview/1720062897?accountid=12832

Gilligan, C. (1982). *In a different voice: Psychological theory and women's development*. Cambridge, MA: Harvard University Press.

Gould, J., & Day, P. (2013). Hearing you loud and clear: Student perspectives of audio feedback in higher education. *Assessment & Evaluation in Higher Education, 38*(5), 554–566. Retrieved from http://0-search.proquest.com.source.unco.edu.unco.idm.oclc.org/docview/1509087941?accountid=12832

Graham, R. (2012, June 24). Carol Gilligan's persistent 'voice.' *The Boston Globe*. Retrieved from https://www.bostonglobe.com/ideas/2012/06/23/carol-gilligan/toGqkSSmZQC3v4KhFyQ5bK/story.html

Ice, P., Curtis, R., Phillips, P., & Wells, J. (2007). Using asynchronous audio feedback to enhance teaching presence and students' sense of community. *Journal of Asynchronous Learning Networks 11*(2). 3–25.

Koehler, M. J., & Mishra, P. (2009). What is technological pedagogical content knowledge? *Contemporary Issues in Technology and Teacher Education, 9*(1), 60–70.

McKenzie, M., & Blenkinsop, S. (2006). An ethic care of educational practice. *Journal of Adventure Education and Outdoor Learning, 6*(2), 91–105. Retrieved from http://dx.doi.org/10.1080/14729670685200781

Merry, S., & Orsmond, P. (2008). Students' attitudes to and usage of academic feedback provided via audio files. *Bioscience Education e-Journal, 11*(1), 1–11. Retrieved from http://0-search.proquest.com.source.unco.edu.unco.idm.oclc.org/docview/61886258?accountid=12832

Meyers, S.A. (2009). Do your students care about whether you care about them? *College Teaching, 57*(4), 205–210. Retrieved from https://unco.idm.oclc.org/login?url=https://search-proquest-com.unco.idm.oclc.org/docview/848216750?accountid=12832

Noddings, N. (1995). *Philosophy of education*. Boulder, CO: Westview Press.

Noddings, N. (2005). *The challenge to care in schools* (2nd ed.). New York, NY: Teachers College Press.

Shadiow, L. K. (2009). The first day of class: How it matters. *The Clearing House, 82*(4), 197–199. Retrieved from http://0-search.proquest.com.source.unco.edu.unco.idm.oclc.org/docview/196888839?accountid=12832

Stone, L. l. (2006). Drawing parts together. *Education & Democracy: Journal of Didactics & Educational Policy, 15*(1), 13–32.

Wolsey, T. D. (2008). Efficacy of instructor feedback on written work in an online program. *International Journal on ELearning, 7*(2), 311–329. Retrieved from http://0-search.proquest.com.source.unco.edu.unco.idm.oclc.org/docview/210332606?accountid=12832

Woodhouse, K. (2012, September 27). Getting grades via video: U-M instructors and students say screencasts provide interactive feedback. *Ann Arbor News.* Retrieved from http://www.annarbor.com/news/for-many-getting-back-a/

Zenger, J., & Folkman, J. (2013, March 15). The ideal praise-to-criticism ratio. *Harvard Business Review.* Retrieved from https://hbr.org/2013/03/the-ideal-praise-to-criticism

CHAPTER 6

A MORALITY OF INCLUSION

A Theoretical Argument for Culturally Consonant Character Education

Chrystal S. Johnson and Harvey Hinton III

ABSTRACT

We offer a theoretical argument in support of a culturally consonant character education approach that seeks to enhance positive outcomes (e.g., academic self-efficacy, school belonging, and civic engagement) among youth of color. We argue that cultural differences are an integral part of character development and that educators who incorporate a culturally consonant character approach further enhance the social fabric of their class communities, strengthen communication between diverse students, and enhance civic engagement, trustworthiness, and reciprocal social relations.

We offer a theoretical argument in support of a culturally consonant character education approach that seeks to enhance positive outcomes (e.g., academic self-efficacy, school belonging, and civic engagement) among youth of color. Character education has served as a means for enriching the moral and civic development of youth in the United States, and it continues to resonate with policymakers, parents, and educators. In fact, 18 states codify character education legislation. An additional 18 states simply promote the value of character development in and outside of school, and 7 states favor character education without formal legislation (Johnson, 2011). Recent research supported claims that character education programs support positive youth development (e.g., Duer, Parisi, & Valintis, 2002; Osler & Hinton, 2015; Skaggs & Bodenhorn, 2006). Duer, Parisi, and Valintis (2002) reported findings that a character education program significantly reduced negative school behaviors such as insubordination, fighting, and truancy. Osler and Hinton (2015) noted increases in civic engagement as a result of a character education program. Survey findings from Skaggs and Bodenhorn's (2006) longitudinal study pointed to noticeable improvement in character-related behavior.

Despite the documented success associated with character education, many of today's character programs articulate a traditional view of character theory and practice that is grounded in Western notions of morality, whereby the moral theories and actions of non-Whites are relegated to a level of depravity.

A rising cultural milieu calls into question the practicality of traditional ideas of character education when preparing thoughtful, engaged youth for a global era. Racial/ethnic diversity is greater in the youth population than in the adult population, and these youth of color overwhelmingly reside in large urban or suburban areas (U.S. Census, 2015). By 2020, youth of color will encompass the majority of the youth population. Current projections point toward the number of White youth enrolled in public and private schools will continue decreasing as the enrollments of Hispanic students and Asian/Pacific Islander students increase (U.S. Department of Education, 2015). This "browning" of youth and youth culture have emboldened educators and researchers to now argue for culturally consonant character development practices to adequately prepare this generation for participatory democratic citizenship (e.g., Johnson, 2007, 2008, 2011; Osler & Hinton, 2015; Siddle-Walker & Snarey, 2004). These researchers systematically challenge schools to find character education approaches that: (a) are inclusive without promoting assimilation, (b) cultivate a sense of belonging while respecting cultural differences, and (c) cherish plural cultural identities without weakening a sense of shared citizenship. Johnson (2011) further contends that such dynamic character education approaches foster cultural identity development while simultaneously reinforcing the place of youth of color in civic engagement on local, national, and global levels.

We reject character education approaches that eschew cultural differences in the character development process. We challenge those character education theorists who argue that context-dependent character is a myth. The exclusion of culture and race from the character process leads to cultural gulfs. Cultural gulfs describe the differences that occur between members of minority and majority groups in their perceptions of belonging and their sense of freedom to express cultural distinctiveness. These cultural gulfs may shrink youth of color's ability to develop habits of mind and heart necessary for life in civil society. The emerging literature on diversity and character education delineate that the culture and race of youth are *sine qua non* to the character development process. As Baldwin (1998) asserted, it "is to history that we owe our frames of references, our identities, and our aspirations" (p. 20). For youth of color, their characteristic spirit and historical narrative tone a distinct character perspective that systematically challenges the legitimacy and usefulness of traditional character development programs.

We argue, therefore, that cultural differences are an integral part of character development and that educators who incorporate a culturally consonant character approach further enhance the social fabric of their class communities, strengthen communication between diverse students, and enhance civic engagement, trustworthiness, and reciprocal social relations (Johnson, 2007). To that end, we put forward the Culturally Relevant Community of Learners and Educators (CRCLE) program as a means for preparing youth of color to assume the mantle of engaged citizen. A pilot program serving urban youth of color in North Carolina and Indiana, CRCLE is a character-embedded, action-oriented approach that focuses on the relational traits and fuses cultural dimensions of diverse racial/ethnic groups in the United States. Later in the chapter, we outline the hallmarks of CRCLE and provide steps that educators can take to implement this culturally consonant character education approach in their classroom. Overall, we hope this research sparks interest in culturally consonant approaches for youth development and provides teacher educators and practitioners with clear methods for implementing character education in diverse classrooms. Before introducing CRCLE, let us briefly examine how the moralities of exclusion call for a culturally sound approach to character education in the United States.

THE MORALITIES OF EXCLUSION, SCHOOLING, AND CHARACTER EDUCATION

The moralities of exclusion structured the education system in the United States, including the scope and nature of character development. Moralities of exclusion is a psychological process where members of a majority group view their own group and its norms as superior to others, thus belittling, marginalizing, excluding, even dehumanizing targeted groups. The targeted group is viewed as undeserving of morally mandated rights and protections. In this case, the categorization of non-Whites as residing on the moral periphery creates a marked otherness between "virtuous" and "debauched," leading to the exclusion of those who are negatively perceived from the moral community. Mills (1997) argued that such exclusion is inherently and explicitly linked to race and racism, which has consistently dominated the cultural-historical domain of schooling in American society. For many generations, most African Americans were denied schooling by the dominant society, by masters in the slave society, or by public authority in the society of free Blacks in the North and South. Exclusion led African Americans to struggle constantly for the right to learn and for the right to be taught in an equal and nonsegregated setting (Raffel, 1998). The conspiracy to keep African Americans in ignorance was pervasive. Most ironic of all, free Blacks were expected to pay taxes for schools they could not attend. Still, they hungered for learning and strove to achieve it in the face of a slavery that survived even in freedom. The claim of Whites that African Americans were academically inept of learning was contradicted by the methodical attempt of Whites to refuse them educational opportunities. As Weinberg (1977) noted, Whites did not fear that African Americans could not learn but that they would.

The moralities of exclusion also extended to the Latino population. The public schools were systematically hostile to Spanish-speaking minorities. In the Southwest, the very existence of Mexican Americans in the schools was resented. School officials converted a language difference into a learning handicap (Raffel, 1998). Even parochial schools failed to protect Spanish language and culture. Neither Puerto Ricans nor Mexican Americans could turn to the Roman Catholic parochial school as a protector of their language and culture. Both in Puerto Rico and Mexico the Church was an upper-class institution with little regard for either the social or cultural interests of the people. Parochial schools tended to serve a narrow circle of children. The U.S. Catholic Church organized few schools for Latino children. Polish immigrants in Buffalo or Chicago sent their children to Polish-language church schools; yet no such option ordinarily existed for the Spanish-speaking minorities. For the indigenous culture, schools, both federal and local, thoroughly excluded indigenous content from the curriculum. Even where many thousand indigenous children attended schools in a relatively compact area—as on the Navajo Reservation—only a tiny proportion of the teachers were themselves indigenous and the curriculum was culturally estranged from the students (Johnson, 2011; Weinberg, 1977).

The morality of exclusion came to define the scope and nature of character education in the United States. Character education was often framed as a response to certain values emphasized in a given context, reflecting the commonly accepted traits of good character and responsible citizenship steeped in Western tradition (Green, 2004; Johnson, 2011). Historically, character education in the United States assumed a White, middle-class, heterosexual position. Puritanical beliefs such as thriftiness, patriotism, and hard work were ingrained in character education discourses and programs. Colonial settlement of the United States gave way to an ideology that erased the moral structures and beliefs of people of color. This thinking led to the creation of the other, who would be perceived outside of the boundary in which moral rules, values, and fairness applied (Mills, 1997).

In spite of this morality of exclusion, some racial minorities chose to culturally appropriate majoritarian character development practices as a means for combating racial stereotypes. Mary McCloud Bethune and Nannie Helen Burroughs approached character development by underscoring innocence, modesty, piety, purity, and domesticity—deemed the ideal (Clark, 2012). These African American women character educationists recognized that a pathway to racial uplift was to make the invention of inferiority vulnerable and to attack the stereotypes by which African Americans, in particular women, were described. In this apartheid, racist environment, Bethune and Burroughs articulated character more in terms of manners, etiquette, and proper behavior than as an internal moral compass (Bair, 2009).

CULTURALLY CONSONANT CHARACTER EDUCATION

Culturally consonant character practice and research, then, stand in contrast to such notions since cultural-historical conditions deliberately shape moral actions and operations. Culture and history determine how people think, believe, and behave. Character practice should be adapted to match the culture and language students bring with them from home. Culturally consonant character education reinforces effective character practice in culturally diverse classrooms. It is rooted in moral philosophy that is inclusive and cultivates a sense of belonging. Culturally consonant character is sustainable, organic, active, thus working toward the creation of culturally grounded citizens woven from varied tapestries. This type of character practice engages and motivates all students. It uses cultural dimensions to bridge the character education cultural gap. Culturally consonant character education accounts for those cultural dimensions that contour character-oriented actions and goals. These cultural dimensions include but are not limited to: (1) spirituality, (2) harmony, (3) affect, (4) expressive individualism, (5) communalism, and (6) social perspective of time (Allen & Boykin, 1992; Boykin, 1986; Green, 2004; Johnson, 2011; Siddle-Walker & Snarey, 2004).

The first dimension, spirituality, denotes a belief in fate or a higher authority that guides an individual's life with an emphasis on the spiritual world instead of the physical. Harmony emphasizes the whole rather than the parts that comprise the whole. It creates a cultural synchronization that affirms the personal and cultural traits children possess (Green, 2004). By treating each student with respect, kindness, and fairness, the teacher builds an interdependent community in which people feel responsible not only for themselves but also for one another (Johnson, 2007; Siddle-Walker, 1996). Affect, the third dimension, places value on feelings and is most clearly illustrated in the explicit sharing of emotions in the classroom.

Expressive individualism values a person's uniqueness and highlights creativity. A very simple example of expressive individualism pertains to an individual's presentation of self to others by way of name choice, dress, and hairstyles (Gay, 2010). Communalism, on the other hand, values the importance of the group over the significance of the individual. From a communalistic perspective, affiliation with a group is a significant part of individual identity, and benefits accrued by individuals are used in the advancement of the group. *Othermothering*, which refers to the ability of African American grandmothers and other mothers to assume a parental role for children with whom they may share no household bond, is a form of communalism. Foster (1993), Beauboeuf-Lafontant (2002), and Johnson (2008) noted the othermothering and social perspective of time in their work. Social perspective of time values social interaction and the building of relationships. The focus of a social perspective of time deemphasizes physical time and highlights the social bonds created and nurtured during an event. Building and sustaining these relationships gives meaning to time. In classrooms, social perspective of time may be enacted by way of socializing in the classrooms; social interactions like talking about topics unrelated to the task at hand while completing it are not only permitted but encouraged.

Culturally Relevant Caring Classrooms and Schools

Youths contribute to their own individual development, their families' well-being, and their communities' civic fabrics. When youths actively improve their communities' well-being, their own development is enhanced and civil society benefits. CRCLE is grounded in evidence-based claims that youth of color benefit from: (a) culturally relevant caring classrooms and school communities, (b) classrooms and pedagogical practice that build positive youth outcomes such as academic self-efficacy and school belonging, and (c) civic engagement. Culturally relevant caring in classrooms and school communities is student centered, contextual, and goal based. Culturally relevant caring recognizes that despite differences in race, gender, and cognitive abilities, all members of the school setting desire caring relationships (Green, 2004). Fluid and complex, caring facilitates moral decisions and ethical behaviors while simultaneously empowering and offering humility (Hoffman, 2000; Noddings, 2002). From a civic and moral perspective, caring engages diverse learners in communal understanding and problem solving. As a youth's self-concept emerges, individual self-interests are redirected toward common goals (Johnson, 2008).

Purposeful Classrooms and Pedagogical Practice

Youth of color benefit from classrooms and pedagogical practice that build positive youth outcomes such as academic self-efficacy and school belonging. Scaffolding positive development among youth of color is essential for sustaining such positive school outcomes. Positive youth development (PYD) focuses on positive sides of developmental trajectories and highlights the potential presence of developmental plasticity or adaptive developmental regulations. CRCLE seeks to capitalize on the idea that youths are resources to be cultivated and that their lives are cultural and historical assets. Theoretically and empirically, the CRCLE concept has been linked to several latent constructs such as confidence, caring, character, and positive social connection (Johnson, 2011; Johnson & Hinton, 2016; Osler & Hinton, 2015).

Academic self-efficacy refers to belief in one's ability to succeed in specific academic tasks and pursuits (Connell, Spencer, & Aber, 1994). Academic self-efficacy beliefs are influenced by multiple factors—the student's personal experiences, the situational context in which the student is operating, and opportunities for the student to engage in efficacious action. Self-efficacy has been found to be a strong predictor of academic outcomes such as motivation, performance, and persistence (Connell, Spencer, & Aber, 1994). Youth of color who perceive themselves capable of doing well academically have higher academic outcomes than their counterparts who report low self-efficacy.

School Belonging

School belonging or school membership has been defined as a sense of acceptance, inclusion, and connection with peers, teachers, and school (Goodenow, 1993) and has been linked with positive academic and behavioral outcomes among adolescents without disabilities (Anderman, 2002). School belonging is also a key factor in promoting motivation, academic attitudes, and school engagement, particularly among low-income youth. It has also been associated with school satisfaction, self-efficacy, perceived competence (Sagy & Dotan, 2001), academic self-efficacy, and grades (Anderman, 2002).

Civic Engagement

Thoughtful and purposefully designed civic engagement activities attached to culturally consonant character practice yield greater learning with youth (Osler & Hinton, 2015). Students with a high civic engagement identity learn more academic content. Through academic praxis (application of theoretical concepts to action), youth shift from being knowledge receivers to idea creators. Abstract concepts come into relief against the background of situation and context as students consider, apply, test, assess, and reevaluate multiple disciplinary approaches to solving an array of human, mechanical, and environmental challenges. Second, civically engaged students learn higher-order skills—including critical thinking, writing, communication, mathematics, and technology—at more advanced levels of aptitude. In efforts to create socially equitable communities, they encounter opportunities to hone innovative approaches that such engagement work requires. By conjoining the academic knowledge and skills necessary to address community needs, students deepen and extend their learning. Third, civic engagement increases students' emotional intelligence and motivates them toward conscientious community action. Youth of color who participate in civic engagement gain interpersonal effectiveness, the ability to collaborate across diverse perspectives, and a sense of self-efficacy for positively impacting individuals, organizations, and communities (Osler &Hinton, 2015).

THE COMPONENTS OF CRCLE

CRCLE is based on five interrelated components: (1) a character-embedded curriculum, (2) deliberative discussion (3) care-based relationships, (4) class community, and (5) civic engagement (see Figure 6.1). Collectively, the components are designed to enhance culturally relevant character development, which may aid in closing the achievement gap between White and Black or Brown learners.

Component 1: Culturally Infused Character Actions

Central to CRCLE is a character-embedded, action-oriented approach that fuses cultural dimensions of diverse racial/ethnic groups in the United States. CRCLE focuses on the following relational traits:

A Morality of Inclusion 81

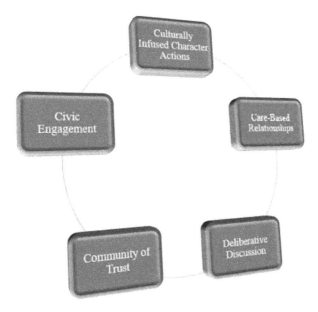

Figure 6.1. Culturally relevant community of learners and educators.

1. Unity. All things are interrelated. Everything in the universe is part of a single whole. Everything is connected in some way to everything else. Unity stresses the importance of togetherness for the classroom and school community, which is reflected in the African saying "I am we" or "I am because we are."
2. Self-determination requires that we define our common interests and make decisions that are in the best interest of our classroom and school community. Youth must actively participate in the development of their own potential. The path will always be there for those who decide to travel it.
3. Collective responsibility reminds us of our obligation to the past, present, and future and that we have a role to play in the school, community, and world.
4. Purpose encourages us to look within ourselves and to set personal goals that are beneficial to the community.
5. Creativity makes use of our creative energies to build and maintain a strong and vibrant classroom and school community.
6. Faith focuses on honoring the best of our traditions, draws upon the best in ourselves, and helps us strive for a higher level of life for humankind by affirming our self-worth and confidence in our ability to succeed and triumph.

7. Harmony emphasizes the whole rather than the parts that comprise the whole. It creates cultural synchronization that affirms the personal cultural traits youth possess. Character traits such as respect, kindness, and fairness maintain harmony.

Component 2: Care-Based Relationships

Caring is oriented toward a moral interdependence, which constitutes the true motive of humanity. Caring seeks the establishment of conditions that encourage goodness, not the direct teaching of virtues (Noddings, 2002). A care-oriented educator expresses moral agency through (1) her knowledge about what she wants students to achieve, internalize, or learn related to principles of right and wrong and (2) how she facilitates such learning as well as her knowledge about what is ethically important for this teacher to do in the course of her pedagogical practice.

Component 3: Deliberative Discussion

Deliberative classroom discussions—those that allow youth to acquire, collaborate, and synthesize knowledge—not only empower youth of color academically but also can help youth respond positively to school. For those reasons, CRCLE seeks to equip youth with the ability to participate in and appreciate forms of deliberative discussion (Hess & McAvoy, 2014).

Component 4: Creating a Community of Trust

Creating a community of trust sounds easy but may be hard for some teachers to implement. A community of trust is built on the application of the culturally infused character education approach outlined in Component 1. Creating a community of trust is meant to foster listening, attention, and appreciation for all members of the classroom. Rules become secondary, as an established trusting environment built on unity, purpose, harmony, and so on directs classroom flow and management (Johnson, 2007).

Component 5: Civic Engagement

The corner stone of CRCLE is civic engagement. Youth who engage with their community learn more academic content. In fact, civic engagement is one way to ensure that no student is left behind. Given the positives associated with civic engagement, it is highly beneficial for youth of color to take part in community activities.

INCORPORATING CRCLE INTO YOUR CLASSROOM

There are several steps teachers can take to incorporate CRCLE into classrooms.

Step 1: Recognize

Educators and learners require and function in caring relationships. Teaching and learning should not engage in exploitation whether through overtesting or superficial multicultural pedagogical practices. A caring classroom environment does not occur in a vacuum. Youth of color need to see caring demonstrated on a regular basis in order to engage in caring acts (Gay, 2010; Ladson-Billings, 2014). Teacher modeling is vital to incorporating caring into the classroom setting. Whether before school, inside the classroom, or after school, educators can exhibit such caring acts as courtesy and hospitality. They can model to students how to dialogue and direct them in deliberative discussions, and educators can include positive emotional support and encourage student responsibility (Noddings, 2002).

Step 2: Set the Tone

Create a classroom environment where youth feel safe asking questions. Allow them to constructively collaborate and develop lifelong learning skills. Implement culturally responsive instruction to scaffold students' comprehension of foundational knowledge and the prerequisite skills/attitudes needed for successful transfer of information (Gay, 2010; Ford, 2010).

Step 3: Build a Cultural Community of Trust

Create a cultural community built on trust. This cultural community highlights difference but builds a classroom harmony that focuses on multicultural and diverse perspectives; it lifts and empowers all children by differentiating instruction. Put into practice, a cultural community of trust supports youth strengths and interests into activities and learning experiences.

Step 4: Allow for Expressive Individualism

The age of high-stakes testing and accountability has led some educators to believe character education focuses on giving learners a voice. Expressive individualism values a person's uniqueness and highlights creativity. A very simple example of expressive individualism pertains to an individual's presentation of self to others by way of name choice, dress, and hairstyles. In the context of teaching, manifestations may include use of instructional strategies to foster ways of learning the content (Allen & Boykin, 1992; Boykin, 1986).

Step 5: Address Cultural and Historical Issues Facing the Community

Generate interest in cultural-historical issues, such as racism and poverty, that confront the communities where youth of color reside. The faces of racism and poverty continue to challenge the principles of democracy. All too often youth of color recognize how racism and poverty influence their school spaces, community design and structure, and available economic opportunities. Few classrooms openly engage youth of color in "color talk" or discuss the status of poor people in the United States (Green, 2004). CRCLE establishes that youth of color need occasions to openly discuss racism and poverty on their terms; for example, an educator may purposefully build a classroom community where stories of racism and poverty are openly shared, respectfully heard, and critically discussed and analyzed.

Step 6: Get Involved

Youth civic engagement is indispensable to democracy. Youth voices and energies are needed to address current problems. Helping youth develop the skills, values, and habits of participation is paramount in a culturally consonant character education program. When youth become involved, the individual and collective capacity among traditionally marginalized groups is strengthened, thus serving as a means to empower (Hess & McAvoy, 2014). Civic engagement opportunities may include community service, neighborhood development, or intergroup dialogue; for example, an educator could have her students deliberate the merits of the #blacklivesmatter movement. Through intergroup dialogue, whereby students critically discuss the issues that led up to this campaign, students will gain understanding of social identity, power, privilege, and oppression through intercultural communication skills and coalition building (Johnson & Hinton, 2016). Such an activity allows diverse students to develop intercultural maturity, recognize differences, and find common ground on some issues.

CONCLUSION

The cultural plurality of the United States is often touted as one of its greatest strengths. Within that plurality, cultural lines between majority and minority groups remain distinct. For members of minority groups, personal fulfillment, happiness, and empowerment may hinge upon their sense of freedom to consistently share their cultural distinctiveness in their lives. However, members of majority groups are not always aware of the critical importance of cultural distinctiveness in the lives of minority individuals and instead consciously or unconsciously advocate assimilation, particularly in the field of character development. As the United States moves toward brilliant diversity, the need to insert culturally consonant character practice seems apparent. Culturally consonant character practice has the potential to enliven character development conversations beyond the pale of White, middle-class, heterosexual voices.

REFERENCES

Allen, B., & Boykin, A., (1992). African-American children and the educational process: Alleviating cultural discontinuity through prescriptive pedagogy. *School Psychology Review*, *21*(4), 586–596.

Anderman, E. M. (2002). School effects on psychological outcomes during adolescence. *Journal of Educational Psychology*, *94*(4), 795–809.

Bair, S. (2009). The struggle for community and respectability: Black women school founders and the politics of character education in the early twentieth century. *Theory and Research in Social Education*, *37*(4), 570–600.

Baldwin, J. (1998). *Baldwin: Collected essays*. New York, NY: Penguin.

Beauboeuf-Lafontant, T. (2002). A womanist experience of caring: Understanding the pedagogy of exemplary Black women teachers. *Urban Review*, *34*(1), 71–86.

Boykin, A. W. (1986). The triple quandary and the schooling of Afro-American children. In U. Neisser (Ed.), *The school achievement of minority children: New perspectives* (pp. 57–92). Hillsdale, NJ: Erlbaum.

Clark, J. S. (2012). Countering the master narratives in US social studies: Nannie Helen Burroughs and new narratives in history education. In C. A. Woyshner & C. H. Bohan (Eds.), *Histories of social studies and race, 1865–2000* (pp. 99–115). New York, NY: Palgrave Macmillan.

Connell, J. P., Spencer, M. B., & Aber, J. L. (1994). Educational risk and resilience in African American youth: Context, self, action, and outcomes in school. *Child Development*, *65*(2), 493–506.

Duer, M., Parisi, A., & Valintis, M. (2002). *Character education effectiveness* (Master's dissertation, Saint Xavier University). Retrieved from ERIC Document Reproduction Service No.ED471100

Ford, D. Y. (2010). Culturally responsive classrooms: Affirming culturally different gifted students. *Gifted Child Quarterly*, *33*(1), 50–53.

Foster, M. (1993). Othermother: Exploring the educational philosophy of black American women teachers. In M. Arnot & K. Weiler (Eds.), *Feminism and social justice in education: International perspectives* (pp. 101–123). Washington, DC: Falmer Press.

Gay, G. (2010). *Culturally responsive teaching: Theory, research, and practice*. New York, NY: Teachers College Press.

Goodenow, C. (1993). The psychological sense of school membership among adolescents: Scale development and educational correlates. *Psychology in the Schools, 30*(1), 79–80.

Green, A. D. (2004). In a different room: Toward an African American Woman's ethic of care and justice. In V. Siddle-Walker & J. R. Snarey (Eds.), *Race-ing moral formation: African American perspectives on care and justice* (pp. 55–72). New York, NY: Teachers College Press.

Hess, D. E., & McAvoy, P. (2014).*The political classroom evidence and ethics in democratic education.* Hoboken, NJ: Taylor and Francis.

Hoffman, M. L. (2000). *Empathy and moral development: Implications for caring and justice.* New York, NY: Cambridge University Press.

Johnson, C. S. (2007). Finding our place: Using cultural historical activity theory (CHAT) and teacher personal theorizing to investigate black theories of character development.*Journal of Research in Character Education, 5*(1), 49–70.

Johnson, C. S. (2008). A culturally consonant tone: African American teachers theorizing on character education policy. *Theory and Research in Social Education, 36*(1), 66–87.

Johnson, C. S. (2011). Addressing the moral agency of culturally specific care perspectives.*Journal of Moral Education, 40*(4), 471–489.

Johnson, C. S., & Hinton, H. (2016). Addressing culturally consonant character development and research. In K. Gonzalez & R. Frumkin (Eds.), *Handbook of research on effective communication in culturally diverse classrooms* (pp. 40–65). Hershey, PA: IGI-Global.

Ladson-Billings, G. (2014). Culturally relevant pedagogy 2.0: a.k.a the remix. *Harvard Educational Review, 84*(1), 74–84.

Mills, C.W. (1997). *The racial contract.* Ithaca, NY: Cornell University Press.

Noddings, N. (2002).*Educating moral people: A caring alternative to character education.* New York, NY: Teachers College Press.

Osler, J., & Hinton, H. (2015). Tri-squared qualitative and mixed methods analysis of perceptions of the effectiveness of the student athelete leadership academy (SALA): A character development and college preparatory program for young African American men. *Journal on School Eduational Technology, 10*(4), 7–22.

Raffel, J. A. (1998). *Historical dictionary of school segregation and desegregation: The American experience.* Westport, CT: Greenwood Press.

Sagy, S., & Dotan, N. (2001). Coping resources of maltreated children in the family: A salutogenic approach. *Child Abuse and Neglect, 25*(11), 1463–1480.

Siddle-Walker, V. (1996). *Their highest potential: An African American school community in the segregated south.* Chapel Hill, NC: University of North Carolina Press.

Siddle-Walker, V., & Snarey, J. R. (2004). Race matters in moral formation. In V. Siddle-Walker & J. R. Snarey (Eds.), *Race-ing moral formation: African American perspectives on care and justice* (pp. 1–14). New York, NY: Teachers College Press.

Skaggs, G., & Bodenhorn, N. (2006). Relationships between implementing character education, student behavior and student achievement.*Journal of Advanced Academics, 18*(1), 82–114.

U.S. Census Bureau. (2013). American Factfinder fact sheet: Selected social characteristics in the United States.
U.S. Department of Education (2015). Institute of Education Sciences, National Center for Education Statistics.
Weinberg, M. (1977). *A chance to learn: The history of race and education in the United States*. Cambridge, England: Cambridge University Press.

CHAPTER 7

ASSESSMENT AS DIALOGUE

Reframing Assessment

Paul Parkison

ABSTRACT

To ask *how teachers and students are doing* is to reclaim the personal view of learning as critically involved with others in the development and definition of ourselves. Overcoming assessment as currently enframed would reinvigorate the relationships between teacher-student and student-student as a reclaiming of the praxis of education. By asking *how teachers and students are doing*, there is advocacy for increased dialogue and dynamism in education and against the passive, compliant reliance on quantitative, mechanical methods of assessment. In this manuscript, the author begins the process of reframing assessment by thinking differently about assessment.

Among the areas of education that have aroused the most resistance over the past five decades is the requirements of assessment. In that time, policies have successfully linked assessment to accountability to such a degree that many educators have lost sight of the idea of assessment as learning and developmentally focused decision making, progress monitoring, and reflective of interest in the world for both teachers and learners. By allowing assessment to be coopted by the paradigm of competition and neoliberal commodification, many educators have lost their ability to step back and examine *how teachers and students are doing* in tasks and studies. The impact has been to depersonalize teachers' and students' involvement with learning experiences, to make learning mechanistic and ritualized rather than deeply personal, generative, and motivated by desire and enduring interest. By eliminating the personal space where the aesthetic and ethical meet in the formation of unique embodiments of humanity, educators have become captive to the restrictive requirements of training, rule following, and compliance that is the current educational system. Many educators have come to view assessment as the primary chains that bind them to this paradigm and foreclose their authentic involvement in the learning experience. Within the world of education, assessment has taken on a mixed but predominantly negative connotation. Assessment is linked to grading and accountability within a high-stakes schooling paradigm. As part of the need to reclaim the space of education that occurs in schools, educators need to reclaim the dialogic space of assessment. The foundation of this space, presented in the seminal work of Paul Black and Dylan Wiliam (2006) as assessment for learning, has largely been marginalized and foreclosed by the hegemony of accountability that is expressed as evaluation and grading. Assessment for learning begins by asking *how teachers and students are doing* from the perspective of students and requires that educators identify political (interconnected and shared) concerns that must be engaged with in order to function as a learning community.

Seeing assessment as an onerous system for the instructor and as an oppressive process for the learner is a significant challenge to learning and collaborative educative experiences. Hearing colleagues push back against processes meant to inform practice as teachers and to provide guidance and feedback to students as learners is disheartening yet understandable. The high-stakes climate of schooling prioritizes questions like:

- How do teachers motivate students to do their best within this high-stakes climate?
- How do educators promote equal opportunity for education for all students?
- How should teachers be held accountable, in a fair manner, for the successes or limitations of their students?

Questions like these foreclose the humanistic interactions of educative experiences and lead to the use of extrinsic motivators to produce instructional and schooling results as teachers struggle to meet the demands of the high-stakes climate. Educators can lose sight of the human interactions that are critical to educative experiences because of the pressures and constraints existing within this foreclosure paradigm.

ASSESSMENT AS DIALOGUE

Assessment as dialogue starts from a different premise: Students and teachers are intrinsically motivated when they are empowered as decision makers (Beane, 2005; Black & Wiliam, 2006; Cornelius-White & Harbaugh, 2010; Glasser, 1986; Jackson, Boostrom, & Hansen, 1993; Riggs & Gholar, 2009). Determining strategies for facilitating, sustaining, and internalizing empowerment among learners is a significant challenge that can be addressed by reclaiming assessment as a process of and in dialogue.

Martin Heidegger (1962) provides a useful frame for reconsidering assessment and the political and ethical role that it plays in schools. For Heidegger, the ethical emerges within the relational condition of care that accompanies human experiences in the world. This care is contextual, specific to the particular space that is inhabited, and it emerges as a consequence of the conceptual frame from which each person starts. The conceptual frame of assessment as high-stakes evaluation, grading, and accountability has the dangerous power of technology. As Heidegger (1977) asserts:

> The essence of technology lies in Enframing. Its holding sway belongs with destining. Since destining at any given time starts man on a way of revealing, man, thus under way, is continually approaching the brink of the possibility of pursuing and pushing forward nothing but what is revealed in ordering, and of deriving all his standards on this basis. Through this the other possibility is blocked, that man might be admitted more and sooner and ever more primally to the essence of that which is unconcealed and to its unconcealment, in order that he might experience as his essence his needed belonging to revealing. (p. 26)

What individuals care about, where they place priorities, enframes the experience they have available to them. The danger of the technology of assessment of learning is the foreclosure of heterogeneous and empowering learning that is possible in every school and classroom.

Establishing balance in foreclosure—a stable, predictable, comfortable position—has become the goal and operational objective of assessment within this climate and culture that is characterized by exclusivity. In today's educational setting, standards are developed to establish predictability and the potential to audit the established guidelines. These standards are meant for "outsiders" who bring the potentiality of being disruptive or destabilizing and should thus be controlled or excluded. Criteria are established—racial, ethnic, socioeconomic, test-score performance, and religious—for membership. Educational attainment equates to exclusivity. Accomplishing success in schools has moved beyond the learning of each individual to include the emotional, cognitive, political, and aesthetic compliance of each teacher and student. The compliance and accountability view of assessment and exclusivity stifles and limits the transformative potentiality of education. This containment affects all Americans and our democracy.

Assessment as dialogue requires that educators unpack the politics of the classroom and reconsider the power dynamic and asymmetry that is often mandated through policy and accountability systems. Traditional classroom politics revolves around a dialectic: student-centered versus teacher-centered. This dialectic asserts a politics that fluctuates between an authoritarian structure where a dominant figure, the teacher, controls all aspects of the classroom and a humanitarian structure where the basic/essential needs of the constituency, the students, direct all aspects of the classroom (Cornelius-White & Harbaugh, 2010). Both structures assume a center or subjective guide to the political relationships in the classroom. The teacher is either the master of their domain or a servant to the masses. The student is either obedient subject or a welfare constituent. In either case, the stakeholders of the classroom do not participate as democratic and collaborative partners. Previous inquiry indicates the adoption by many preservice teachers of a participant-subject rather than a citizen identity and political stance (Parkison, 2009). The technology of assessment of learning forecloses all other potentialities—potentialities that Jean-Francois Lyotard (1988) would call *differends*.

What counts as legitimate content and data for decision making, progress monitoring, and legitimate educational reflection—the objects of assessment—depends upon the enframing technology that establishes the foundation upon which the system or paradigm rests. Common sense relies upon a contextual framework and enframing technology. The taken-for-granted is embedded within a set of assumptions that depend on a specific ideological perspective. Education has been captured by the current assessment regime by fetishizing learning in the form of measurable, standardized, and anticipated outcomes. This fetishizing of learning also marginalizes significant segments of the American population by linking a person's social, political, and economic worth to his or her production of learning markers or benchmarks.

I'D RATHER NOT ASSESS: ASKING HOW WE ARE DOING

> Being genuinely alive is always having one's attention turned to this or that, turned to something as to an end or a means, as relevant or irrelevant, inter-

esting or indifferent, private or public, to something that is in daily demand or to something that is startlingly new. All this belongs to the world horizon, but there is need of special motives if the one who is caught up in such a life in the world is to transform himself and is to come to the point where he somehow makes this world itself his theme, where he conceives an enduring interest in it. (Husserl, 1965, p. 166)

Assessment as dialogue—asking how students and teachers are doing—assumes a different ethical and political paradigm for the classroom. Assessment as dialogue requires a shift in perspective that fundamentally changes classroom politics through the adoption of an alternative enframing technology. Instead of establishing a center, either subjective or objective, assessment as dialogue asserts a transgredient relational interaction as a beginning and collaborative space (Bakhtin, 2008; Davis, Sumara, & Luce-Kapler, 2008). This shift in perspective premises all human experiences of the world upon collaboration. Individuals are able to utilize collective, or intersubjective, worldviews to create meaning. Ludwig Wittgenstein (1974) called these intersubjectively constructed horizons language games. Within the horizon of experience, people utilize dialogically developed spaces and institutions, language games, to create meaning. By shifting from an objective/subjective political structure to an intersubjective political structure, the classroom becomes empowering, democratic, and collaborative.

Approaching assessment from a dialogical orientation has significant implications for the normative outcomes to be addressed and achieved. Mikhail Bakhtin (2008) recognizes dialogue as composed of emotional-volitional, axiological perspectives that seek responses from other positions that can embody a space of shared, but not necessarily conflict-free, exchange. Dialogue, within this perspective, is a way of being rather than a technique or type of communication (Rule, 2011). Dialogue becomes creative embodiment, a generative presence, that actively engages and accompanies responses from diverse axiological positions (Nielsen, 2002). Creating spaces in which the generative presence of these diverse axiological positions can emerge and be embodied in action is a collaborative, social enterprise. Generative presence that has potentiality within assessment as dialogue is relational—it is about being positioned in relation to multiple others and to multiple future potentialities. As educators take a position, they embody a potentiality for themselves and for others. This position carries responsibility (Levinas, 1981), answerability (Bakhtin, 1990), or concernful thrown-ness (Heidegger, 1962) that has the power of generating, originating, producing, or reproducing possibilities. An educator's bearing, carriage, or air as a person within the eternally recurring moment of presence makes the difference. How teachers and students occupy a relationship determines its generativity. An educator's presence is an opportunity and choice every time. These recurring choices are spaces for assessment: dialogic spaces in which teachers and students intersubjectively participate in decision making, progress monitoring, and reflective practice.

Asking how teachers and students are doing opens a space for the consideration and discussion of what education could be: learning, play, study, reflection, ethics, production, destruction, compliance, dissent, and so forth. Educators play a critical role in moving education out of the oppressive, fetishized assessment paradigm as it currently exists. Even though teachers feel they are captives of this same system through the mythology of accountability, it is incumbent upon them to break education out of its enframing as mechanized rituals of testing, accreditation, certification, and the commodification of learning. Educators must cease being the implementers of compulsive teaching and communicators of passive submission to external authorities. The foreclosure paradigm depends upon this type of capitulation for its hegemony.

Abandoning the fetishized version of assessment that currently controls education does not mean that there would no longer be standards, expectations, or knowledge. The habits that hold society together as a collection of connected individuals would receive greater emphasis in the open-ended question of how teachers and students are doing. Generative interconnectivity of society and its constituent communities requires the promotion of the dynamism and vitality of connective habits within communities. Enabling this space of "how are teachers and students doing" involves opening an interstice between expectation and experience. Opening a space for assessment as dialogue enables the generation of differentiation rather than association, which has the potential to produce something new and unexpected. Within a space of interstice that characterizes assessment as dialogue, there is a moratorium rather than a foreclosure. The outcomes are contingent and negotiated as the connective habits of a community open the space for becoming.

Sustainability of communities depends upon the cultivation of good habits and an openness to new, heterogeneous ways of knowing and doing. Resistance to bad habits (standards, expectations, or knowledge constructs) requires educators to recognize the role they play in naturalizing authority by dictating the "normal" and holding onto the taken-for-granted historical and conservative patterns of thought and ways of life. This alternative enframing turns assessment to become a search for the unexpected, a cynicism toward common sense, and an activation of wonder and imagination. Good habits are formed when they are generated with sustainability or generative interconnectivity as the intention. They are supported when learning becomes a process of students becoming that has space for difference—becoming is heterogeneous in its outcome (Foucault, 1970; Hroch, 2014; Nietzsche, 1966, 1982). In this alternative enframing, the break in the homogenization, or habituation of expectations, that characterizes assessment in the foreclosure paradigm becomes a source of transformation and generative education.

A dialogical perspective encourages the consideration of the complex interrelationship of events and relationships within a given system. By strategically opposing the categories that symbolize a specific form of being with the naïve self-acceptance of those categories as legitimate, dialogue provides a technology to deconstruct the system and problematize the taken-for-granted assumptions on which the system rests. Currently, within assessment as accountability, the technology categories and criteria of learning become mutually legitimating by deferring credibility to other categories within the system. This reification occurs when one category is supported by another, which then supports the original category, creating a tautological system that resists challenge. In this manner, the categories can be mutually incompatible without creating a crisis in reasoning. The enframing of this technology lies with the relationships between categories, with the system, not with the categories themselves. A collateral consequence of a shift to assessment as dialogue is the reclamation of tools like standardized assessments, forced-response test items, and other commonly used assessment of learning strategies. These mechanisms of foreclosure are repositioned as voices in the dialogue rather than the required language game in which assessment must occur. By problematizing the reification of categories through the dialogic perspective, it becomes possible to create a space for alternative dialogue concerning the function of the system of assessment being considered. In this process, educators expose the *differend* that is assessment as dialogue.

Assessment as dialogue positions the learner and learning in a different technological frame. Students are encouraged to reflect on and develop their skills and proficiency with established academic skills like information processing and documentation, cooperation and collaboration, and self-regulation (Dean, Hubbell, Pitler, & Stone, 2012). The time spent developing the students' awareness of these competencies is significant but essential to the students' development as independent learners and participants in the assessment dialogue. The students need to be able to reference this listing of academic learning skills, objectives, and goals to help them determine their personal learning progress and goals. They should be encouraged to consider the areas of learning that they identify as limitations in their self-assessment.

Pedagogically, assessment as dialogue leverages moments that emerge when the expected outcome and the singular experience fracture—when a space is opened as interstices between expectation and experience. This space represents the spark of curiosity, wonder, and confusion necessary for education, learning, and dialogue to begin. Fracturing the anticipated and the singular hinges on the potential for heterogeneous, dynamic, and fluid events. This fracturing happens when testing, evaluation, and accountability no longer hold as the hegemonic enframing of the education context. When educators no longer respond to occurrences in the classroom in a habitual way, these are affirmative moments when the unexpected, the excluded, is let in. The excluded is not a deficit or void but a multiplicity of experiences that are incomprehensible and require negotiation in transgredient.

Another integral part of assessment as dialogue involves student-generated rubrics and individualized task lists (Au, 2009; Berliner, 2011; Black & Wiliam, 2006; Parkison, 2015; Riggs & Gholar, 2009; Wiggins, 1993). Allowing students to determine the standards by which they should be evaluated creates a climate in which fairness, understanding of expectations, and personalized learning goals come together to create intrinsic motivation and a collaborative dialogic space. The collaborative establishment of desired learning is a difficult adjustment for all the stakeholders. Once a performance task is determined, a basic task list is collaboratively developed. The difference in this technology involves setting the relative assessment value of each subtask through dialogue rather than by mandate from outside the relationship. The students establish the desired learning and proficiency for each subtask within a performance task. This process takes some time for the students to become familiar with the expectations—theirs and the other stakeholders in the classroom (parents, teachers, fellow students, community members, …). Most students are not used to having this type of power within their classrooms. As the students became acquainted with the collaborative technology that is assessment as dialogue, they demonstrate greater awareness of their responsibility in the successes and limitations they experience, enable, and facilitate within the classroom.

Assessment as dialogue shifts the enframing away from the technologies of testing, grading, and accountability toward a focus on inquiry as enduring interest in the world. By refocusing on students' independence and empowerment as learners and away from high-stakes accountability, it is possible to influence students' and teachers' sense of self-efficacy and enhance internal locus of control—the sense of agency as ethical and political learners. As students struggle to find identity and a sense of empowerment, it is critical that teachers and schools embody frameworks or schemas through which the students can learn the requisite skills of an independent, autonomous inquirer. Assessment as dialogue within the classroom is a result of cultural adjustments: The students have to be empowered as learners, the teacher needs to recognize their expertise in learning processes as well as content, and the desired learning needs to be context specific. Building relationships among and between stakeholders that would help assessment as dialogue emerge takes time and structure.

Teachers should feel confident in the impact that taking time to facilitate experiences of these processes and learning skills can have on the climate of the classroom and the empowerment of the students.

ENDURING INTEREST IN THE WORLD

Enduring interest in the world, the political choice of what is important and valuable, is what characterizes humankind and grants meaning to life and learning. Asking how teachers and students are doing requires that educators identify political (interconnected and shared) concerns that must be engaged with in order to function as individuals and communities. Educators must also be able to recognize, judge, and discriminate among choices as they present themselves with regard to what is best or most important. The discrimination between varied choices is political engagement and the proper role of assessment as decision making, progress monitoring, and reflective practice for both teachers and learners. To abdicate this engagement is to abdicate a claim to the abilities that enable individuals to be self-directed in the process of becoming.

The tension that exists in the attempt to ground education within a hegemonic accountability-driven assessment system creates pressure on teachers and learners. By engaging in the processes of intersubjective knowing and interacting with the world-horizon as an ideal, that generative educational experience is constituted and exists. As educators adopt an intersubjective look forward into the future, toward an ideal potentiality, purpose in education enters into dialogue. Jan, a Czech philosopher and activist associated with the Charter 77 Movement (1976–1992), offers his theory of three movements of human existence: (1) receiving, (2) reproduction, (3) transcendence. In dealing with the distinction between a thing and a lived experience, between an object and a subject, Patocka (1989) unveils the essential character of an entity (like a teacher or learner) that acts through its own identity. For Patocka, identity is an absolute reality. The use of phenomenological reduction proves to be a method of access to this identity and of understanding through the world in its everydayness.

Patocka looks to Edmund Husserl's (1965) transcendental turn as an attempt to ground and justify faith in the totality of the world:

> The world as a whole is ever-present, and then always as a horizon; this horizontal given-ness is something original. Nor is horizon any particular perspective and anticipation. Those are possible only on the basis of it. Hence it might be possible to deduce that though consciousness is a constant anticipation, it can carry out this anticipatory role only on the condition that it accepts something like a global given-ness of the world which is

> prevenient, is not exhausted in anticipations or reducible to the verification of the particular. (Patocka, 1989, p. 221)

He finds an intersubjectively constituted horizon as the source of all experience and of all identity. It cannot be objectively verified without that verification being reducible to a subjectively constituted horizon—an ideological commitment. The significance here is the turn toward an open grounding of meaning on intersubjectively constructed existence within a global world-horizon as an ideal. The intersubjective everyday, free of thematic framing and concealment, becomes the horizon for self-manifestation and identity.

A depersonalized and technocratic schooling system, governed by a system of standards, testing, and accountability, characterizes a totalizing regime that excludes the horizon for self-manifestation and identity. This totalizing regime leaves space for only constrained critical questions for teachers: addressing issues of raising test scores, reducing achievement gaps, measuring response to interventions, and providing differentiated instructional procedures to remediate the failed students, teachers, and schools. Curricula are developed to facilitate equality of capability among students in the mode of consumption that make the current schooling regime viable in the realm of education (Migone, 2007).

The escape from the foreclosure paradigm takes the form of a sacrifice. The phenomenon of sacrifice represents an authentic break with and engagement in the world as an ideal. The sacrifice of assessment of learning is an attempt to redefine the world in such a way as to open the way for authentic manifestations of identity. In such a movement of sacrifice, teachers and students are acting both in identity and for identity. The sacrifice represents the willful, resolute, concerned action of the constitution of the intersubjective horizon—in the sacrifice educators attempt to teach from and toward an ideal. Again, Patocka (1989) helps explain:

> Whatever, though, might be the case in this respect, it seems to us that radical sacrifice is the experience of our time and of the time just passed, an experience which might lead to a transformation in the way we understand both life and the world—a transformation capable of bringing our outwardly rich yet essentially impoverished age to face itself, free of romantic underestimation, and thereby to surpass it. (p. 339)

In sacrifice, educators have a phenomenal expression of Being, free of thematic and ideologically enframed orderings and conceptions. This theme of sacrifice is vitally linked to humanity's authentic potentiality-for-being-its-self that finds embodiment and expression in asking how teachers and students are doing, in educator's heterogeneous responses to experiences.

Seyla Benhabib illuminates the politics of this type of heterogeneity in her discussion of Jurgen Habermas's *Theory of Communicative Action* (Habermas, 1987). Benhabib (1986) writes:

> The pathologies of the lifeworld arise in three domains: in the sphere of cultural reproduction, the consequence is a loss of meaning; in the sphere of social integration, anomie emerges; and as regards personality, we are faced with psychopathologies. Since each of these spheres contributes to the reproduction of the other two, the crises phenomena are in fact more complex: loss of meaning in the cultural domain can lead to the withdrawal of legitimization in the sphere of social integration, and to a crisis of education and orientation in the person. Anomie can imply increasing instability of collective identities, and for the individual, growing alienation. (pp. 249–250)

The facilitation of the production of a diverse range of critical, creative, and generative habits here takes precedence over the bad habits identified with restrictive requirements of training, rule following, and compliance that characterize the current assessment as accountability system within the foreclosure paradigm.

To ask how teachers and students are doing is to reclaim the personal view of learning as critically involved with others in the development and definition of identity. Overcoming assessment as currently enframed would reinvigorate the relationships between teacher-student and student-student as a reclaiming of the praxis of education. Asking how teachers and students are doing is to advocate for increased dialogue and dynamism in education and against the passive, compliant reliance on quantitative, mechanical methods of assessment and instruction. Educators need to begin the process of reframing assessment by thinking differently about assessment. Reframing assessment as dialogue will lead to shifting the ground upon which educators think assessment from the repetition of the same (homogeneous) to the process of generating difference through deterritorialized responses (Deleuze & Guattari, 1987; Hroch, 2014).

Accepting the critical task of education—facilitating an enduring interest in the world—is to think differently about students, to see them as people in the process of becoming. Seeing students as people in the process of becoming requires educators to move beyond (outside of) education's current assessment focus on accumulation and exchange of information in which what is learned effectively sustains the habituated circulation of knowledge and the maintenance of the status quo. Thinking about students as people in the process of becoming means valuing learning as a process of transformation, the process of coming to think differently, and becoming other in the process. Accepting the critical and transformative task of education requires supporting thinking differently from the fetishized learning norms and facilitating the production of a diverse range of critical, creative, and generative ideas that promote students' desiring and experiencing of joy in expressing their emerging capacities.

REFERENCES

Au, W. (2009). *Unequal by design: High-stakes testing and the standardization of inequality.* New York, NY: Routledge.

Bakhtin, M. (1990). *Art and answerability* (M. Holquist, V. Liapunov, Eds., & V. Liapunov, Trans.). Austin, TX: University of Texas Press.

Bakhtin, M. (2008). *The dialogic imagination.* Austin, TX: University of Texas Press.

Beane, J. A. (2005). *A reason to teach: Creating classrooms of dignity and hope.* Portsmouth, NH: Heinemann.

Benhabib, S. (1986). *Critique, norm, and utopia: A study of the foundations of critical theory.* New York, NY: Columbia University Press.

Berliner, D. (2011). Rational responses to high stakes testing: The case of curriculum narrowing and the harm that follows. *Cambridge Journal of Education, 41*(3), 287–302.

Black, P., & Wiliam, D. (2006). Assessment for learning in the classroom. In J. Gardner (Ed.), *Assessment and learning: An introduction* (pp. 9–25). London, England: SAGE.

Cornelius-White, J. H., & Harbaugh, A. P. (2010). *Learner-centered instruction: Building relationships for student success.* Los Angeles, CA: SAGE.

Davis, B., Sumara, D., & Luce-Kapler, R. (2008). *Engaging minds: Changing teaching in complex times* (2nd ed.). New York, NY: Routledge.

Dean, C. B., Hubbell, E. R., Pitler, H., & Stone, B. (2012). *Classroom instruction that works: Research-based strategies for increasing student achievement* (2nd ed.). Alexandria, VA: Association for Supervision and Curriculum Development.

Deleuze, G., & Guattari, F. (1987). *A thousand plateaus: Capitalism and schizophrenia* (B. Massumi, Trans.). London, England: Athlone Press.

Foucault, M. (1970). *The order of things: An archaeology of the human sciences* (L. M. Choses, Trans.). New York, NY: Vintage Books.

Glasser, W. (1986). *Control theory in the classroom.* New York, NY: Harper & Row.

Habermas, J. (1987). *The theory of communicative action.* Cambridge, England: Polity Press: Blackwell.

Heidegger, M. (1962). *Being and time* (J. Macquarrie & E. Robinson, Trans.). New York, NY: Harper & Row.

Heidegger, M. (1977). *The question concerning technology and other essays* (W. Lovitt, Trans.). New York, NY: Harper Torchbooks.

Hroch, P. (2014). Deleuze, Guattari, and environmental pedagogy and politics. In M. Carlin & J. Wallin (Eds.), *Deleuze and Guattari, politics and education* (pp. 49–75). New York, NY: Bloomsbury.

Husserl, E. (1965). *Phenomenology and the crisis of philosophy: Philosophy as rigorous science and philosophy and the crisis of European man* (Q. Lauer, Trans.). New York, NY: Harper Torchbooks.

Jackson, P. W., Boostrom, R. E., & Hansen, D. T. (1993). *The moral life of schools.* San Francisco, CA: Jossey-Bass.

Levinas, E. (1981). *Otherwise than Being, or beyond essence*. The Hague, The Netherlands: Nijhoff.
Lyotard, J.-F. (1988). *The differend*. Manchester, England: Manchester University Press.
Migone, A. (2007). Hedonistic consumerism: Patterns of consumption in contemporary capitalism. *Review of Radical Political Economics, 39*(2), 173–200.
Nielsen, G. M. (2002). *The norms of answerability: Social theory between Bakhtin and Habermas*. Albany, NY: State University of New York Press.
Nietzsche, F. (1966). *Beyond good and evil: Prelude to a philosophy of the future* (W. Kaufmann, Trans.). New York, NY: Vintage Books.
Nietzsche, F. (1982). Twilight of the idols. In F. Nietzsche & W. Kaufmann (Eds.), *The portable Nietzsche* (pp. 463–563). New York, NY: Penguin Books.
Parkison, P. (2009). Social studies education and preservice teacher preparation: Confronting the participant-subject paradigm. *Teacher Education & Practice, 22*(4), 414–435.
Parkison, P. (2015). Rubrics reframed: Reappropriating rubrics for assessment and learning,. In M. Tenam-Zemach & J. Flynn (Eds.), *Rubric nation: Critical inquiries on the impact of rubrics in education*. Charlotte, NC: Information Age Publishing.
Patocka, J. (1989). Introduction of the study of Husserl's phenomenology: Chapter 6—The first explanation of the phenomenological reduction. In E. Kohak (Ed.), *Jan Patocka: Philosophy and selected writings* (pp. 215–228). Chicago, IL: University of Chicago Press.
Patocka, J. (1989). Nebezpeci technizace ve vede u E. Husserla a bytostine jadro techniky jako nebezpeci u M. Heideggera. In E. Kohak (Ed.), *Jan Patocka: Philosophy and selected writings* (p. 331). Chicago, IL: University of Chicago Press.
Riggs, E. G., & Gholar, C. R. (2009). *Strategies that promote student engagement: Unleashing the desire to learn* (2nd ed.). Thousand Oaks, CA: Corwin Press.
Rule, P. (2011). Bakhtin and Freire: Dialogue, dialectic and boundary learning. *Educational philosophy and theory, 43*(9), 924–942. doi:10.1111/j.1469-5812.2009.00606.x
Wiggins, G. P. (1993). *Assessing student performance: Exploring the purpose and limits of testing*. San Francisco, CA: Jossey-Bass.
Wittgenstein, L. (1974). *Philosophical grammar* (A. Kenny, Trans.). Los Angeles, CA: University of California Press.

VOLUME 20, NUMBER 2

EDITOR'S NOTES

THE CLAIMS OF CHILDREN'S VOICES

Michelle Tenam-Zemach

In attempting to weave together a cohesive narrative that will seamlessly connect an eclectic set of manuscripts, I was dumbstruck at the thought of how I will accomplish this task. How would I offer our readership a meaningful introduction to seven interesting, contemporary but unique chapters? In discussing my challenge with Editor, Chara Bohan, she insisted that my job was to discuss an issue of relevance, one that I found compelling and meaningful as it relates to the field of education. In reflecting on Chara's words, I fell upon my recent musings of what I have been grappling with lately: The Parkland shootings.

Living in sunny South Florida represents several challenges. We are a diverse community rich in various languages, cultures, and opinions about an array of topics. As I reflect, ponder, and watch events unfold around the Marjorie Stoneman Douglas (MSD) school shooting, I have conflicting feelings and thoughts. On the one hand, I have viewed in awe the responses from the students who survived the attack, responses that reflected the diverse needs of their community. On the other hand, from the moment the pundits, community members, and politicians began discussing the events that took place, I could not help but think "how much of what I am witnessing is a result of the privilege of a few?" I also could not help but wonder why those who were tragically impacted by the actions of Nicolas

Cruz, the Parkland shooter, are in such bewilderment as to how this could happen to *them*, in *their* community, and why they consider themselves immune to students like Cruz who are mentally ill (for an interesting reaction to the shooting, listen to this local news recording by Michael Udine, one of the Broward County Commissioners and former Mayor of Parkland (https://soundcloud.com/wlrn/643am-broward-commissioner-michael-udine-speaks-about-parkland-shooting).

As anyone paying attention to these events would notice, these children have had a substantial impact on several debates raging in this country, most notably, the issue of gun control. The survivors of the shooting, all of whom are teenagers, are highly engaged as change agents. In a span of merely 3 months, the students from MSD have created a movement armed with their knowledge of how to effectively use social media to impact change. They have demonstrated grit, determination, and most importantly, a sense of confidence (although some might say arrogance; see "After Parkland," 2018) that they can in fact effect positive change around the issues of gun control and issues of mental health.

Armed with their harrowing experiences, intellect, and unbounded energy, these students will stand up to anyone no matter their status or wealth. This boldness was first exemplified at a gun rally that was held within days after the shooting. Emma Gonzalez, a senior at MSD, clutching her AP Government notes and chanting "BS!" gave a speech that has had over 3 million views on YouTube ("Florida Student to NRA," 2018). A similar sense of outrage and conviction among these youth took place at a *CNN* townhall where MSD students, and other Parkland residents, were filled with anger, moral outrage, and some might say, disrespect, fearlessly confronted three U.S. Senators and a spokeswoman for the NRA, on the issue of gun control. Another example of these students demonstrating their tenacity was in their organization of a march in Washington, DC; they used their knowledge of social media to encourage others to attend their "March for Our Lives Rally," an event where people from around the nation converged on the Mall in the hundreds of thousands (and this does not factor in concurrent marches that occurred in cities all over the country and world). They also used social media to encourage companies, successfully I might add, to boycott a Fox TV host, Laura Ingraham, because of comments she made against one of their own, David Hogg, a senior at MSD (Wootson, 2018). They even helped to pass gun control legislation in the state of Florida (Astor, 2018). The list of their accomplishments as agents of change represents the voices of these children in a myriad of contexts.

One cannot help but be amazed by the power and conviction of these children. But as I watch these events unfold, as I watch documentaries about these students lives ("The Parkland Diaries," 2018), as I read article after article (Alter, 2018; Burch, 2018), and as I talk to friends in the Parkland community, I wonder how much of what I am witnessing is occurring because of a confluence of events that ultimately center on the privilege of a few. I wonder "why now; why this particular school, community and group of kids?" and my answer keeps returning to the issues of privilege and their access to a quality education. I have no readily available data to suggest that I understand why these children can affect so much change so soon and so swiftly. Perhaps it is simply a confluence of events that have led us to think "enough is enough." But, for me, as an educator, when I listened to Emma Gonzalez read her AP Government notes at the gun rally, I said to myself "why aren't all children afforded the type of education Emma is offered?" And what other affordances have students like Emma, those coming from an affluent area like Parkland, been given that have led to these shifts in discourse. I ponder these questions and many others, all of which center on the issues of privilege and the tragic state of our nation when it comes to issues of education, gun control, and the mentally ill.

Hence, I again return to lamenting the state of education, and curriculum, in this country. I realize that the voices of these children must be heard and respected. As educators, part of that process is joining them in their struggle to shift the rhetoric to one that focuses on humanity, no matter the color of a student's skin, the altar to which he/she/they worship, or the amount of privilege they have or lack. We, as educators, must support these children in their fight to change the world, and not by agreeing to be armed with guns in classrooms but by demanding real change. We see pleas for change in education occurring in the current teacher strikes around the country. But we must do more. Now is the time for all those who deeply care for our society and the role that we educators play in that society to stand OUR ground and be a part of the movement of the youth who inspire us and fight for all of us. Perhaps, we need to learn from our students how to utilize social media more effectively to impact change. Or, perhaps we should be forming grassroots partnerships with students in our schools. Despite the mechanism of interaction, what is relevant is that we listen, hear, and join the chorus of their voices so that these children continue to be heard. Yes, how we each choose to engage in this struggle may differ; nevertheless, we must all contribute to these children's voices, and we must all be heard.

This brings me to the chapters in Issue 2 of *CTD*. All of these *CTD* chapters provide of platform for the voices of people in education. Given the eclectic nature of the chapters in this year's journal, finding a way to connect them in Issue 2 presented a challenge. Looking at the chapters more broadly, I established two categories, empirical and conceptual chapters. In that vein, in Curry, Reeves, McIntyre, and Capps' empirical study, they utilize NAEP assessment data to investigate the differences among fourth-grade students reading achievement scores as they relate to teacher quality variables (e.g., teacher preparation route, degree earned, etc.). While their findings are mixed, their study reinforces the notion that those who prepare teachers for the classroom require a deeper understanding of the variables that produce a teacher capable of impacting student performance. In quite a different empirical analysis, Schneider interviews two finalists for the Presidential Award for Excellence in Mathematics and Science Teaching to uncover their experiences with self-regulating their instruction. Schneider's study demonstrates that these teachers lived experiences are rather similar as they relate to self-regulation processes and that both teachers are committed to providing "highly effective" math instruction to their students.

Continuing with the affordance of allowing voices in education to be heard, Masko offers readers a school-based perspective of student-teacher relationships and interactions. In her qualitative study, she investigates how these complex relationships intersect with school climate in an urban middle school. Using Nodding's (1984) theory of care, Masko generates several themes that place care at the center of teacher-student relationships. Her work further reinforces the importance of caring relationships between students and teachers. Consider how such positive relationships might have the power to reduce school violence. In another chapter, Perrotta offers an insightful analysis of how middle and secondary students' social identities influence their manifestation of historical empathy through analysis of a marginalized historical figure Elizabeth Jennings. Perrotta found that there is a gap in students' historical empathy regarding differences of diverse students, and these disparities impact their demonstration of historical empathy. Care and empathy are two affective qualities that could change our violent society.

Zajdel and Conn's chapter explores the impact of corporate branding on a school, a teacher, and the larger community. Focusing on the embedded presence of the implicit curriculum and the school ecology, they analyze the ways corporate brands, in this case McDonald's, permeate multiple spaces of a school. Their eye-opening study suggests that as educators, we all need to consider the influence of corporations on teachers' day to day lives and the impact their presence has on students. Clearly, schools are microcosms of the larger society.

While the aforementioned chapters offer analysis of data to support the need for additional educational research in various arenas, Tanguay Bhatnagar, Barker, and Many offer a model for professional learning of teacher educators. This type of professional development model is critical in teacher education, where teacher educators are responsible to prepare teacher candidates who will eventually teach culturally and linguistically diverse students. The model synthesizes several components to facilitate teacher educators' capacity to work with their students and potentially improve their performance in diverse classrooms. An insightful piece, I consider this model a hopeful one to help faculty in colleges of education find ways to work collaboratively to develop infrastructure that supports faculty understanding of culturally responsive teaching and learning.

A quite different chapter in Issue 2 by Aaron Zimmerman also offers a conceptual discussion, one focused on the aesthetic dimension to mathematical inquiry. He argues that it is conceivable for teachers to underscore this dimension, despite working in a standards-based mathematics context. He does admit that this curricular approach demonstrates "unique challenges to early-career teachers," but he nevertheless urges novice educators to confront those challenges and find ways to appreciate the aesthetic dimension of mathematics. Zimmerman's chapter reminds me that, again, all educators, despite the ways they interact with and within the education system, they face a myriad of challenges. This perspective returns me to my position that we all must do more to improve education for all those involved, and that would be everyone in some manner or another. While none of the chapters in Issue 2 directly relate to the Parkland shooting, issues of privilege, or gun violence in this country, each of them offer insight into various aspects of schooling that can help us improve what we know and do in schools. As I continue in this work as Associate Editor, I hope to further explore the intersectionality of the role of privilege in education, and students' self-empowerment. *Curriculum and Teaching Dialogue* provides a space for readers and members of AATC to delve deeply in relevant and meaningful work that broadens and shifts our understanding of curriculum and teaching. In the end, all voices in education need to be heard.

REFERENCES

After Parkland: Marco Rubio claims next generation is arrogant. (2018, February 28). *News & Guts*. Retrieved from https://www.newsandguts.com/parkland-marco-rubio-claims-next-generation-arrogant/

Alter, C. (2018, March 22). The school shooting generation has had enough. Retrieved from http://time.com/longform/never-again-movement/

Astor, M. (2018, March 8). Florida gun bill: What's in it, and what isn't. Retrieved from https://www.nytimes.com/2018/03/08/us/florida-gun-bill.html

Bromwich, J. E. (2018, March 27). Parkland students find themselves targets of lies and personal attacks Retrieved from https://www.nytimes.com/2018/03/27/us/parkland-students-hogg-gonzalez.html

Broward County Commission Michael Udine Speaks about Parkland Shooting. (2018, February 15). Retrieved from https://soundcloud.com/wlrn/643am-broward-commissioner-michael-udine-speaks-about-parkland-shooting

Burch, A. D. S. (2018, March 29). Parkland activist got some college rejections. He'll Majorin 'Changing the World.' Retrieved from https://www.nytimes.com/2018/03/29/us/parkland-students-college-admission.html

Florida student to NRA and Trump: 'We call BS.' (2018). *CNN*. [Video File]. Retrieved from https://www.youtube.com/watch?v=ZxD3o-9H1lY

Noddings, N. (1984). *Caring: A feminine approach to ethics and moral education* (2nd Ed.). Berkeley & Los Angeles, CA: University of California Press.

The Parkland diaries—never again—young voices out loud. (2018, March 23). *iGloobeINFO*. [Video File]. Retrieved from https://www.youtube.com/watch?v=baOHujAs35s

Wootson, C. R. (2018, April 1). David Hogg rejects Laura Ingraham's apology: 'A bully is a bully.' Retrieved from https://www.washingtonpost.com/news/arts-and-entertainment/wp/2018/03/31/laura-ingraham-takes-an-easter-break-amid-david-hogg-controversy-and-advertiser-revolt/?noredirect=on&utm_term=.953634504bee

CHAPTER 1

DO TEACHER CREDENTIALS MATTER?

An Examination of Teacher Quality

Daphney Leann Curry, Emily Reeves, Christina Janise McIntyre, and Matthew Capps

ABSTRACT

This study investigated the type and level of teacher credentials that impact fourth-grade reading achievement as reported by the National Assessment of Educational Progress. Data analyses revealed a significant statistical difference existed among fourth-grade reading achievement scores for the following teacher quality variables: National Board Professional Teaching Standards status ($p < .001$), teacher preparation route ($p < .001$), and degree earned ($p < .05$). No statistical difference existed among reading achievement scores for college major/minor.

BACKGROUND

Over the past 50 years, the teaching profession in general has endured many shifts in practice, research, and policy. Educator preparation programs (EPPs) are under increased scrutiny questioning their ability to prepare preservice teachers. This study examined the impact of National Board Professional Teaching Standards (NBPTS) status, teacher preparation route, level of education, and college major/minor on fourth-grade reading achievement data as scored on National Assessment of Educational Progress (NAEP).

Several studies indicate a child's teacher as an important factor that accounts for some of the variation in achievement, outside of student and family background variables (Darling-Hammond, 2010; Rice, 2003; Wendel, 2000). High-quality teachers, not commercial reading programs, impact students' reading achievement (Allington, 2006; Darling-Hammond, 2006); however, differences in specific characteristics or credentials that make a high-quality teacher exist (Pretorius, 2012).

National Board Certification (NBC) is an advanced teaching certification available to teachers with at least 3 years of experience. NBC teacher recipients are required to demonstrate high levels of content and pedagogical knowledge in their field. Cavalluzzo (2004) examined connected student and teacher data sets in the Miami–Dade County public school system to investigate the impact NBC and other teacher qualification variables (e.g., teaching experience, type of certification in mathematics, advanced degree, and undergraduate institution) have on student learning outcomes. Teachers with NBC were shown to have a small increase in student achievement when compared to similar teachers without NBC. Vandevoort, Amerin-Beardsley, and Berliner (2004) reported increased student achievement gains for students with NBC teachers in their investigation of 14 school districts in Arizona. The authors used survey data from principals and teachers as well as student achievement data and found academic gains of 1.3 months for students taught by NBC teachers.

Evidence of the impact of teacher certification and teaching experience on students indicates that uncertified teachers and teachers with nonstandard certification routes (e.g., Teach for America) had a negative influence on student learning gains. Teach for America (TFA), provides a nontraditional path to certification by enlisting recent college graduates, often with no teaching experience, to teach in high-need areas in the United States. Overall, TFA teachers had lower student achievement scores ranging from 0.5 to 3 months lower than teachers with full certification; however, TFA teachers with full certification were not statistically different than non-TFA teachers (Darling-Hammond, Holtzman, Gatlin, & Heilig, 2005). Decker, Mayer, and Glazerman (2004) also investigated the math and reading achievement gains of students with TFA teachers with opposite results. The data set used included approximately 2,000 students in grades 1 through 5 from 100 classrooms in the United States. A control group was comprised of students with teachers from traditional and alternative certification programs, as well as uncertified teachers. The authors reported TFA teachers had a positive influence on student math achievement when compared to the control group. Gains in student math achievement were greater when compared to novice teachers in the control group; however, achievement gains in reading were not statistically significant.

Goe (2007) conducted a research synthesis for the National Comprehensive Center for Teacher Quality designed to examine the teacher quality attributes that impact student achievement. Goe limited the synthesis to research that linked teacher quality attributes to student achievement as measured by standardized test scores. Goe reported a positive correlation between student achievement and a teacher's content area knowledge and certification in secondary mathematics. In addition, several studies examined by Goe revealed a positive correlation between a teacher's degree and certification in mathematics and student achievement in high school. However, Goe reported no evidence to support a connection between advanced degrees and student achievement. Several studies in the synthesis revealed that advanced degrees have a negative impact on student achievement (Monk, 1994; Rowan, Correnti, & Miller, 2002; Clotfelter, Ladd, & Vigdor, 2006).

DESIGN AND METHODOLOGY

This study investigated the effects of NBPTS status, teacher preparation route, level of education, and college major/minor on fourth-grade reading achievement using causal-comparative research. Specifically, this study explored potential differences in students' reading achievement scores as a function of NBPTS status, teacher preparation route, level of education, or college major/minor. Independent variables were examined using collected teacher background survey information and fourth-grade reading NAEP scaled scores.

NAEP Reading Assessment

As specified by the NAEP, or "Nation's Report Card," Reading Framework, the Main NAEP reading assessment measures reading skills and comprehension (e.g., in-school and out-of-school reading experiences) of literary and informational texts for grades 4, 8, and 12 (National Center for Education Statistics [NCES], 2013a). Reading achievement results are reported at the national and state level, and reported scores represent overall reading achievement at the aggregate level and do not identify the individual achievement of schools or students. For the purposes of this study, Main NAEP assessment data was used.

Sample

Student and school samples are drawn from each state, the District of Columbia, and Department of Defense schools (NCES, 2013a). National Main NAEP assessment samples are selected using probability samples to ensure students and schools selected represent all subpopulations of public and nonpublic U.S. schools (NCES, 2013a). The number of participating schools and students for each cycle depends on the number of content areas and test items assessed. Approximately 30 students per content area assessed are chosen for each participating school (NCES, 2013a). On average, 100 schools from participating states are selected for Main NAEP assessments per cycle. Student samples for each school range from 30 to 150 students depending on school size and content areas assessed.

Participants

Participants for this study were a nationally representative sample of fourth-grade students and their teachers from public and private schools that participated in the 2007, 2009, 2011, and 2013 Reading Main NAEP (NCES, 2013a). Archival data from the last four NAEP testing periods were retrieved using the NAEP Main Data Explorer. We included demographic data including teacher background, training, and instructional practices information in the analysis (NCES, 2013b).

Instrumentation

NAEP uses a variety of instruments to measure the reading and comprehension skills of fourth-grade students in U.S. schools including both literary and informational texts. The NAEP Reading Framework specifies assessment of the following content areas: literary text, fiction, literary nonfiction, poetry, informational text, exposition, argumentation and persuasive text, and procedural text/documents (NCES, 2009). In addition, the Main reading assessment provides a measure of reading cognitive processes (e.g., locate/recall, integrate/interpret, critique/evaluate) by text type and vocabulary knowledge. Teacher background and instructional practices information were collected and reported for the 2007, 2009, 2011, and 2013 NAEP cycle.

DATA ANALYSES

Data were collected on NBPTS status to determine the impact of earning and/or receiving certification through the National Board Certification for Professional Teaching Standards (NBPTS) in at least one content area on fourth-grade reading scores. Data were categorized into one of three criteria: (a) NBPTS, (b) working on NBPTS, or (c) NBPTS not earned. Descriptive data for each category of NBPTS are provided in Table 1.1. Evidence indicates a significant difference in fourth-grade reading achievement depending on teachers' NBPTS status [$F(2,365) = 25.546, p < .001$, $n_p^2 = .122$] with a medium effect size (Cohen, 1988). Post-hoc analysis was calculated utilizing Tukey's honest significant difference (HSD) test. Researchers selected this methodology due to the increased critical value utilized to determine whether an observed difference between any two means is significant. Other methodologies, such as Bonferroni, rely on an adjusted level of significance and increase the likelihood of a Type I error. Although any post-hoc test runs the risk of an error, those associated with Type II are potentially less damaging than those associated with Type I (Huck, 2012).

Post-hoc comparison using the Tukey's HSD test indicated students' performance on the reading assessment is lower ($p < .001$) when teachers are pursuing NBPTS ($M = 212.9857, SD = 9.18488$) than when teachers do not have NBPTS ($M = 220.7584, SD = 7.4095$). In addition, student performance on the reading assessment is lower (p < .001) when teachers are pursuing NBPTS ($M = 212.9857, SD = 9.18488$) than those teachers who do have NBPTS ($M = 220.2282, SD = 7.81035$). Furthermore, no significant difference ($p > .05$) in fourth-grade reading performance existed between the students whose teacher has NBPTS and those students whose teachers do not.

Table 1.1.
Descriptive Statistics of NBPTS Classification

	N	Mean	Std. Deviation	95% CI for Mean		Minimum	Maximum
				Lower Bound	Upper Bound		
No	149	220.7584	7.4095	219.5589	221.9579	192	238
Yes	149	220.2282	7.81035	218.9638	221.4926	179	236
Working Toward	70	212.9857	9.18488	210.7957	215.1758	193	232
Total	368	219.0652	8.4477	218.1993	219.9312	179	238

To determine the impact of certification route (alternative certification versus a traditional route) on reading achievement, we collected data through NAEP and categorized the data by state. NAEP describes a traditional route as teacher preparation provided through a college or university with teacher education programs. Descriptive statistics for each preparation route are provided in Table 1.2. Evidence indicates that students score higher on fourth-grade reading achievement $t\,(241) = -5.3$, $p < .0010$ when their teacher goes through a traditional certification route ($M = 221$, $SD = 6.4$) as opposed to an alternative certification ($M = 216$, $SD = 9.2$). Results indicate a large effect size ($n_p^2 = 0.62$) for preparation route (Cohen, 1988).

Table 1.2.
Descriptive Statistics for Preparation Route

	N	Mean	Std. Deviation	Std. Error Mean
Alternative	138	216.0290	9.27436	0.78949
Traditional	153	221.0392	6.44805	0.52129

Participants in the data collection were asked to indicate whether they received a major, minor, or no emphasis in the area of elementary education as a part of their undergraduate coursework. We collected data by state and categorized the data to one of three criteria: (a) a major in elementary education, (b) a minor in elementary education, or (c) no elementary education background. We used this data to determine impact on reading achievement scores.

Descriptive data for each category are provided in Table 1.3. Results indicated no significant difference [$F\,(2,608) = 2.927$; $p = .054$, $n_p^2 = .009$] existed in the fourth-grade reading achievement scores of students regardless of whether or not their teachers have a major in elementary education, a minor in elementary education, or no emphasis in elementary education. The effect size (.009) is considered small (Cohen, 1988).

Participants in the study were asked to indicate the highest degree earned on the following scale: high school diploma, associate, bachelor, master, specialist, doctorate and professional degree (e.g., MD, LLB, JD, and DDS). None of the participants responded as teaching with a high school diploma or associate degree. Descriptive data for each category of education are provided in Table 1.4. Results indicated that degree earned does make a significant difference on reading achievement scores [$F\,(4,578) = 4.329$, $p = .002$, $n_p^2 = .029$] with a small effect size (Cohen, 1988).

Table 1.3.
Descriptive Statistics for Elementary Education Major at Undergraduate Level

	N	Mean	Std. Deviation	95% CI for Mean Lower Bound	95% CI for Mean Upper Bound	Minimum	Maximum
No Elem Educ	204	219.9853	6.87931	219.0356	220.935	194	236
Elem Educ Major	204	221.6471	6.99915	220.6808	222.6133	201	239
Elem Educ Minor	203	220.2118	8.57347	219.0253	221.3983	190	240
Total	611	220.6154	7.54556	220.0159	221.2149	190	240

To determine where significant differences occur, we conducted a post-hoc analysis (Tukey's HSD). Results indicated that students whose teacher earned a master's degree performed significantly ($p < .05$) higher than students whose teacher earned only a bachelor's degree. In addition, evidence suggested that earning a professional degree results in students who perform significantly higher ($p < .05$) than those who earn only a bachelor's.

Table 1.4.
Descriptive Statistics for Degree Earned

	N	Mean	Std. Deviation	95% CI for Mean Lower Bound	95% CI for Mean Upper Bound	Minimum	Maximum
Bachelor	204	219.2157	6.47865	218.3213	220.1101	197	234
Master	204	221.7059	7.12186	220.7227	222.689	200	238
Specialist	169	220.7751	9.15068	219.3855	222.1648	192	245
Doctorate	3	222.6667	5.50757	208.9851	236.3482	219	229
Professional	3	231.3333	16.80278	189.5929	273.0737	213	246
Total	583	220.6192	7.70075	219.9928	221.2456	192	246

SUMMARY AND DISCUSSION OF FINDINGS

This study investigated the potential impact of NBPTS status, teacher preparation route, college major/minor, and degree earned on fourth-grade reading achievement as reported by the NAEP. Data analyses revealed a significant statistical difference existed among fourth-grade reading achievement scores for the following teacher quality variables: NBPTS status ($p < .001$), teacher preparation route ($p < .001$), and degree earned ($p < .05$). No statistical difference existed among reading achievement scores for college major/minor.

No significant difference existed between those fourth graders with teachers who have NBPTS and those who do not, reinforcing findings from McColsky et al. (2006) and Sanders, Ashton, and Wright (2005), who were also unable to find significant differences between NBPTS and non-NBPTS teachers. However, research investigating the impact of NBPTS on student achievement has produced conflicting results (Cavalluzzo, 2004; Vandevoort et al., 2004), with many studies finding positive gains in student reading achievement when teachers achieve NBPTS status. The difference may be in other content or grade areas, considering this study only investigated fourth-grade reading achievement. Conversely, results of this study indicated statistically significant results where students with teachers working toward NBPTS performed significantly lower ($p < .001$) than students with teachers who have earned or have not earned NBPTS status.

Teacher preparation route (e.g., traditional vs. alternative certification) had a significant positive impact ($p < .001$) on fourth-grade reading achievement but only for students whose teachers entered the profession through a traditional route (e.g., college or university teacher preparation program). The research investigating the impact of teacher preparation route on student achievement has produced mixed results (Decker et al., 2004). In recent years, policymakers and researchers have scrutinized the quality and type of teacher preparation routes available (Darling-Hammond, 2000), calling into question the value of traditional teacher preparation programs. Alternative certification programs may devalue teacher professional status and lessens the teaching profession to a trade. Results from this study support previous research (Darling-Hammond et al., 2005) findings emphasizing the value of traditional teacher preparation programs, specifically student teaching and professional methods courses in producing highly effective teachers. A limitation of this study is the research available on teaching experience primarily investigated math achievement of middle and high school students. These findings indicate a need for more research in other content areas and grade levels.

Other significant findings that emerged are that a degree earned had a positive impact on fourth-grade reading achievement where students whose teachers earned a master's degree performed significantly ($p < .01$) higher than students whose teachers earned a bachelor's degree. Small sample size made it impossible to determine whether a professional or doctorate impacted fourth-grade reading achievement. In contrast to current research, the degree earned had a positive impact on student performance. Available research has failed to link advanced degree status to improved student achievement in content areas (Carr, 2006). While these findings add to our understanding of the relationship of teacher quality and student performance, a possible recommendation for further study is to expand the research to include student achievement data for all content areas tested (e.g., math, science, reading, and social studies). This would allow the research to ascertain how teacher quality variables impact student performance across all content areas.

REFERENCES

Allington, R. L. (2006). *What really matters for struggling readers: Designing research-based programs*, (2nd ed). Boston, MA: Pearson/Allyn and Bacon.

Carr, M. (2006). *The determinants of student achievement in Ohio's public schools*. Columbus OH: Buckeye Institute for Public Policy Solutions.

Cavalluzzo, L. C. (2004). *Is National Board Certification an effective signal of teacher quality?* Alexandria, VA: The CAN Corporation.

Clotfelter, C. T., Ladd, H. F., & Vigdor, J. L. (2006). Teacher-student matching and the assessment of teacher effectiveness. *The Journal of Human Resources, 41*(4), 778–820.

Cohen, J. (1988). *Statistical power analysis for the behavioral sciences*. New York, NY: Routledge Academic.

Darling-Hammond, L. (2000). Teacher quality and student achievement: A review of state policy evidence. *Education Policy Analysis Archives, 8*(1), 1–44.

Darling-Hammond, L. (2006). *Developing learning-centered schools for students and teachers*. Thousand Oaks, CA: SAGE.

Darling-Hammond, L. (2010). *Evaluating teacher effectiveness: How teacher performance assessments can measure and improve teaching*. Washington, DC: Center for American Progress.

Darling-Hammond, L., Holtzman, D. J., Gatlin, S. J., & Heilig, J. V. (2005). Does teacher preparation matter? Evidence about teacher certification, Teach for America, and teacher effectiveness. *Education Policy Analysis Archives, 13*(42), 1–47.

Decker, P. T., Mayer, D. P., & Glazerman, S. (2004). *The effects of Teach for America on students: Findings from a national evaluation*. Princeton, NJ: Mathematical Policy Research.

Goe, L. (2007). *The link between teacher quality and student outcomes: A research synthesis*. (Research Brief). Washington, DC: National Comprehensive Center for Teacher Quality. Retrieved from ERIC database. (ED521219)

Huck, S. (2012). *Reading statistics and research*. Boston, MA: Pearson.

McColsky, W., Stronge, J. H., Ward, T. J., Tucker, P. D., Howard, B., & Lewis, K. (2005). *Teacher effectiveness, student achievement, and National Board Certified teachers*. Arlington, VA: National Board for Professional Teaching Standards.

Monk, D. H. (1994). Subject area preparation of secondary mathematics and science teachers and student achievement. *Economics of Education Review, 13*(2), 125–145.

National Center for Educational Statistics. (2009). *Reading framework for the 2009 NAEP*. Retrieved from http://www.nagb.org/content/nagb/assets/documents/publications/frameworks/reading09.pdf

National Center for Educational Statistics. (2013a). *NAEP Nations report card*. Retrieved from https://www.nationsreportcard.gov/reading_2011/

National Center for Educational Statistics. (2013b). *NAEP Teacher Background Questionnaire*. Retrieved from http://nces.ed.gov/nationsreportcard/pdf/bgq/teacher/2013_BQ_Teacher_G04_RM.pdf

Pretorius, S. G. (2012). The implications of teacher effectiveness requirements for initial teacher education reform. *Journal of Social Sciences, 8*(3), 310–317.

Rice, J. K. (2003). *Teacher quality: Understanding the effectiveness of teacher attributes*. Washington, DC: Economic Policy Institute.

Rowan, B., Correnti, R., & Miller, R. J. (2002). *What large-scale, survey research tells us about teacher effects on student achievement: Insights from the prospects study of elementary schools*. Philadelphia, PA: Consortium for Policy Research in Education.

Sanders, W. L., Ashton, J. J., & Wright, S. P. (2005). *Comparison of the effects of NBPTS certified teachers with other teachers on the rate of student academic progress*. (Final Report). Arlington, VA: National Board for Professional Teaching Standards.

Vandevoort, L. G., Amerin-Beardsley, A., & Berliner, D. C. (2004). National board certified teachers and their students' achievement. *Education Policy Analysis Archives, 12*(46), 1–117.

Wendel, T. (2000). *Creating equity and quality: A literature review of school effectiveness and improvement*. Kelowna, BC: Society for Advancement of Excellence in Education. Retrieved from http://education.devenir.free.fr/Documents/CreatingEquity.pdf

CHAPTER 2

TEACHING MATHEMATICS MASTERFULLY

Instructional Self-Regulation in Two PAEMST Finalists

Melissa Peterson Schneider

ABSTRACT

In this phenomenological study, two finalists for the Presidential Award for Excellence in Mathematics and Science Teaching (PAEMST) are interviewed with the objective of uncovering their instructional self-regulation experiences and processes. Both finalists teach in a school where the majority of students come from poverty and approximately half are learning English. This study reveals common lived experiences about the participants' use of self-regulation processes to provide highly effective mathematics instruction.

Teachers who develop their abilities to reflect upon, act in the moment of, and anticipate the success or challenges of their instruction determine professional growth, demeanor, and motivation for the profession. How teachers develop these abilities may be vital to understanding and promoting the growth of authentic and effective teaching craft. The nature of self-regulation as it is experienced and perceived by teachers of elementary-level mathematics at a suburban Title 1 school in the Denver, Colorado, area was explored in this phenomenological study. A purposive sample of two teachers, both of whom have been recognized as national finalists for the prestigious Presidential Award for Excellence in Mathematics and Science Teaching (PAEMST), were interviewed. For the purpose of this study, self-regulation will generally be defined as one's use of impulse control, metacognition, and decision making based on long-term goal outcomes (Sinatra & Pintrich, 2010). Using Williams and Hill's (2012) resource for investigating social science phenomena, trustworthiness was established through the integrity of the data, stability between subjectivity and reflexivity, and clarity in sharing the results and their connection to research and practice. From 36 codes, six themes emerged: (a) negotiation of goals, (b) reflection, (c) management of influences, (d) confidence, (e) high expectations, and (f) the ability to deconstruct self-regulation in teaching practices.

The central research question in this phenomenological study is: What role does self-regulation have in driving the innate teaching abilities of two nationally recognized elementary mathematics teachers in their poverty-majority, limited English-speaking classes? This study will benefit teachers, instructional mentors, educational staff developers, and most importantly students, as the shared self-regulatory processes and experiences of two highly successful teachers are elicited, examined, and described.

REVIEW OF THE LITERATURE

The use of effective self-regulation strategies can take time to sharpen and utilize in classroom environments where there is a myriad of demands on a teacher to hypothesize students' unique and collective learning needs (Kelaher-Young & Carver, 2013). Research about self-regulation as it pertains to goal management, multiple goal management, and strategic disengagement from goals discusses the dilemma experienced by individuals in deciding what internal and external resources to exhaust or employ when keeping to a long-range overall goal (Shah, 2005). Teacher self-regulation is a complex, multidimensional construct, as confirmed in a 2009 study that developed a way to measure it through nine different factors: (a) goal setting, (b) intrinsic interest, (c) performance goal orientation, (d) mastery goal orientation, (e) self-instruction, (f) emotional control, (g) self-evaluation, (h) self-reaction, and (i) help-seeking (Capa-Aydin, Sungar, & Uzuntiryaki, 2009). In the case of educating elementary-age students at risk for low academic achievement due to the latent matters found in high poverty and low language ability populations, a challenge exists in how best a teacher might maintain focus on essential learning goals, such as student mastery of state standards in mathematics (Edwards, Esmonde, Wagner, & Beattie, 2017).

Parrish (2010) summarized her transformational experience in student questioning during a mathematics lesson by thinking in the moment about the type of questioning that was being used in a lesson. By knowing what types of questions could be asked and subsequently what instructional actions could simultaneously be employed by the responses, Parrish could intentionally guide her students to appropriate mathematical practices. Similarly, the National Council of Teachers of Mathematics (2014) asserted that teachers need to apply a focus to their pattern of questioning to increase their awareness of student thinking and open the learning task to different student perspectives.

Smith and Stein (2011) assert five essential practices for the successful teaching of mathematics: (a) anticipating, (b) monitoring, (c) selecting, (d) sequencing, and (e) connecting. These practices are considered steps that can be taken when planning for, teaching, and reflecting on a lesson. Each of these steps requires careful thought processes by the teacher, and authors Smith and Stein promote the intentional planning of mathematical moments in the classroom, discussing how the teacher can be in control of these and how not to rely on their spontaneous occurrence but rather through the five research-based practices presented in their work.

Hall and Simeral (2015), through the study of coaching practices and self-reported teacher thinking habits, articulate stages of a teacher's thinking and reflective development about their practices and instructional planning. The authors present a self-reflection questionnaire and scoring ranges placed on a progressive continuum, useful for determining at which stage a teacher may be thinking through lessons, the actions taken during lessons, and anticipation of student learning. A progression of four stages a teacher experiences in thinking and acting is presented in the course of the book: (a) the unaware stage, (b) the conscious stage, (c) the action stage, and (d) the refinement stage (Hall & Simeral, 2015). Through the study of one's thinking and instructional decision making, the highest level, the refinement stage, is deconstructed for the purpose of building a beginning teacher from the unaware stage, characterized by the absence of spontaneous instructional decision making and confusion over the prioritization of learning goals while teaching.

In the literature reviewed, no studies reported the combination of expert mathematics instruction accompanied by a level of teacher self-regulation as it is defined here. While teacher self-regulation discussed in the literature often agreed with themes found in this study, such as forethought, performance control, and self-reflection (Zimmerman, 2002), deep descriptions of in-the-moment, expert-level teacher self-regulation specifically tied to mathematics instruction was not found in the literature. Consequently, this study focused on how two nationally recognized teachers in mathematics employed and experienced successful self-regulation habits for the benefit of student learning.

METHOD

A phenomenological approach was used to study the lived experiences of two teachers and the role self-regulation plays in their approach to teaching, other shared aspects of their metacognition, and decision making while teaching. This approach is most suitable for understanding the common experiences of individuals in order to develop deeper understanding about the details of the phenomenon, as well as to develop practices (Creswell, 2013).

Sample

A purposive sample of two teachers participated in this phenomenological study. Both participants were recruited for their common finalist status in the 2016 PAEMST competition. According the PAEMST (2018) website, this award is given annually by the president of the United States to one teacher from each of the 50 states. The application process requires essay responses to reflective questions, demonstrated service to the profession, videotaped lessons by the nominee demonstrating teaching practices, and instructional plans for further lessons with accompanying defense of teaching practices. Both participants were White, female, and in their early 30s. Additionally, both participants had completed their master's degree in education, and each had taught elementary grades for 9 years, the length of their teaching career. Both teachers taught in the same Title 1 elementary school in which 86% of the approximately 330 kindergarten through fifth-grade students qualified for free and reduced lunch, and 47% were identified as having limited or no English proficiency. Three percent of the students in the school were identified as gifted and talented, while approximately 15% were identified for special education services.

Research Design

Phenomenological studies are characterized by their inquiry-based design in which the researcher typically uses an interview approach to draw out the lived experiences of individuals about a phenomenon that is articulated by the participants (Creswell, 2014). It is important to intentionally choose participants who have experienced the phenomenon being investigated (Creswell, 2013). In the case of this study, the researcher had worked with both participants in the capacity of colleague and instructional coach and served as mentor of one participant for the PAEMST application process. Over the course of 4 years, the researcher and two participants planned, taught, and reflected upon instruction, observing one another's instruction and studying best practices in mathematics education as a professional learning community within their school. The researcher was aware of the degree of self-regulation that seemingly manifested in the math instruction of these participants having had years of prior experiences working with them.

A unique characteristic of effective phenomenological research lies in the value of the interview questions to capture a lived experience from participants that is not explained by theory (Streubert & Carpenter, 1999). Studying the self-regulation experiences of nationally recognized teachers of mathematics allows for a personal teaching experience to be explored and described in a way that typical studies investigating instructional self-regulation or metacognition have not yet covered. Additionally, this research employs the use of bracketing, a process used by researchers in phenomenological studies to separate one's beliefs, feelings, and perceptions in an attempt to be more accurate in one's conveyance of the lived experiences of others (Creswell, 2013). As a past mathematics instructional coach, former PAEMST nominee, and former colleague of the participants, I decided that it was necessary to both recognize and make efforts to bracket those experiences.

PROCEDURE AND DATA COLLECTION

Following approval from the University of Denver's Institutional Review Board, the two qualifying participants were informed of the study and asked to participate. Both participants gave their informed consent prior to the study, and each gave permission to use their first names, Sarah and Lindsey. Both participant interviews were conducted several weeks apart at two public coffee shops.

Data Collection

Each participant was interviewed once for 60–90 minutes and asked to verbally respond to nine interview questions (see Appendix). Interviews were tape-recorded and transcribed verbatim. Both participants were offered the opportunity of member checking to verify the accuracy of their interview responses, but each declined, saying they did not have the time and that they trusted the transcription and interpretation process. Nonetheless, both Sarah and Lindsey were sent the transcriptions and final interpretations via e-mail to read if and when they desired.

General background information on each participant was collected at the commencement of the interview. This information included age, teaching experiences, including schools and grade levels taught, and degrees completed. Participants were compensated with a $50 gift card.

Data Analysis

The interviews were each transcribed in order to "highlight significant statements, sentences, or quotes that provide an understanding of how the participants experienced the phenomenon" (Creswell, 2014, p. 82). It was the researcher's intent to capture the phenomenon in a highly descriptive write-up based on the common textural, structural, and emotional themes found in the interview transcriptions. Common word use, repeated phrases and ideas, as well as commonalities in examples provided by each participant were treated as codes contributing to themes in a cross-case analysis.

Results

In collecting basic information about Sarah and Lindsey, it was noteworthy that both participants had been teaching the same amount of time, were about the same age, and had attended the same university for one of their degrees. Lindsey had spent 5 years teaching upper elementary grades at a neighboring school district in a predominantly White, middle-class school prior to teaching in her current position. Sarah also shared a similar background of beginning her teaching career at a predominantly White, middle-class elementary school for a year in a neighboring school district. Both Sarah and Lindsey had been teaching in their current positions, at the time of the study, for 8 and 4 years, respectively.

From the two verbatim transcripts, 36 codes were found that were consolidated into six themes that helped to shape the phenomenon being studied: self-regulation experiences as a process for teaching students mathematics.

Theme 1: Negotiation of Goals

This theme simultaneously captures the navigation of instructional goals and student learning while in the moment of teaching:

Sometimes when a kid's sharing, I find myself wanting to jump in and add to what they're saying, and sometimes I make the decision to do it; other times I have to think, no, not yet, that's not going to help their understanding. So that's kind of the academic part. Also there's the part about what kind of choices the kids are making behaviorally, ones I need to intervene around because they're derailing the lesson, or is my intervening going to take us off track more because the whole class is off-track, too. So, I think there are all the academic decisions that happen, but then also just the things teachers have to deal with in regards to what the kids are doing. (Sarah)

… like knowing when to add an action to a word so they understand it, we do a lot of TPR (total physical response). If I say "add," my kids are great about motioning that it's going to get bigger; if I say "subtract," they'll motion that it's going to get smaller. They have that muscle memory for words, and I can anticipate the front-loading of vocabulary, not just academic but also the content piece … then moving into a lesson thinking about the stages of mathematical learning and thinking, and being able to provide an "in" for all learning. So even though I know that one of my students wouldn't need a number rack, it wouldn't hurt him to use it; whereas another student is not going to be able to access anything I'm teaching without it. I think it's really reading your classroom. I think of when the kids write me an answer on their whiteboards and flash it to me, if 90% of my room is getting it, I'm feeling good about moving on in the lesson, and then I know that there's these three over here that we need to add one more problem for and maybe the next one those three come with me and we sit and do it together because I know that the rest of my class can do it independently; so I really focus. (Lindsey)

Theme 2: Reflection

This theme captures the reflection on practices and development of one's own teaching expertise:

I think being a master teacher comes with a lot of practice and, you know, like a lot of bad lessons that you reflect on and do differently the next time. You are just always getting better. (Sarah)

I wish I could go back to my first years, the hardest part is that when you do something instinctively, it is hardest to explain why you're doing it, it's hard to put that into words. Um, I think when I came to this school and these kiddos were not responding to the ways I used to teach, it was a huge learning curve for me, and I had to realize it wasn't them, it was me … and thinking how can I change what I'm doing so they can access anything I'm trying to give them, anything at all … I mean like if you walk away with even the littlest bit of something from that lesson, I called that a success in the beginning. So I think one of my self-regulation processes that I use before I even go into a lesson ... is anticipating where they're at, and I think that comes through in looking at your data and seeing where they're at, and carrying that to the lesson and what you're asking them to do. (Lindsey)

Early on in my teaching, I didn't know everything I know now. I didn't know how to facilitate a discussion. I didn't know as much about how to build kids' understanding. There probably was more, uh, me just doing problems in front of them or not having that overall plan for the lesson, so I couldn't make those decisions in the moment quite like I can now, um, or things would throw me off. You know, crisis in the school, something gets canceled, something gets changed; I didn't always know what to do then. I didn't always know what to do then and how to adjust. (Sarah)

Theme 3: Management of the Quality of Instruction

This theme captures threats or boosts to self-regulation processes while teaching:

The changing in classes stands out to me because ... this year, I have two classes and they are very different, within the same day. And then compared to last year, I had a very large class, but they understood how to have conversations around math (well, they liked to talk), so they kind of got that! So to come into this year, I have one class that with practice can do that, like they are with it. Then the other class, it's a major struggle for them, so I've had to deliberately think about how to get in certain participation structures, like they thrive more on "person A talks, now person B talks," whereas the other class I can just say, "Talk to your neighbor, talk to your partner," and it just naturally happens. And with one group, math strategies come up that are supposed to come up; the other group, a lot of times, they have one or two strategies, and that's all. So I have to decide, do I say, "I saw someone in the other class do this; what do you think they were thinking?" Or, you know, I have to make different instructional decisions for that group. Um, and I think anytime you get new materials or new standards, you kind of have almost a little bit of a setback until you become more familiar and you know the materials and you're better able to judge. I mean like last year with the new materials, it felt like the lessons were too long, and we never finished, and I haven't felt that way at all this year because I know where we're headed. So, I feel okay about what to skip and where to stop, and I never worry about finishing. (Sarah)

The other adults who have been in my room that have interrupted my highest functioning degree of self-regulation are the ones that didn't have the content knowledge or developmentally appropriate practice knowledge, and I ended up having to teach them at the same time if I could, or I did damage control. (Lindsey)

I think it depends a lot on the adult and the relationship you have with that person. Um, especially in math, I always worry that you don't want someone to jump in and ruin the trajectory of where you're trying to get, you know; you don't want them to introduce the standard algorithm too soon or that kind of thing. And so, I've had adults in my room that I am very comfortable with, and when they jump in, I am able to say, "Not yet, don't do that," or "Why are you writing for the kid; let them do their own work."And I think other adults that I've worked with understand, like they know there's a learning path somewhere so they just trust that. (Sarah)

Theme 4: Confidence

This theme captures the display of conviction by the participant in her craft of teaching, a display of self-efficacy:

So, I feel okay about what to skip and where to stop, and I never worry about finishing. (Sarah)

It always is worth it, and I stand strong in making those little decisions because I always weigh it out because I want them to learn the big stuff. (Lindsey)

I think back to my first year of teaching, and if something changed, I didn't know what to do; but now, I've got like plan B, C, and D in case I need to go there. (Sarah)

I wanted to be a better learner ... I wanted to be better at my job, and I wanted to be the best teacher I could be for my kids, and if you're not willing to do that, then internally that is a huge block. (Lindsey)

Theme 5: High Expectations

This theme captures the expectation for all students and teachers to learn and deliver at a high level:

Regardless of where I was, I would still have that plan of where I want things to go and what things I am looking for. I feel like I try, even though I know the kids aren't coming from the background of having that knowledge, I still have the expectation that the kids will meet the learning standard. But, I think where I may need to do a little extra work is in formalizing their language. You know, they get up, and they start talking about math, and they don't have the words. So I still let them share, you know, their model is still up there, but I might have to do more re-voicing of what they're saying to get some of the proper vocabulary in that they're not using, because I want to model words that I hope they will eventually use. And I think that's true to some extent in any classroom; I just know with our kids that there are more words they don't know or more concepts that they've never had exposure to. Um, and also the embedding of vocabulary instruction in the lesson is important for all kids, but especially for our kids; vocabulary is key to them having access, even if it's not about math, so they can tell what's going on. I mean, like we have lessons with story problems that have cake-pops in them, so the word cake-pop has to be incorporated in some way. And it can be quick and easy, like here's a picture of a cake-pop. (Sarah)

I don't think other middle-class White classrooms do nearly as much student talking as we do, but for our English learners, you know you have to. Again, it's just good teaching for everyone. (Lindsey)

You have to be able to implement models or strategies or manipulative materials that give everybody access to the content, and you have to have flexibility. I mean, if you scan your room and you see that half of your class doesn't get it, then there is something wrong, and you have to deviate from the plan. And if you don't get to the end of the lesson today, that's fine, come back and hit it tomorrow. But whatever was the block in that moment, it's important that you took the time to address it to help your students get from A to B, because you know they can do it. (Lindsey)

Theme 6: Ability to Deconstruct Self-Regulation in Teaching Practices

This theme captures the participant's ability to deconstruct their expert level use of self-regulation processes to a beginner level, giving suggestions for step-by-step processes, and also reflecting on how they experienced the development of their own self-regulation:

If you're trying to develop a habit, I think that having that very specific (decision making) structure could be a good thing to introduce to somebody, and like I said, not for the whole lesson, but let's pick a problem in the lesson where we are really going to use the structure. (Sarah)

… let go of feeling perfect in exchange for being more present with your kids. Don't worry about how the lesson looks or sounds like, it won't be a perfect show; nothing is. Just get into connecting with your kids. It's part of your everyday life as a teacher, and you will get used to it. Be real and in the moment and you will become a better teacher every year and the self-regulation will grow. (Lindsey)

You have to take baby steps; it takes years. One thing would be thinking about just pacing a lesson; there's a lot to think about. Perhaps start with thinking about how much time you want to spend on every activity. That's a very simple way to start. It's not the depth we want to go to, but at least we're thinking about it. The goal is to have this overall plan and then to be able to make decisions within it. Um, so then maybe after that, just picking a piece of the lesson and really thinking, okay, what do we want shared? What do we want to come out of this, and how are we going to look for it? And not necessarily the whole lesson; it might be one problem that we are going to make those decisions around or one chunk of the lesson that we are going to make those decisions around. Maybe it's just realizing I can identify the strategies I want shared, and then the next go-around is, I can identify *and* sequence them in a way that makes sense for students. You know, kind of building that up over time from feeling like I can pace it to I can make deeper decisions about each chunk, little by little, not all at once. (Sarah)

DISCUSSION

Through the exploration of interview findings in these six themes, a current of intense focus through the practices of these two teachers was shared. The deep knowledge they each possessed about their goals and connecting with students with the fewest amount of distractions penetrated their teaching craft. The ability they had to break down this phenomenon for a beginner teacher suggested a level of expertise. Through their stories and experiences, the teachers captured the essence of the self-regulation phenomenon that fuels their teaching.

Both Sarah and Lindsey spoke confidently to the negotiation of goals, claiming to have made the best choices for students and their instruction at the same time. Confidence was just a small piece of what the teachers possessed that allowed them to stand strong through their lessons each day, and their confidence was built by a level of reflection that was steeped in humility and thoughtfulness on their pasts as beginner teachers and their professional development experiences along their career paths. Managing influences to self-regulation, both positive and potentially negative, took energy from both teachers as they allocated attention to manage other adults in the room as well as balance the demands of implementing new math materials. The agreed-upon high expectations for what makes good teaching existed, no matter if students were from poverty or language-deficit backgrounds. Their opinions about masterful teaching for all students advocated a standard of equity and a passion for math learning that went beyond the classroom and into students' futures. Both teachers exhibited high levels of commitment and vision to their vocation.

In the last theme described, the ability for Sarah and Lindsey to deconstruct their expert-level abilities to self-regulate and manage seamless instructional delivery, and explain it to a new teacher, was captured. Both teachers were able to suggest starting points that incorporated all of the other themes present: reflection, management of influences, negotiation of goals, confidence, high expectations, and ability to deconstruct self-regulation in teaching practices. This suggests that all six themes need to be present to effectively cultivate the high-functioning degree of self-regulation possessed by Sarah and Lindsey. While new teachers will benefit from the stories and advice offered in this study, staff developers, teacher mentors, and even materials designers may want to dig deep into what has been gleaned about the preservation of a teacher's ability to manage influences and self-regulate.

Sarah and Lindsey each possessed a unique reflective nature, both having chosen to teach and stay teaching in a Title 1 school, preferring it to other experiences for increased accountability and rigor in teaching demands that were present in that position. Both participants claimed that their teaching was better than it had ever been in a middle-class predominantly White school and also claimed that this "better" level of teaching is what should be available to all students. In the end, the initial working definition of self-regulation for this study was added to by Lindsey to include a heavy degree of anticipation and mental rehearsal, a form of *pre*-reflection so to speak, that would be worthy of further investigation.

Implications for Teaching and Curriculum

From a supervisory, coaching, or collegial level, probing into the self-regulation experiences and processes of an expert-level teacher's instructional habits could be a resourceful and efficient way for others to understand what makes their teaching so highly successful. In the case of the beginning teacher, tapping into the deconstruction of self-regulation, as articulated by Sarah and Lindsey, may help to shape a trajectory of excellent teaching practices, thinking, and actions. Additionally, knowing the common threats to one's authentic self-regulation processes can help supervisors and instructional coaches protect and be aware of the level of instructional product being offered to students.

Sarah and Lindsey were able to confidently articulate why and how their teaching craft had evolved to the level of awareness that it had, through their experiences in instructional self-regulation. Asking teachers about their own self-regulation experiences and how they feel it connects to their instructional success may be a motivating and insightful process by which teachers, instructional coaches, or supervisors can learn more about themselves as educators and their practices.

Limitations

While this study was limited to mathematics instruction, investigating these instructional experiences within the context of teaching other content areas may allow for the drawing out of more self-regulatory experiences and processes. The sample size in this study was small, having only recruited two PAEMST finalists to explore their lived experiences. The demographics of the sample were essentially homogenous, having two White female teachers of similar age, with highly similar educational preparation and years of experience and teaching at the same school. Having a more diverse sample, albeit age, race, educational preparation, experience level, or differences in schools taught, may offer more variety in experiences reported within such a study.

Future Research

Within this phenomenological study, experiences with instructional self-regulation have been identified. From this research, it can be recommended that a masterful teacher's instructional self-regulation processes are capable of being developed, reflected upon, utilized, compromised, and enriched. If even the best teachers routinely face changes in classroom make-up, adult personnel coming and going from classrooms, curriculum materials, and even the change in one's teaching craft over the course of time, how can self-regulation be tracked, developed, and maximized for the greatest student success? How can the themes of reflection, confidence, navigation of instructional goals, high expectations, the ability to deconstruct self-regulation in teaching practices, as well as the management of outside influences be further articulated to develop this phenomenon fully? Further research with more PAEMST finalists and other master-rated teachers is needed to determine if there is a definitive relationship between excellent mathematics or science teaching and one's self-regulatory experiences in instruction. While this study was limited to mathematics instruction, investigating these instructional experiences in the context of teaching in other content areas may allow for more generalizations to be drawn.

REFERENCES

Capa-Aydin, Y., Sungur, S., & Uzuntiryaki, E. (2009). Teacher self-regulation: Examining a multidimensional construct. *Educational Psychology, 29*(3), 345–356. doi:10.1080/01443410902927825

Creswell, J. W. (2013). *Qualitative inquiry and research design: Choosing among five approaches* (3rd ed.). Thousand Oaks, CA: SAGE.

Creswell, J. W. (2014). *Research design: Qualitative, quantitative, and mixed methods Approaches* (4th ed.). Thousand Oaks, CA: SAGE.

Edwards, A. R., Esmonde, I., Wagner, J. F., & Beattie, R. L. (2017). Learning mathematics. In R. E. Mayer & P. A. Alexander (Eds.), *Handbook of research on learning and instruction* (pp. 57–80). New York, NY: Routledge.

Hall, P., & Simeral, A. (2015). *Teach, reflect, learn: Building your capacity for success in the classroom*. Alexandria, VA: Association for Curriculum and Supervision Development.

Kelaher-Young, A. J., & Carver, C. L. (2013). Shifting attention: Using learning self-assessment tools during initial coursework to focus teacher candidates on student learning. *Teacher Education Quarterly, 40*(4), 111–133.

National Council of Teacher of Mathematics. (2014). *Principals to actions: Ensuring mathematical success for all*. Reston, VA: Author.

Parrish, S. (2010). *Number talks: Helping children build mental math and computation strategies*. Sausalito, CA: Math Solutions.

Presidential Award for Excellence in Mathematics and Science Teaching. National Science Foundation. (2018, 10 March). www.paemst.org

Shah, J. Y. (2005). The automatic pursuit and management of goals. *American Psychological Society, 14*(1), 10–13.

Sinatra, G. M., & Pintrich, P. R. (2010). *Intentional conceptual change*. New York, NY: Routledge.

Smith, M. S., & Stein, M. K. (2011). *Five practices for orchestrating productive mathematics discussions*. Reston, VA: National Council of Teachers of Mathematics.

Streubert, H. J., & Carpenter, D. R. (1999). *Qualitative research in nursing: Advancing the humanistic imperative* (2nd ed.). New York, NY: Lippincott.

Williams, E. N., & Hill, C. E. (2012). Establishing trustworthiness in consensual qualitative research studies. In Hill, C.E. (Ed.), *Consensual qualitative research: A practical resource for investigating social science phenomena* (pp. 175–185). Washington, DC: American Psychological Association.

Zimmerman, B. J. (2002). Becoming a self-regulated learner: An overview. *Theory into Practice, 41*(2), 64–70. doi:10.1207/s15430421tip4102_2

APPENDIX:
INTERVIEW PROTOCOL

Thanks so much for agreeing to this interview. The reason why I asked you to participate in this interview is to hear about your experiences and perspectives in the use of self-regulation strategies while teaching mathematics. The permission form that you signed means that I can record our discussion so that I can listen to it later and use it to write a report. I will ask the questions and I may take some notes of the conversation.

Do you have any questions? Let's get started.

1. You are a nationally recognized teacher of elementary mathematics. Please tell me the following: How long have you been teaching? What is your educational background in? When did you complete your degree(s)? Where have you taught, what grade levels, and for how long? What were/are the demographics of each place you taught (socioeconomic and ethnic)? How old are you?
2. While I know you are very humble about this honorable status of being chosen as a PAEMST Finalist, talk to me for a moment about what you feel makes a master teacher of elementary mathematics.
3. First, I'd like to hear your thoughts about the role of self-regulation in your teaching. When I refer to self-regulation, I am talking about your internal use of impulse control, metacognition, and decision making based on long-term goal outcomes (such as student mastery of learning standards).
4. How have self-regulation strategies been useful in your teaching of mathematics to elementary-age children coming from poverty and language-deficit backgrounds?
5. Please describe a time when your use of self-regulation in teaching was less frequent or different in some way than it is now.
6. What impact does change (for example, change in classes from year to year, change in materials, change in schools or districts and/or demographics taught, change in teammates, change in grade level taught, change in student needs, change in your education level) have on your use of self-regulation strategies?
7. What impact does having another adult(s) in the classroom have on your ability to self-regulate while you teach?
8. How do you manage cases where you feel distracted or that your self-regulation abilities are compromised or interrupted?
9. What do you think has been the single most impactful way that you've professionally developed yourself that has impacted your ability to self-regulate while teaching?

10. Now I'd like to wrap up the interview by making sure I didn't miss anything. Has our discussion brought up any other issues about the use of self-regulation strategies while teaching elementary mathematics to children of high poverty and low language abilities that you'd like to talk about?
11. I'll be transcribing this interview in the next couple of weeks. Out of all the things we've talked about today—or maybe some topics we've missed—what should I pay most attention to? What should I think about when I read and write about your interview?
12. Would you be interested in receiving a copy of the transcript? Please feel free to call or e-mail me any time if you think of anything else that you'd like to tell me about what we've talked about today.

CHAPTER 3

"KEEP IT REAL & LOVE 'EM UP"

Student-Teacher Relationships in an Urban Middle School

Amy L. Masko

ABSTRACT

This chapter describes a qualitative study investigating how student-teacher relationships intersect with school climate in an urban middle school. Findings indicate that care is at the center of the relationships, which establishes a climate in the school that teachers describe as having a "family atmosphere." The implications of this research further the discussion in the field of urban education about the function of high expectations that are grounded in caring relationships between students and teachers.

Students and teachers spend the majority of their waking hours with each other throughout the academic year. This qualitative study of student-teacher relationships is an attempt to understand some aspect of the quality of that time, with the ultimate intention of understanding how positive relationships between teachers and students can improve the experience of schooling for everyone, but most particularly for marginalized students. I spent 7 months in the school observing in classrooms and interviewing teachers and students about the nature, extent, and quality of their relationships with each other and how they impact the climate of the school. I utilized an assets-perspective, where I was keenly aware of the cultural strengths that the students and teachers bring to the school context.

School reform literature has focused on several themes over the years, including charter schools and other aspects of school choice, as well as curriculum reform, such as Problem Based Learning and Place-Based Education, among others. However, Usher and Kober (2013) point out that there has been a significant aspect of student success that has been overlooked in the literature: student motivation. They identify four themes of student motivation that occur in their analysis of the literature, the final of which is relatedness. They define relatedness as providing a sense of belonging or approval from a person of social importance. My study furthers the research on student motivation, relevant to relationships with teachers. Students are asked in this research to identify a teacher(s) with whom they have a connection or a relationship as a starting point to the inquiry of characteristics of strong student-teacher relationships. In this sense, they helped determine the direction of the study.

The literature on school climate often focuses on administrative and teacher input, and while I interviewed teachers, this research centers around student voice about the climate of their school and the quality of their relationships with their teachers. Student voice is often left out of discussions about school reform and improvement, as many researchers have noted (Burke, Collier, & McKenna, 2014; Mitra, 2003). Burke et al. (2014) state that what is often missing in policy decisions "is any attempt to actually engage students in the kinds of intimate opportunities to really do the work of fostering the business of ideas about schooling" (p. 5).

Review of the Literature: School Climate, Student-Teacher Relationships, and Academic Achievement

Research reveals a clear link between school climate, student-teacher relationships, and academic achievement. School climate has been described as the lived embodiment and experience of how a school is organized, how people relate to each other, and the kinds of relationships that are institutionally supported (Sherblom, Marshall, & Sherblom, 2006). Sergiovanni (2000) calls a school culture the "normative behavior that holds a school together" (p. 1). The two terms, culture and climate, are often seen as two parts of a complex, interacting whole (Sherblom et al., 2006).

A study of 490,000 Californian high school students indicated that those who reported a higher perception of a positive school culture achieved a higher GPA, regardless of family structure (O'Malley, Voight, Renshaw, & Ecklund, 2015). In another study, Holgaard, Kovac, Overby, and Hougen (2015) determined that academic achievement is positively affected when students perceived the school climate to be task oriented and aimed toward civic virtue, and negatively affected when school climate is competitive in nature. Sherblom et al. (2006) found a correlation between teacher positive perceptions of school culture and student math and reading achievement. This positive relationship between school climate and student achievement was found at the elementary level, as well (Johnson & Stevens, 2006).

One factor of school climate that is understudied is student motivation (Usher & Kober, 2013). Reform literature prominently focuses on standardized testing, accountability, teacher quality, and school management, yet ignores student motivation (Usher & Kober, 2013). A report by the Institute of Medicine (2004) highlights the fact that you cannot legislate motivation. They state, "increasing motivation is unlikely to be accomplished by policy decisions" (p. 14), but rather by creating "a set of circumstances in which students take pleasure in learning and come to believe that the information and skills they are being asked to learn are important and meaningful for them and worth their time" (p. 14). Essentially, the report argues that student motivation increases when the climate of teaching and learning has a focus on quality, meaningful instruction. Furthermore, the likelihood that students will be engaged and motivated in their learning increases as family, teachers, and their peers support students' personal involvement in learning (Institute of Medicine, 2004). In other words, the attitudes of those involved in the students' academic life, including their peers, have a direct influence on student motivation. Fortunately, there has been some movement in the notion of "peer disapproval of high grades" (Debruin-Parecki & Teel, 2012, p. 72) as a factor in discouraging achievement among students of color, as Fordham and Ogbu (1986) discuss in their seminal study on peer influences on achievement of academically successful African American students. Debruin-Parecki and Teel (2012) found that peer disapproval was a larger factor when students flaunted their high grades, producing a more nuanced understanding of intersection of peer influence on achievement.

As Sherblom et al. (2006) point out, effective schools have a climate and culture of high academic expectation, effective administrative support, and a shared mission among teachers and staff. This chapter explores the student-teacher relationship in developing a school climate of high expectations toward achievement and considers its impact on the work of school reform.

CONCEPTUAL FRAMEWORK: THE ETHICS OF CARE

While this study did not begin with the intention to investigate the role of care in schools, it quickly emerged as a category in the data, and I decided to investigate how care manifests in these relationships. Care is at the center of the strong student-teacher relationships. Noddings describes the ethics of caring in her seminal 1988 article:

> A relational ethic, an ethic of caring, differs dramatically from traditional ethics. The most important difference for our present purpose is that ethics of caring turn the traditional emphasis on duty upside down. Whereas Kant insisted that only those acts performed out of duty (in conformity to principle) should be labeled moral, an ethic of caring prefers acts done out of love and natural inclination. (p. 219)

This definition is useful in considering how care manifests in schools, as it operationalizes the term within natural boundaries of nurture and love. There is significant research that continues to apply, challenge, and refine Noddings's care theory for cultural responsivity among other factors (see Beauboeuf-Lafontant, 2002; Delpit, 2013; Garza, 2009; Gay, 2000); however, this research, while remaining cognizant of the contributions of the field to continually refine Noddings's ideas, remains grounded in her foundational theory as the conceptual framework because it is fluid enough to discuss the complexities that arose in my data.

METHODOLOGY

I conducted a qualitative study, utilizing ethnographic methodology to investigate how students and teachers relate to each other. Specifically, I investigated positive teacher-student relationships in order to understand what qualities and traits exist in those relationships. Is there something to learn about school climate and school connection for students from examining positive relationships with teachers?

The Setting

The middle school is located in a midsize, low-income, Midwest community of approximately 37,000 residents. The middle school is over 61% African American, 21% White, 13% Latino, and approximately 5% other. The school is 100% free and reduced lunch and has a 14% proficiency rate, as measured by state exams. I am using the term *urban* to describe the school, as that is the term used within the district. As Milner (2012) points out, the term is often code for low-income schools populated by students of color, yet we do not have a definition of the term in our field. While this district is located in a midsized town, it is very poor and very segregated. It is a largely African American city, surrounded by White communities. However, in one of my early meetings with the principal, we discussed the term urban. He stated that, while they certainly have problems associated with large urban districts, it operates socially as a small town. For example, if a child misbehaves and is in his office, he might say something like, "What is your aunty going to say about this?" While this may be something common a principal might say, the child in this school knows that Mr. Hunt goes to the same church as his aunty and their relationship is that of neighbor as much as a family-school relationship. He said that people tend to settle in this town, so everyone knows everyone's families, and many went to school in the same building their children and grandchildren currently attend. In this sense, it has a stable community that supports each other in strong social bonds, which is unlike an urban center, which might have much more transient populations. I use the term urban in this study because it is the term used by the district, but clearly it is not an urban school.

Data Collection and Analysis

I conducted classroom/school observations for approximately 7 months of the academic year, as well as interviews with students and the teachers they identified. I interviewed eight seventh- and eighth-grade students who represented a range of academic success within the school. Students were selected by the administration to be representative of the spectrum of success to struggle, using the following criteria: high/medium/low grades, school leaders, and high/low discipline rates (suspensions and detentions). I asked those students to identify any teachers with whom they felt a connection. They identified 13 teachers from a variety of subject matters. Some teachers were identified by more than one student, and some were identified by only one. Either way, I included every teacher the students named as one with whom they felt a positive connection. One teacher declined to participate due to her busy schedule ($N = 20$).

I interviewed the teachers twice and students three times (twice individually and once in a small focus group) to try to identify specific traits of their relationships. The three interviews focused on the following: (a) student-teacher relationships/connections, (b) qualities of good teaching (as identified by the students), and (c) school climate. I also observed these teachers' classrooms one to three times throughout the year. I transcribed the interviews, taking care to capture the participants' verbatim language. I analyzed the data hierarchically, organizing it into topics, categories, and finally into themes (Creswell, 2011). I coded the data using analytic memos. I expanded the analysis to visual diagrams, which allowed me to triangulate the themes across participants within group (students, for example) and between groups (students and teachers, for example). All names in this research are pseudonyms.

Findings

The climate: The school, the students, and the teachers. The climate of the school is impacted by the students' and the teachers' relationships. The following vignette, composed from my field notes, describes the tone in the school on the day after a high school student (a former student of the middle school) was shot and killed:

> The school, while always friendly and warm, is particularly loving today. Students are hugging each other and the teachers. I walk up the stairs to observe Ms. Washington's class and Mr. Hunt (the principal) gives me a quiet smile. He is hugging three girls, their heads reaching just under his chin. No one is crying. They are just hugging. Other students are walking by, heading to class. This space is safe. This staff is warm, and these students are here to share in their grief together.

While hugging was not a daily occurrence that I witnessed, it also was not rare. Although the teachers described the school as "a little chaotic," "disorderly in the hallway," "lively and energetic" [laughing], "immature," or even "crazy," they also described it like Mr. Kamp, a relatively new White teacher, did: "It's a family. It's community-focused. Lots of great relationships with students. Sometimes I think with some students, this is one of the few places they feel safe." Perhaps Ms. Washington, an African American teacher, summed up the two sometimes opposing descriptions best: "The kids are very comfortable with each other. We hear them. They are loud, so we hear them with their dialect. They are comfortable here. It's a relaxed atmosphere. A family atmosphere. I think we've accomplished that." This quote is a good example of the tension that is discussed at length in the literature on race, language, and schooling (see Perry & Delpit, 1998; Wheeler and Swords, 2006; Young, Barrett, Young-Rivera, & Lovejoy, 2014). Loudness and dialect, in Ms. Washington's quote, may indicate that school is a comfortable place for the students to be their fully raced selves rather than being a disparaging comment about the use of home dialects in a formal school setting, which often would require students to adopt two identities—one at school and one at home (see Phelan, Davidson, & Yu, 1993). Indeed, while the vignette I shared about the hugging in the hallway was not a typical day, I think the tone it describes is fairly typical.

The students described the school in similar ways as the teachers, actually. Shaylee stated, "I think it's really decent. It's just a handful of kids that act like they got no home training or something. It's just a few teachers who have to put enthusiasm in the way they teach." Jakyle, in describing the climate said:

> Disrespectful. Yeah. Poor language. It's a lot of kids in this school who care about their work. I know I do. Because when I first got here, I thought the work was gonna be easy. I got all Fs. I was playin' around. But I'm gonna stay after school the whole month. I can't afford to do 7th grade again. I know I ain't stupid.

Tiana quickly added: "And we have a lot of kids who help. If they see a kid struggling, there will be one or two kids who help." Marcus, pointing through the window to the secretaries' desks, quickly added at the end of an interview, when I asked if there was anything else I should know about the school climate, "They the best secretaries in the world right there." Areon also jumped in: "We got the best principal, too."

The eight students ranged from excellent students, such as Tiana, to students who struggled, like Jakyle, who said this when asked if he put effort into his work (a trait he indicated was a way to show teachers that students care about them): "Not in all of my classes. I'm gonna have to go to summer school. I'm failing two of my classes. Mr. Kamp and Mr. Freeman. Mr. Kamp, he get on my nerves too much, so I don't even try in his class."

Interestingly, the 12 teachers were also quite variable. Some of the teachers were quite serious and strict. I would describe Ms. Kent and Ms. Felt as having similar styles. They were both White women who were serious in their demeanor and fairly strict. Both teachers kept their students busy in class, but Ms. Felt's class moved at quite a rigorous pace. Mr. Jones, a White older teacher, was a joker. I would describe his teaching as performance. The first observation was in his class, where he gave a lecture about the Roman Empire, the feudal system, Huns, lords and fiefdom, nobles and serfs. He taught through story and connected to the students' lives through discussion of their friends, popular music, movies, and teachers who play favorites. I wrote after the lecture: "Great story! Strong content knowledge. Everyone was engaged."

Ms. Washington, an older African American teacher, was a very sweet, gentle teacher. She spoke softly to the students and thanked them several times each class for various behaviors, such as handing in papers or putting their books away. On the opposite end of the spectrum, Ms. Sherman-Smith, also African American, was firm and strict with students in nearly every interaction I witnessed. In fact, when I interviewed her, she said, "I'm shocked that anyone put my name into this research. I won't give myself rave reviews. It's always shocking to me when a student wants to come back to me. I describe my relationship ... [pause] ... I'm motherly. I love you, but I'm about business. A mother-business relationship."

Of the 12 teachers, three were White men, and nine were women—six White, three African American. The principal was a White male. There was only one White male student in my study: David. The rest were African American or biracial—four boys and three girls.

The academics: Strong content knowledge and teaching for understanding. I cannot say that all of the teachers who were identified had strong content knowledge, but I can confidently say that it was a common theme. Admittedly, some of the teaching that I witnessed focused more on discipline and classroom management than on content. However, I recognize that because there were so many teachers identified in this study, I was not able to embed myself for a significant time in any one teacher's classroom. If I had, I might have seen more of a mix of solid academic instruction along with discipline. I did, however, witness many teachers with strong content knowledge throughout my observations.

Regardless of my observations, content knowledge and teaching for understanding emerged as strong themes from the student interviews. David describes his theory of why Ms. Mavis is such a good math teacher: "Ms. Mavis speaks it out so you ... in a meaning you will get it. I think she studies math. She does the lesson and then teaches it the next day, I think." In his mind, she must practice the lesson she's teaching the students the night before. In my observation of Mr. Jones's class, I was enraptured by his lecture on the Roman Empire, as were his students, as I looked around the room. He was an excellent storyteller, and it was clear that his knowledge of this historical period was deep. A student, in talking about another social studies teacher, Ms. Felt, described her lesson about one of George Washington's speeches. He said that she made him feel like he was there, in the square, listening to Washington.

In addition to deep content knowledge as a mark of a good teacher, students also recognized the ability to teach in a manner and to a degree that students understand. Marcus described one of his teachers in this way: "When she teaches, she makes sure we understand what she teach. Like after she teach, she takes a whole 5 or 6 minutes to answer our questions to make sure we understand." Jakyle concurs with this notion in his analysis of Ms. Sherman-Smith's teaching:

> She explains about the question you ask her. Some other teachers will answer your question, but then they go back to teach what they wanted to teach. Ms. Sherman-Smith, she does explain the answer to you in words that you can understand. After you understand, then she goes back to teaching what she have to teach. They [other teachers] quicker with they answers, and you don't understand what they said because sometimes they get mad, they ignore what you said, and they go back to teaching what they want to teach.

Ms. Sherman-Smith is the teacher who said that she was surprised that she was included in the research because she doesn't give herself "rave reviews" about her ability to form relationships with students. This study demonstrates that relationships between teachers and students are complex, and Ms. Sherman-Smith is a case in point. She is strict. Her demeanor with students is firm. As she said, "I'm about business." And while she was identified by only one student initially as a teacher he "connected with" or who "really got him," Ms. Sherman-Smith's name came up in interviews with numerous students when they were describing characteristics that made a teacher a good teacher. The trait of teaching content well and making sure that students understand before moving on to new content was identified not just as good teaching but as caring. As Tiana states, "If they ask you if you got what they're teaching you and make sure you understand, then you know they care."

The relationships: Care at the core. Care was a strong theme emerging from the data, both from teachers' perspectives and students'. Although I did not ask teachers any specific questions about the notion of care, nearly every teacher addressed it in their interviews. Students also raised the issue in their first two interviews, so I dedicated the final focus group interview to the concept of care.

Noddings (2005) states that

> a caring relationship is, in its most basic form, a connection or encounter between two human beings—a carer and a recipient of care, or cared-for. In order for the relation to be properly called caring, both parties must contribute to it in characteristic ways. (p. 15)

She does acknowledge that the relationship is not often equal, and as such the cared-for "receives the caring and shows that it has been received" (p. 16). In this research, the teacher is the carer and the students are the cared-for.

It should be noted that while the following sections focus on specific themes within the ethic of care, students sometimes indicated that some teachers did not seem to care about them. While I chose to focus my interviews on what positive student-teacher relationships look like in this school rather than to ask questions about the negative or uncaring relationships, students often explained their concepts of care in opposition to teachers who did not seem to care. They identified being yelled at in class as well as being sent out of the class or to the principal's office as indications that the teacher did not care. They also indicated that moving on too quickly from a concept before the students understand it was illustrative of "not-caring." One student indicated that he could tell teachers who cared about students because they made sure the students understood before they moved on, but many teachers "teach what they want to teach," indicating that the curriculum was a stronger drive than student understanding.

Students identified several characteristics of care, which I was able to categorize into the following four themes: (a) being a warm demander, (b) showing understanding to students' lived experiences, (c) teacher-as-parent, and (d) honest and clear communication.

Warm demander. In characterizing her relationship with students, Ms. Mavis stated,

> They know I'm here if they need me. They know I expect a ton from them. And they know I love them. I'm a parent. My role is a parent. But one that is removed enough to talk through their bad decisions.

Ms. Warren's perception of her relationships with students mirrors Ms. Mavis.

> I am a very tough teacher. I expect a lot out of my kids. The program we run is very rigorous. I spend a lot of time defending science to them. They don't think they need it. So, I convince them they do. They respond if I set the bar high.

Ms. Sherman-Smith responded similarly when she described why she believes that students perform for her: "I demand that you do your best. I demand that you see something in yourself that you don't even know exists." Ms. Sherman-Smith, Ms. Warren, and Ms. Mavis are warm demanders, which Delpit (2013) describes as teachers who "expect a great deal of their students, convince them of their own brilliance, and help them to reach their potential in a disciplined and structured environment" (p. 77). Delpit's model of a warm demander is a model of care. Indeed, even students recognize it as such. Shaylee described good teaching as "pushing kids to go harder, even if they don't want to." Jakyle stated, "Even though I still be gettin' in trouble, I still like [school] because the teachers don't mess with you for no reason. They do it because they want to help you learn." He later went on to highlight Ms. Sherman-Smith specifically, stating, "Like Ms. Sherman-Smith, she mean at the same time she actually help me. When you don't listen to her, she turn mean." Jakyle and Shaylee recognize that challenging students and demanding that they listen in order to learn are ways to express care. Geneva Gay (2000) also supports this model of high expectations as a model of care within a framework of cultural competency when she states that "caring teachers are distinguished by their high performance expectations, advocacy, and empowerment of students" (p. 62).

Understanding. In addition to this model of warm demander, students and teachers both talk about being understanding. Marcus describes Mr.

Jones: "He know when I'm upset. He know not to play with me. He know when I'm not in the mood." (How?) "I don't know. He just look at me. And he know when something's wrong with me. Like when I'm feelin' sick." Tyrone concurred with those sentiments when describing why he feels he has a good relationship with Coach Brit: "Everything I'm going through, he understands because he sits down and talks with me. He gets me more. He let me change in his bathroom when people were bullying me and stuff."

The teachers said similar things about the importance of understanding the students. Ms. Shelby explained, "I think it's also talking to them on their level. If there is something that happened in your life that you can relate to their life, that, to me, is huge." Coach Brit agreed:

> It took me two and a half years working here to fully understand every kid has a different dynamic. Or even every day because you don't know what's going on at home. It took me a while. I try to talk to them. Let them know I care. Let them know I [understand] a lot more about them than they think I do.

Nearly every teacher spoke about the need to be understanding to the students. Sometimes this referred to connecting with students on a personal level, as Ms. Shelby and Coach Brit describe. On other occasions, it was meant as having patience with students' behaviors or lack of effort due to their lives outside of the classroom. Ms. Felt explained it like this:

> I would say their whole families and whole lives contribute to [the school climate]. They're not walking in here in isolation. Some kids have stability and they walk in here ready. And some kids have a lot of instability. So, they might sit here and do nothing or they might lash out. They come wrapped up with all their stuff, and we all know it.

Ms. Felt is a teacher that I categorized as a "warm demander," based on my observations and the students' descriptions of her demeanor. However, this quote is one I want to analyze as representative of the tension that is always present between being understanding and lowering expectations as a result of teacher empathy. Some researchers who write about urban schools have raised concerns about teacher attitudes that are grounded in a deficit model that sees the challenges that children who grow up in poverty experience as personal deficiencies, and as a result, these teachers lower their expectations (Delpit, 2013; Gorski, 2013). My awareness was heightened in order to be constantly cognizant of this perspective throughout this research.

Many teachers said things similar to Ms. Felt. Although it is difficult for me to evaluate whether this deficit perspective resulted in lower expectations for students and reduced rigor at the school, overall it remains a concern for me. However, I can speak to Ms. Felt's rigor and expectations. She was described by students as being serious, having deep content knowledge, and "giving real-world examples" to help students learn. After one of my observations in her class, I wrote in my field notes: "Rigorous pace, packed curriculum, very organized teacher." Many of the teachers, however, stated similar sentiments, and I remain concerned that teachers in urban schools sometimes hold lower expectations for their students, which typically results in lower achievement (Delpit, 2013). In asking the students what they liked about school, Tiana responded that she likes that teachers give them work they think they can do, and Areon added, "They give us the easiest work we can do." Tiana may have been suggesting that teachers challenge the students or that the work is easy, but Areon's addition to that conversation went unchallenged by Tiana. This sentiment about easy work was not an uncommon comment among the students, either.

However, none of the teachers identified in this study were singled out by any students for being easy. In terms of pedagogy, some of the teachers in this study were singled out for knowing their content, making sure students understand, for patiently answering questions, for being hard, and/or providing "real-world" examples. As Mr. Kamp points out, "There's a fine line between working with kids' behaviors and putting up with too much." Perhaps Tiana has identified that fine line when she explains her standards for good teaching: "Encouragement and sympathy. If every teacher does it, then the students will feel safe and cared for." While it is important for teachers to recognize the unique and often challenging context of their students, it is critical to hold high standards, offer a rigorous curriculum, and encourage their students to succeed. And perhaps most important is to follow the advice of Ms. Washington. When I asked her if she could identify any traits that make a good teacher, she said: "Efficacy. [They have to] believe that they can make a difference in a student's life. They have to like kids."

Teacher-as-parent. The final category of caring that I want to discuss is that of teacher-as-parent. Ms. Sherman-Smith described herself as a "business-mother," and Ms. Mavis described herself as a "parent." Ms. Washington stated, "You have to be willing to be more than a teacher—a mom or aunty or granny, depending on your age." Ms. Warren said, "I kinda treat them like my own kids. I was hard on my kids…. So, I guess I bring that mommy to school." And finally, Coach Brit said, "With the boys, I try to relate from a fatherly standpoint. And I can discipline them and relate to them." The kids concurred. Marcus stated, "Ms. Kent is like my mom at school. She checks my grades. If one of my grades is down, she asks me about it. She just makes sure I stay on track. She makes me do all my work." This notion of teacher-as-parent, most specifically mother, is a key component of Noddings's (2005) ethics of care. She states:

> Some of the most fascinating work in contemporary feminist theory is devoted to the study of women's experience and its articulation. It seems likely that women's traditional experience is closely related to the moral approach described in ethics of care. Women, more often than men, have been charged with the direct care of young children, the ill, and the aged.... Women have learned to regard every human encounter as a potential caring occasion. (p. 24)

And in Noddings's (1984) earlier work, she further describes care as the approach of the mother.

> The view to be expressed here is a feminine view. This does not imply that all women will accept it or that men will reject it; indeed, there is no reason why men should not embrace it. It is feminine in the deep classical sense—rooted in receptivity, relatedness, and responsiveness. (p. 2)

Beauboeuf-Lafontant (2002) also discusses the maternal role in her study of exemplary Black women teachers. "The concept of othermothering is germane to education because teaching in the African-American [sic] community, as in other ethnic groups, has been dominated by women since the turn of the 20th century" (p. 77). In these interactions of care described here, we can see evidence of Noddings's feminine ethics of care in both the female and male teachers' descriptions of themselves as "mother," "parent," or "father," as well as Beauboeuf-Lafontant's iteration of a womanist experience of caring. In addition to the teacher-as-parent, students also identified clear communication and honesty as traits of care.

Honesty and clear communication. Caring was also recognized by teachers and students in the form of honesty. Ms. Sherman-Smith describes how she forms relationships with students: "I am matter of fact with them. I just detest lies. I'm very frank with them. 'I'm not trying to be harsh, but I have to be honest with you...'" Ms. Mavis advises that a good teacher needs to "Keep it real. 'You're working my nerves.' I pull them aside and ask them why they act the way they do." This description was in relation to discipline, but she also described being honest when talking to students about the purpose of learning. "Just keep it real. Don't make education this lofty thing in the sky. It keeps you from being dumb."

Students discussed clarity in communication as an important aspect of care. David described the qualities of a good teacher to include "good communication. Like if you need help and she won't just yell at you like 'Go sit down!'" Areon described two teachers he can relate to: "Ms. Kent and Ms. Felt. Because they get what I be saying, like Ms. Kent might know where I be coming from when I'm speaking. Talking about a paper or something. We can communicate easy. Easier than some teachers." Students seemed to interpret clear communication as a key component of good teaching. They also recognized that a lack of clear communication often resulted in negative student-teacher interaction. Many students talked of teachers yelling because they did not seem to understand that the students needed clarification in order to understand.

Mr. Jones, in describing the job said:

> The kids are going to be the biggest challenge of your life, but it's also going to be the most rewarding thing you will do with your life. There is tremendous support for fostering good, healthy relationships with kids. The philosophy is love them up. It's the key to getting them to pass. Obviously, it's got to be paired with good instruction, but if you were to make a list, top to bottom, to get kids to succeed, love them up would be number one, good instructional techniques would be number two.

Ms. Washington concurred, "You have to have a caring spirit to work here. And if you're not willing to do that, you shouldn't work here, because our kids deserve that. I really think this should be an oath for teachers."

SUMMARY AND IMPLICATIONS

This study examined how the relationship between teachers and students manifested in an urban middle school and influenced the school culture. The school has very low achievement, as measured by state standardized tests, which is something the principal was concerned about. When planning the study with Mr. Hunt, we discussed discipline issues, achievement, and student-teacher relationships. The questions that emerged from that discussion focused on how to help the most marginalized students stay connected to school. Mr. Hunt wondered if there were some solutions to discipline issues and low achievement in student-teacher relationships. He asked, "Is there something we can learn about teachers who have good relationships with students that we can then teach to other teachers?" In other words, how do the students who get in trouble a lot and do not seem to like school connect with teachers? Are there identifiable traits that can be taught through professional development? These questions directed the design of the study, yet the answers I found were not quite as delineated as Mr. Hunt and I might have hoped when we were in the planning stages. However, what this study demonstrates is that student-teacher relationships are multifaceted and involved. Students connect with teachers with a variety of different personalities and teaching styles.

The only common traits that the research exposed were for teachers to (a) be caring, (b) know their content, and (c) teach it so that students understand. Yet within those traits, the data also demonstrates a complexity that suggests these things look different for each teacher and student. For one child, a caring teacher had strict classroom discipline and regularly checked his grades, yet for another student, the teacher could tell when he was having a bad day and just gave him space. I was struck by these differences not only as I pored over my data, but also as I read the literature on student-teacher relationships, and each study indicates different factors as important to the relationships. For example, in Garza's 2009 study of Latino and White high school students' perceptions of care, he identifies different traits.

> Caring teachers (a) provide scaffolding during a teaching episode, (b) reflect a kind disposition through actions, (c) are always available to the student, (d) show a personal interest in the student's well-being inside and outside the classroom, (e) and provide affective academic support in the classroom setting. (p. 310)

While I might argue that our themes are simply organized differently and "teaching for understanding" might be similar enough to "provide scaffolding during a teaching episode," I found that I would have difficulty organizing my data into these specific themes. Care theory has been discussed, critiqued, reiterated, and refined in the literature for many different contexts over the 30 years since Noddings's seminal 1988 article, but I argue that her foundational theory of care provides the flexibility, fluidity, and plasticity that is needed for discussions of complex human interactions between teachers and students.

As Coach Brit reminds us, "Every kid has a different dynamic." This is true for teachers, too, which indicates, then, that each individual relationship would have its own dynamic. Relationships are certainly complex. Noddings (1984) cautions about this when she says, "If we can understand how complex and intricate, indeed how subjective, caring is, we shall perhaps be better equipped to meet the conflicts and pains it sometimes induces" (p. 12). Ms. Shelby explains some of the pain in student-teacher relationships when she describes the school climate. "A place like this—I mean our kids come with a lot of baggage. And you do take that home with you. You worry about them. You take that secondary trauma home, and it's hard." Teachers who define their job in definitions of care, like these teachers clearly do, would be wise to engage in self-care in order to avoid burnout and live their careers in a state of wellness rather than fatigue and stress. It may be necessary for school districts to implement some programs in well-being for teachers and staff.

While this study certainly demonstrated that students and teachers formed quality relationships at this school, I am left wondering if it has any impact on student achievement. This school has an achievement rate of only 14%, as measured by state standardized tests. However, the literature suggests that schools with a positive school culture show higher achievement (Holgaard et al., 2015; O'Malley et al., 2015; Johnson & Stevens, 2006; Sherblom et al., 2006), and this school certainly has a positive school culture. While students discussed being "pushed" or challenged as a quality of a caring teacher, as well as teaching in a way for students to understand the content, there were several unanswered questions about how those qualities translate to actual achievement. A follow-up study to this might investigate the impact of curricular pacing, content knowledge, and teaching for understanding on student achievement, in a mixed-method designed study. That said, I recognize that these are limiting measures of achievement. For example, in Howard's (2013) comprehensive analysis of Black male learning, achievement, and experience with schools, he calls on achievement to be measured differently, for curriculum to be dramatically transformed, and for teachers to transform their practices to better connect with the cultural lives of Black adolescent males. Perhaps a study into the achievement, as measured by the state standardized test scores, could lead to work in reform of curriculum to be more culturally responsive to this specific community.

The most important implication of this study is to remember that caring relationships between students and teachers are critical to quality education. In considering the original guiding question of this research—how can teachers help the most marginalized students to connect to school?—we would be wise to listen to Mr. Jones: "I have rarely met a kid who doesn't like school who feels loved."

REFERENCES

Beauboeuf-Lafontant, T. (2002). A womanist experience of caring: Understanding the pedagogy of exemplary Black women teachers. *Urban Review, 34*(1), 71–86.

Burke, K., Collier, B., & McKenna, M. (2014). *College student voices on educational reform.* New York, NY: Palgrave Macmillan.

Creswell, J. W. (2011). *Educational research: Planning, conducting, and evaluating quantitative and qualitative research* (4th ed.). Upper Saddle River, NJ: Pearson.

Debruin-Parecki, A., & Teel, K. M. (2012). *Making school count: Promoting urban student motivation and success.* New York, NY: Taylor and Francis.

Delpit, L. (2013). *"Multiplication is for white people": Raising expectations for other people's children.* New York, NY: The New Press.

Fordham, S., & Ogbu, J. (1986). Black students' school success: Coping with the "burden of 'acting white.'" *Urban Review, 18*(3), 176–206.

Garza, R. (2009). Latino and White students' perceptions of caring behaviors: Are we culturally responsive to our students? *Urban Education, 44*(3), 297–321.

Gay, G. (2000). *Culturally responsive teaching.* New York, NY: Teachers College Press.

Gorski, P. (2013). *Reaching and teaching students in poverty: Strategies for erasing the opportunity gap.* New York, NY: Teachers College Press.

Howard, T. C. (2013). How does it feel to be a problem? Black male students, schools, and learning in enhancing knowledge base to disrupt deficit frameworks. *Review of Research in Education, 37*(1), 54–86.

Holgaard, R., Kovac, V. B., Overby, N. C., & Hougen, T. (2015). Academic self-efficacy mediates the effects of school psychological climate on academic achievement. *School Psychology Quarterly, 30*(1), 64–74.

Institute of Medicine. (2004). *Engaging schools: Fostering high school students' motivation to learn.* Washington, DC: National Academies Press.

Johnson, B., & Stevens, J. J. (2006). Student achievement and elementary teachers' perceptions of school climate. *Learning Environments Research, 9*(2), 111–122.

Milner, H. R. (2012). But what is urban education? *Urban Education, 47*(3), 556–561.

Mitra, D. L. (2003). Student voice in school reform: Reshaping student-teacher relationships. *McGill Journal of Education, 38*(2), 289–304.

Noddings, N. (1984). *Caring: A feminine approach to ethics and moral education* (2nd Ed.). Berkeley & Los Angeles, CA: University of California Press.

Noddings, N. (1988). An ethic of caring and its implications for instructional arrangements. *American Journal of Education, 96*(2), 215–230.

Noddings, N. (2005). *The challenge to care in schools: An alternative approach to education.* New York, NY: Teachers College Press.

O'Malley, M., Voight, A., Renshaw, T. L., & Ecklund, K. (2015). School climate, family structure, and academic achievement: A study of moderation effects. *School Psychology Quarterly, 30*(1), 142–157.

Perry, T., & Delpit, L. (1998). *The real Ebonics debate: Power, language, and the education of African American children.* Boston, MA: Beacon Press.

Phelan, P., Davidson, A. L., & Yu, H. C. (1993). Students' multiple worlds: Navigating the borders of family, peer, and school cultures. In P. Phelan & A. L. Davidson (Eds.), *Negotiating cultural diversity in American schools* (pp. 52–60). New York, NY: Teachers College Press.

Sergiovanni, T. J. (2000). *The lifeworld of leadership: Creating culture, community, and personal meaning in our schools.* San Francisco, CA: Jossey-Bass.

Sherblom, S. A., Marshall, J. C., & Sherblom, J. C. (2006). The relationship between school climate and math and reading achievement. *Journal of Research in Character Education, 4*(1-2), 19–31.

Usher, A., & Kober, N. (2013). Student motivation: An overlooked piece of school reform. *Education Digest, 78*(5), 9–16.

Wheeler, R. S., & Swords, R. (2006). *Code-switching: Teaching Standard English in urban classrooms.* Urbana, IL: National Council of Teachers of English.

Young, V. A., Barrett, R., Young-Rivera, Y., & Lovejoy, K. B. (2014). *Other people's English: Code-meshing, code-switching, and African American literacy.* New York, NY: Teacher's College Press.

CHAPTER 4

A STUDY OF STUDENTS' SOCIAL IDENTITIES AND A "HISTORICAL EMPATHY GAP" IN MIDDLE AND SECONDARY SOCIAL STUDIES CLASSES WITH THE INSTRUCTIONAL UNIT "THE ELIZABETH JENNINGS PROJECT"

Katherine Perrotta

ABSTRACT

The purpose of this study is to examine whether middle and secondary students' social identities impact exhibition of historical empathy through analysis of an underrepresented historical figure with the instructional unit "The Elizabeth Jennings Project." Major findings show that evidence of a "historical empathy gap" exists with regard to disparities on how students of diverse racial affiliations, English language proficiency, gender identities, and learning abilities impact demonstration of historical empathy.

Historical empathy (HE) is an important aspect of social studies instruction that is shaped through students' analyses of the historical context of documents, investigations of the perspectives of authors of documents, and making affective connections to content and/or personal experiences (Huijgen van Boxtel, van de Grift, & Holthuis, 2017; Endacott & Brooks, 2013; Yilmaz, 2007). Although considerable scholarship exists about pedagogies that promote the cognitive aspects of HE in middle and secondary social studies, there is limited research about how subjective conditions, such as students' social identities that include racial, gender, and ethnic affiliations, foster HE (Brooks, 2011; Colby, 2009–2010; Dulberg, 2002; Epstein & Shiller, 2005). As debates concerning issues such as civil liberties, race, gender rights, and immigration persist in the 24/7 news cycle, social media, and legislative bodies persist, understanding whether students' social identities impact demonstration of HE is critical for educators to promote historical thinking skills, civic engagement, and participation in this democratic society (VanSledright, 2001).

PURPOSE OF STUDY AND RESEARCH QUESTIONS

The purpose of this study is to analyze whether the students' social identities impact demonstration of HE through source analysis about antebellum civil rights activist Elizabeth Jennings with the instructional unit "The Elizabeth Jennings Project" (EJP). The question that frames this research is as follows:

> Do students' social identities reveal insights about whether racial, gender, and/or ethnic affiliation(s) impact demonstration of HE through engagement of an instructional unit about Elizabeth Jennings as an underrepresented historical figure in middle and secondary social studies classes? If so, how? If not, why?

Endacott's (2010) recommendations for further scholarship on whether the affective aspects of HE are shaped through source analysis about underrepresented historical figures inspired me to focus on Jennings as the curricular focus of this study. Jennings was ejected from a streetcar in New York City in 1854 due to her race. Although she successfully sued the Third Avenue Railway Company for violating common carrier laws, which stipulated the accommodation of paying passengers on public conveyances, she remains a relatively obscure historical figure (Hewitt, 1990; Perrotta & Bohan, 2013). Traditionally, the mainstream social studies curriculum has focused on Eurocentric narratives, hence rendering the histories of minorities and women as "add-ons" in the curriculum (Loewen, 1995; Kincheloe, 2001, pp. 249, 258). As a result, examination of whether students' social identities impact their demonstration of HE through analysis of an underrepresented historical figure may be a way to promote "social understandings" (Gutsell & Inzlicht, 2012) that combat "a ubiquitous lack of awareness of how ... minority groups fought for and achieved civil rights" (Perrotta & Bohan, 2013, p. 14).

LITERATURE REVIEW

This literature review highlights several features about the subjective aspects of HE regarding defining social identities, HE assessment, and connections to curricular initiatives, which this study aims to contribute.

Social Identities and Historical Empathy

Practitioners and researchers must be aware of what students' social identities are and how they are determined to effectively understand how these subjectivities impact demonstration of HE. As stated previously, students' social identities include family cultures, language abilities, biases, life experiences, and attitudes toward primary and secondary source research. Additionally, Brown and Capozza (2016) contend that social identity is impacted by the emotional significance one places on belonging to a group (p. 16). This is an important point with regard to understanding how social identification may impact demonstration of HE. For example, students who identify with minority groups may experience anxiety with regard to his or her social affiliations and/or interactions with other groups, whereas students who are part of a majority group may exert their need for belonging by perpetuating biases and prejudice against others (Brown & Capozza, 2016, pp. 8, 17–18).

Although friction can arise between groups, such tensions can serve as teachable moments in which students of different social affiliations can demonstrate HE. One way these aims can be achieved is through analysis of counterstories. The implementation of counterstories, or "unofficial" histories of underrepresented individuals and groups, as "powerful literature" that "problematize[s] ethical decisions" can facilitate "moral motivation ... within the agent or within interactions" that can promote cognitive and emotive elements of HE (Noddings, 2002, pp. 1–2; Stinson, 2008; Tyson, 2006). Brown and Capozza (2016) contend that when intergroup interactions are facilitated "on equal footing" and entrenched in "cooperative activity" to understand diverse perspectives, anxieties and prejudices may decrease and empathy may increase (p. 20). In short, the inclusion of counterstories in curricula, such as the EJP, may promote HE by encouraging empathetic interactions among students of diverse social identities.

Assessment

Another major concern with regard to the subjective nature of HE pertains to assessment. According to Cunningham (2009), evaluating students for HE proficiency is difficult due to the fact much of the cognitive and emotive elements of HE "happens in the minds of students" (p. 694). Moreover, another factor that poses challenges when evaluating students' demonstration of HE pertains to misconceptions that HE involves only using one's imagination and feelings to understand historical contexts and perspectives (Lee & Shemilt, 2011, p. 40). In order to clarify this misconception, Endacott and Brooks (2013) assert that HE is "a dual-dimensional, cognitive-affective construct" (p. 41). Studies by Barton and Levstik (2004), Kohlmeier (2005), Brooks (2008), Jensen (2008), and Metzger (2012) show that the intellectual and emotive elements of HE are interdependent skills that can be considered when applied to a variety of pedagogical tasks such as Socratic seminars, debate, narrative writing, and film analysis, hence demonstrating that HE is not purely an imaginative or emotional act.

Furthermore, Endacott (2014) and Lee and Shemilt (2011) argue that successful frameworks for assessing HE skills should focus on the process in which students engage in cognitive and affective tasks. For example, Dulberg (2002), Lee and Ashby (2001), and Lee and Shemilt (2011) provide frameworks that emphasize this progression by highlighting that lower levels of HE demonstration occur when students base historical interpretations on generalizations, stereotypes, and judgments of the past based on present-day terms; whereas students who demonstrate higher levels of HE are able to discern how the past is different from the present. Although these frameworks are comprehensive measurement tools of the cognitive aspects of HE, they are limited with regard to evaluating how students' social identities impact their displays of HE. As a result, effective frameworks need to include ways to assess for the dual-dimensional aspects of HE that "extend beyond the cognitive aspects of how we think historically" (Endacott, 2010, p. 6).

Connections to Current Pedagogical and Curricular Initiatives

Despite challenges with regard to identifying students' social affiliations and assessing for HE demonstration, current pedagogical and curricular initiatives support the promotion of HE in social studies. For example, the National Council for the Social Studies (NCSS) College, Career, and Civic Life Framework for Social Studies Standards (C3 Framework) states, "Historical understanding requires developing a sense of empathy with people in the past whose perspectives might be very different from those of today" (NCSS, 2013, p. 47). Furthermore, the Common Core Standards for History/Social Studies connect with the curricular goals of HE with regard to student analysis and application source evidence to determine historical contexts and perspectives and making historical arguments (National Governor's Association Center for Best Practices, 2010). Although the EJP connects to the curricular goals of the C3 Framework and CCS, Wright and Endacott (2016) caution that "the focus on narrow performance criteria for tasks such as written historical argumentation may result in a disconnect between the instrumental ends of the [common core] and the broader purposes of history education" (p. 309). Consequently, practitioners must consider how to foster the cognitive and affective aspects of HE and connect students' social identities to content without solely accommodating instruction to test objectives.

METHODOLOGY

Case study methodology was implemented for this investigation of whether students' social identities impacted demonstration of HE in middle and secondary social studies classes. A case study provides "theoretical insight, and for examining the fine detail of social life" (Prior, 2003, p. 153), such as a classroom. Case study methodology was selected for this research for several reasons. First, the study site provided a small sample size of student participants that was conducive for the researcher to ascertain deep insights about whether students' social identities impacted demonstration of HE through her observations of their engagement in the EJP during class lessons and focus group interviews. Second, this methodology builds upon Endacott's (2010) case study recommendations with regard to gaining greater understandings of whether engaging students in historical inquiry about underrepresented historical figures such as Elizabeth Jennings can promote the affective aspects of HE.

Data Collection and Analysis

Several data collection protocols were implemented in this study. First, I collected students' work samples from the EJP and applied the Historical Empathy Measurement Rubric (HEMR) to determine evidence of HE demonstration. These work samples included K-W-L Charts, first-and third-person narrative writing assignments, a document-based question (DBQ) essay, and notes taken from DBQs for an in-class debate. I adapted the HEMR from Lee and Shemilt's (2011) Five-Level Framework, which is a comprehensive measurement of the cognitive and emotive elements of HE based upon three decades of scholarship on HE pedagogies and assessment (Brooks, 2008; Endacott, 2010; Foster, 2001; Lee & Ashby, 2001; Portal, 1987; Shemilt, 1987). I used the HEMR as the measurement tool for this study because it provides a range of HE demonstration based on a five-level scale. These five levels included:

> **Level 1:** No evidence of HE; students view the past as dysfunctional and/or based on distortions about past peoples and events.
>
> **Level 2:** Some evidence of HE; students do not view the past as "inferior" but use generalizations to explain the past as being dysfunctional when compared to the present.
>
> **Level 3:** Moderate level of HE demonstration; students make generalizations about the past that are based on stereotypes without the views that the past is inferior to the present.
>
> **Level 4:** Moderate to high level of HE demonstration; students can understand positions of the past by explaining perspectives in historical context, but base these understandings from a presentist lens.
>
> **Level 5:** Highest level of HE demonstration; students recognize that the past is different from the present, that people in the past made decisions based upon the times, and do not view the past from a presentist lens.

Conceptualizing why a student who performs at a Level 1 demonstrates lower levels of HE versus a student who scores at a Level 5 is a major aspect of assessing for HE. A student who performs at a Level 1 views the actions and perspectives of people in the past as nonsensical or illogical, whereas a student who performs at a Level 5 comprehends why people in the past held certain points of view given the context of the times. For example, the EJP addresses the issues of racial discrimination in the antebellum North. There were people living in New York City, such as Mayor Fernando Wood, who disagreed with abolition and proposed secession from the Union to maintain cotton trade with the Confederacy during the Civil War (Burrows & Wallace, 1999). A student who performs at a Level 1 may express that Wood's position on slavery was wrong without considering the socioeconomic and political context of the antebellum period and Civil War with regard to why someone living in the North, where slavery was abolished, would support the Confederacy. A student at a Level 5 would be able to identify and explain how the economic and racial context of the antebellum period shaped people's perspectives on controversial issues such as slavery and make judgments on those perspectives without viewing the past from today's standards.

A major concern that practitioners must keep in mind when using the HEMR or any sort of measurement tool to assess for HE, particularly when teaching topics like slavery, is not condoning wrongdoings in the past. Scholars caution that HE is not sympathy, especially for the "wrong" people in history (Lee & Ashby, 2001, p. 22; Noddings, 2002). Seixas and Peck (2004) state, "Meaningful history cannot entertain a relativism that disallows our condemnation of brutal slave owners, enthusiastic Nazis, and marauding conquistadors" (p. 113). Hence, teaching HE does not involve sympathizing with oppression, genocide, racism, and crimes against humanity. Instead, HE entails teaching with multiple sources with different perspectives in order for students to deepen their understanding of how and why people's decisions in the past impact their conceptualizations of the past and relevancy of historical content to their lives, community, and world.

Furthermore, I conducted three focus group sessions with eight students in each group after teaching the last lesson of the EJP in order to gain deeper insights about whether students' social identities impacted their demonstration of HE. The school administrator and I chose the students who participated in the focus group sessions, which lasted 45 minutes each. I used Sellers, Smith, Shelton, Rowley, and Chavous's (1998) Multidimensional Model of Racial Identity (MMRI) criterion as a model for creating semistructured interview questions for the focus group sessions. This model was used because Sellers et al. recommend that scholars use the MMRI as a means to understand students' social identities that pertain to "significance and meaning of ethnic group membership" (p. 19). Since the MMRI is designed to elicit insights about the racial identity of African American students, the MMRI was developed to include broader questions to connect to students' diverse demographic backgrounds as seen in Table 4.1.

Several data analysis protocols were implemented in this study. First, the EJP assignments were graded based on the HEMR and averaged to ascertain whole-class data with regard to demonstration of HE from engagement in the EJP. Second, the HEMR data was disaggregated based on the students' demographics in order to assess whether students' social identities impacted their demonstration of HE. Third, the focus group data was analyzed in order to distinguish patterns with regard to whether students' social identities influenced their responses to the EJP materials. Two independent reviewers evaluated the students' EJP assignments in

Table 4.1.
Student Focus Group Questions

Question	Responses
How do you identify yourself with regard to race and/or ethnic background?	
What were your thoughts about Elizabeth Jennings at the start of this unit?	
Do you think your participation in the EJP influenced your understanding of yours and others' positions?	
Prior to these lessons, did you think race and inequality were problems in the United States?	
Prior to these lessons, did you think race and inequality were problems in your community?	
Do you or anyone you know have any experiences with racial inequality? If so, explain.	
Think about some recent events in the news in the United States. Do you think there are similarities to the challenges Elizabeth Jennings faced?	
What do you think can be learned from Jennings that is helpful to understanding race and/or inequity?	
Have your views on race and inequality changed after learning about Elizabeth Jennings?	

order to ensure the reliability of the HEMR for student demonstration of HE. Frequent member checks with the school administrator and participating students were conducted in order to ensure the accuracy of the HEMR and focus group data analyses.

Instrumentation

There were five lessons of the EJP that were taught over the course of 5 days during 45-minute periods. Colby's historical narrative inquiry model (2009–2010) guided and aligned with the design of these lessons, which focused on the activation of prior knowledge, comprehension of secondary sources on historical content, document analysis, narrative writing, and asking questions and drawing conclusions in order to foster HE among middle and secondary students. Lesson One involved a small group and a whole-class discussion of prior knowledge about matters of civil rights using a K-W-L graphic organizer. Students examined primary and secondary sources about Elizabeth Jennings in Lessons 2 and 3 and wrote first- or third-person narratives using evidence from these sources to support their arguments. An in-class debate was conducted during Lesson 4, where students were assigned to argue whether Jennings was justified in her actions using source evidence. Students completed the "L" column of the K-W-L graphic organizer as an individual reflection, then shared what they learned in a class discussion during Lesson 5 to conclude the unit.

Study Site and Participants

The participants in this study were students at Shore Institute. Shore Institute is a private coeducational school in a large metropolitan region in the Northeast. Shore Institute was selected as the study site as a sample of convenience because I was acquainted with the principal and related to one of the faculty members at the school. Shore Institute's small class sizes and relative diversity were conducive for ascertaining insights about whether students' social identities impacted demonstration of HE through engagement of the EJP. There were 13 students in a combined 7th- and 8th-grade class, 9 students in the 11th-grade class, and 12 students in the 12th-grade class. The summarized demographic information that was provided by the study participants is highlighted in Table 4.2.

Table 4.2.
Summarized Study Participants' Demographic Information

Total # of Students	Male	Female	Asian(a)	African American	White (Non-Hispanic or Latino) (b)
29	78.57%	21.42%	25%	17.85%	39.28%
(a)	Students who identified as Indian, Bangladeshi, Pakistani, or the Asian Subcontinent were counted as Asian.				
(b)	Students who identified as being of Middle Eastern descent were counted as White.				

Role of the Researcher and Subjectivities

I had an emic role in this study: I taught the classes, conducted the focus group sessions, had significant influence over implementation of pedagogies, and determined what questions to ask during the focus group sessions. Furthermore, I spent years researching Elizabeth Jennings and developing the EJP as a graduate student. The emic nature of my role presents a significant limitation to this research, as having an etic role in this study might have yielded different results. Consequently, my ability to be completely objective was not possible.

FINDINGS

These HEMR scores show that students demonstrated midlevels of HE when they engaged in the cognitive acts of activating prior knowledge with the K-W-L chart, writing first- and third-person narratives based on primary and secondary source analyses, and citing document evidence in an in-class debate about whether Jennings was justified in her actions against the Third Avenue Railway Company. The summarized HEMR scores are seen in Table 4.3.

Table 4.3.
Summarized Findings of Whole-Class Data (Scores Out of 5-HEMR)

Grade	K-W-L Chart	1st- or 3rd-Person Narrative Writing	Debate	Overall Score
7th & 8th	2.64	2.6	2.77	2.67
11th	2.8	2.5	2.9	2.733
12th	2.45	2.3	2.27	2.34

Although these HEMR scores show that students were proficient in demonstrating their academic understandings of the content of the EJP, the whole-class data was limited with regard to evaluating whether students' social identities impacted their demonstration of HE. Once the whole-class data was disaggregated based on students' demographic information, a "historical empathy gap" emerged as seen in Table 4.4. Next, the focus group data was analyzed in order to gain further insights about why white students had higher HEMR scores as compared to students of color, women, students with special needs, and English language learners (ELLs). The focus group data included in the analysis of findings are cited as "Field Notes."

Race

African American students scored lower than their White peers on the formal skills assessed in the EJP assignments, such as narrative writing, but were more proficient in making affective connections to content during class

Table 4.4.
Summarized Data of Students' Averaged HEMR Scores Based on Demographics

Student Demographics	# of Students	Averaged HEMR Score
African American	5	2.54
White	9	2.868
Hispanic	6	2.775
Asian	9	2.54
Male	22	2.66
Female	7	2.2
Special Education	11	2.35
General Education	18	2.88
English Language Learners	4	2.17

discussions, the debate activity, and focus group sessions. White students predominately expressed throughout the EJP their beliefs that Americans are equal and free today and that attitudes of racism are "outdated," "evil," and "stupid" (Field Notes, January 8, 2016). One White student stated, "There is no more slavery, so we are free" (Field Notes, January 8, 2016). However, African American students raised contemporary issues of discrimination during the implementation of the EJP more frequently. For instance, an African American student highlighted the examples of Trayvon Martin, Dylan Roof, and Eric Garner, stating, "Racism holds us back from advancement ... racism and prejudice will never go away" (Field Notes, January 8, 2016). The identification of these cases is important, for many White students did not make these current connections to issues with race in the EJP activities. As a result, these responses support the existence of a historical empathy gap with regard to how the social identities and experiential knowledge of students of color impacted their affective connections to content, whereas White students possessed stronger cognitive skills when demonstrating understanding of the cognitive aspects of historical understanding through analysis of the EJP documents.

Special Needs Students

One-third of the students in this study were identified as having learning or emotional special needs and had an individualized educational plan (IEP). Many of the special needs students verbalized their thoughts about the EJP content during class discussions, in-class debate, and focus group sessions more effectively than in the written assignments. For example, one student with an IEP raised the issue of representation in curricula, noting "textbooks decide what's important, and let's face it, there were probably thousands of people like Jennings who were kicked off trains" (Field Notes, January 8, 2016). This statement evidenced her HE demonstration with regard to issues pertaining to historical figures that are represented in school textbooks. These findings suggest, that similar to students of color, special needs students exhibit stronger affective elements of HE when given assignments that connect to their life experiences and demographic affiliations.

Gender

The historical empathy gap was particularly significant between the male and female students in this study. A major reason for this discrepancy was that there were almost five times more boys than girls enrolled in the participating classes. The only instance where matters of gender were raised during the implementation of this study occurred during the 12th-grade focus group session. One female student remarked that "power" played a role in Jennings's case, stating, "If I were in her situation, I'd raise awareness, because women are not weaker than men" (Field Notes, January 8, 2016).According to Noddings (2002) and Kornfeld (1992), the inclusion of feminine perspectives and sources about women may promote HE and "contextual thinking" among male and female students (p. 28). I might have elicited greater insights about whether students' gender impacted their displays of HE had the MMRI and EJP lessons contained specific questions about gender.

English Language Learners (ELLs)

ELLs yielded the lowest on the HEMR. Similar to the demonstration of HE among special needs students, ELLs strongly displayed HE through class discussions and the focus group sessions instead of written assignments. For instance, an ELL student who identified as Asian stated, "We moved a long way from racial segregation, but I believe there is a lot of racism towards all races and Muslims" (Field Notes, January 8, 2016). When I asked the student to clarify this statement, he/she was referring to "things being said" leading up to the 2016 presidential primaries (Field Notes, January 8, 2016).I conducted a member check with the school administrator about the ELL students' HEMR scores and focus group responses. He noted that the students "scored overall levels higher than anticipated," particularly due to the fact many of these students were new arrivals to the United States (Field Notes, July 15, 2016). The school administrator's observations were insightful, as several of these students came from Communist or former Communist countries in Eastern Europe and Asia, where human rights issues are still a problem. Consequently, ELL's HEMR scores suggest that their experiential knowledge and cognizance of current events impacted their demonstration of HE.

DISCUSSION

The evidence indicates a historical empathy gap in this study, highlighting that students' social identities impact demonstration of HE. The HEMR data show that White students possessed stronger cognitive skills identifying historical context and perspectives of authors in sources in the EJP. However, students of color, special needs students, and ELLs demonstrated stronger affective responses to content, particularly during the focus group sessions and EJP activities that involved verbal responses. These findings may suggest that instructional units like the EJP that contain assignments and assessments that connect to students' social identities as well as learning ability and language proficiency may promote HE and close the historical empathy gap.

LIMITATIONS

There were limitations to this study. First, the HEMR was not an effective measurement of whether students' social identities impacted their demonstration of HE. As a result, a rubric that includes criteria to evaluate for evidence of students' affective responses to content may provide insights into how students develop the cognitive and emotive skills of HE through analysis of underrepresented historical figures. Second, the focus group questions were initially designed to elicit students' perspectives about race. Questions that probe for insights about other social affiliations such as gender, ethnic affiliation, and religion may provide more data about how students' social identities contribute to demonstration of HE and why a historical empathy gap exists.

RECOMMENDATIONS FOR FUTURE RESEARCH

There are two major areas for future research that may serve to close the historical empathy gap and probe for greater understandings on how students' social identities impact demonstration of HE. First, there is little scholarship on effective pedagogical factors that promote HE among special education students. Harris-Murri, King, and Rostenberg (2006) contend that the implementation of response-to-intervention (RTI) strategies, such as thorough evaluation of services and differentiated instruction, may be effective methods to promote HE for special needs students. More research on the implementation of RTI strategies may help close the historical empathy gap for special needs students.

Second, there is a lack of research on effective strategies that can promote HE among ELLs, women, and students of color. Cruz and Thornton (2013) note that effective methods for ELL social studies instruction include providing students the opportunity to analyze culturally relevant curricula that can support exhibition of the cognitive and affective elements of HE. Furthermore, Kumagai and Lypson (2009) assert that matters of multicultural education "must go beyond the traditional notions of 'competency' (i.e., knowledge, skills, and attitudes). It must involve the fostering of a critical awareness—a critical consciousness—of the self, others, and the world" (p. 782). As a result, further scholarship is needed to gain insights on whether the implementation of culturally relevant curricula and counterstories promotes HE by providing students with the opportunity to assess "whose knowledge matters most" (Buras, Randels, Salaam, & Students at the Center, 2010, p. 1).

CONCLUSION

The findings of this study demonstrate that students' social identities, which include racial, gender, and ethnic affiliations, as well as language proficiency and learning abilities, can impact demonstration of HE. Students who identified as White demonstrated stronger cognitive skills pertaining to written proficiency in the EJP assignments, whereas minority students displayed greater affective connections to experiential knowledge, hence evidencing a historical empathy gap. Further research is needed to address how the inclusion of differentiated assignments, holistic assessment tools, counterstories, and culturally relevant curricula, and broader interview protocols can elicit deeper understandings about how students' social identifications impact their demonstration of HE. By understanding the role students' social identities play in the exhibition of the cognitive and affective elements of HE, practitioners and scholars may be better equipped to promote the curricular and pedagogical aims of current social studies initiatives that foster greater civil engagement in social studies classrooms across the country.

REFERENCES

Barton, K. C., & Levstik, L. S. (2004). *Teaching history for the common good.* Mahwah, NJ: Lawrence Erlbaum Associates.

Brooks, S. (2008). Displaying historical empathy: What impact can a writing assignment have? *Social Studies Research and Practice, 3*(2), 130–146.

Brooks, S. (2011). Historical empathy as perspective recognition and care in one secondary social studies classroom. *Theory and Research in Social Studies Education, 39*(2), 166–202.

Brown, R., & Capozza, D. (Eds.). (2016). *Social identities: Motivations, emotional, and cultural influences.* New York, NY: Routledge.

Buras, K. L., Randels, J., Salaam, K. Y., & Students at the Center. (2010). *Pedagogy, policy, and the privatized city: Stories of dispossession and defiance from New Orleans.* New York, NY: Teacher's College Press.

Burrows, E. G., & Wallace, M. (1999). *Gotham: A history of New York City to 1898.* New York, NY: Oxford University Press.

Colby, S. R. (2009–2010). Contextualization and historical empathy: Seventh-graders' interpretations of primary documents. *Curriculum & Teaching Dialogue, 12*(1&2), 69–83.

Cruz, B. C., & Thornton, S. J. (2013). *Teaching social studies to English language learners* (2nd ed.). New York, NY: Routledge.

Cunningham, D. L. (2009). An empirical framework for understanding how teachers conceptualize and cultivate historical empathy in students. *Journal of Curriculum Studies, 41*(5), 679–709.

Dulberg, N. (2002, April). *Engaging in history: Empathy and perspective-talking in children's historical thinking.* Paper presented at the annual meeting of the American Educational Research Association, New Orleans, LA. ERIC Document Reproduction service, No. ED 474 135, 1–48.

Endacott, J. L. (2010). Reconsidering affective engagement in historical empathy. *Theory and Research in Social Education, 38*(1), 6–49.

Endacott, J. L. (2014). Negotiating the process of historical empathy. *Theory and Research in Social Studies Education, 42*(1), 4–34.

Endacott, J. L., & Brooks, S. (2013). An updated theoretical and practical model for promoting historical empathy. *Social Studies Research and Practice, 8*(1), 41–58.

Epstein, T., & Shiller, J. (2005). Perspective matters: Social identity and the teaching and learning of national history. *Social Education, 69*(4), 201–204.

Foster, S. J. (2001). Historical empathy in theory and practice: Some final thoughts. In O. L. Davis, E. A., Yeager, & S. J. Foster (Eds.), *Historical empathy and perspective taking in the social studies* (pp. 167–181). Lanham, MD: Roman and Littlefield.

Gutsell, J. N., & Inzlicht, M. (2012). Intergroup differences in the sharing of emotive states: Neural evidence of an empathy gap. *Social Cognitive and Affective Neuroscience, 7*(5), 596–603.

Harris-Murri, N., King, K., & Rostenberg, D. (2006). Reproducing disproportionate minority representation in special education programs for students with emotional disturbances: Toward a culturally responsive response to intervention model. *Education & Treatment of Children, 29*(4), 779–799.

Hewitt, J. H. (1990). Search for Elizabeth Jennings: Heroine of a Sunday afternoon in New York City. *New York History*, *71*(4), 387–415.

Huijgen, T., van Boxtel, C., van de Grift, W., & Holthuis, P. (2017). Toward historical perspective taking: Students' reasoning when contextualizing the actions of people in the past. *Theory and Research in Social Education*, *45*(1), 110–144.

Jensen, J. (2008). Developing historical empathy through debate: An action research study. *Social Studies Research and Practice*, *3*(1), 55–67.

Kincheloe, J. L. (2001). *Getting beyond the facts: Teaching social studies/social sciences in the twenty-first century.* New York, NY: Peter Lang.

Kohlmeier, J. (2005). The power of a woman's story: A three step approach to historical significance in high school world history. *International Journal of Social Education*, *20*(1), 64–80.

Kornfeld, E. (1992). The power of empathy: A feminist, multicultural approach to historical pedagogy. *The History Teacher*, *26*(1), 23–31.

Kumagai, A. K., & Lypson, M. L. (2009). Beyond cultural competence: Critical consciousness, social justice, and multicultural education. *Academic Medicine*, *84*(6), 782–787.

Lee, P., & Ashby, R. (2001). Empathy, perspective taking, and rational understanding. In O. L. Davis, E. A. Yeager, & S. J. Foster (Eds.), *Historical empathy and perspective taking in the social studies* (pp. 21–50). Lanham, MD: Roman and Littlefield.

Lee, P., & Shemilt, D. (2011). The concept that dares not speak its name: Should empathy come out of the closet? *Teaching History, 143, Constructing Claims,* 39–49.

Loewen, J. W. (1995). *Lies my teacher told me: Everything your social studies textbook got wrong.* New York, NY: Touchstone.

Metzger, S. A. (2012). The borders of historical empathy: Students encounter the Holocaust through film. *Journal of Social Studies Research*, *34*(4), 387–410.

National Council for the Social Studies. (2013). *The college, career, and civic life (C3) framework for social studies state standards: Guidance for enhancing the rigor of K–12 civics, economics, geography, and history.* Silver Springs, MD: NCSS. Retrieved from http://www.socialstudies.org/sites/default/files/c3/C3-Framework-for-Social-Studies.pdf

National Governors Association Center for Best Practices, Council of Chief State School Officers. (2010). *Common core state standards: English language arts standards- History/social studies, grades 6-12.* Washington DC: National Governors Association Center for Best Practices Council of Chief State School Officers. Retrieved from http://www.corestandards.org/ELA-Literacy/RH/introduction/

Noddings, N. (2002). *Educating moral people: A caring alternative to character education.* New York. NY: Teacher's College Press.

Perrotta, K. A., & Bohan, C. H. (2013). Nineteenth century Rosa Parks? Assessing Elizabeth Jennings' legacy as a teacher and civil rights pioneer in antebellum America. *Vitae Scholasticae: The Journal of Educational Biography*, *30*(2), 5–23.

Portal, C. (1987). Empathy as an objective for history teaching. In Portal, C. (Ed.), *The history curriculum for teachers* (pp. 89–99). London, England: Falmer Press.

Prior, L. (2003). *Using documents in social research.* Los Angeles, CA: SAGE.

Seixas, P., & Peck, C. (2004). Teaching historical thinking. In A. Sears & I. Wright (Eds.), *Challenges and prospects in Canadian social studies* (pp. 109–117). Vancouver, British Columbia, Canada: Pacific Educational Press.

Sellers, R. M., Smith, M. A., Shelton, J. N., Rowley, S. A., & Chavous, T. M. (1998). Multidimensional model of racial identity: A reconceptualization of African American racial identity. *Personality and Social Psychology Review, 2*(1), 18–39.

Shemilt, D. (1987). Adolescent ideas about evidence and methodology in history. In Portal, C. (Ed.). *The history curriculum for teachers* (pp. 39–61). London, England: Falmer Press.

Stinson, D. W. (2008). Negotiating sociocultural discourses: The counter-storytelling of academically (and mathematically) successful African American male students. *American Educational Research Journal, 45*(4), 975–1010.

Tyson, C. A. (2006). Research, race, and social education. In K. C. Barton (Ed.), *Research methods in social studies education: Contemporary issues and perspectives* (pp. 39–56). Greenwich, CT: Information Age.

VanSledright, B. A. (2001). From empathic regard to self-understanding: Im/positionality, empathy, and historical contextualization. In O. L. Davis, E. A. Yeager, & S. J. Foster (Eds.), *Historical empathy and perspective taking in the social studies* (pp. 51–68). Lanham, MD: Roman and Littlefield.

Wright, G. P., & Endacott, J. L. (2016). Historical inquiry and the limitations of the common core state standards. *Journal of Social Studies Research, 40*(4), 309–324.

Yilmaz, K. (2007). Historical empathy and its implications for classroom practices in schools. *The History Teacher, 40*(3), 331–337.

CHAPTER 5

ADVERTISING "GENEROSITY" IN SCHOOLS

Do You Want Fries With Your Curriculum?

Joseph Zajdel and Daniel R. Conn

ABSTRACT

In this study, we explore corporate branding as an implicit curriculum and its embedded presence in the school ecology. We discuss ways in which corporate brands infiltrate schools through false generosity in an effort to make sense of the realities of teaching and learning in the presence of embedded branding and advertising. The study concludes by discussing themes of commercial normativity and modeling consumption.

Marketing and advertising are ubiquitous in society, from television commercials to radio spots, online promotions, billboards, logos, storefronts, branding, musical jingles, and so forth. One particular strategy known as *cradle-to-grave* marketing seeks to *grow customers* by developing them during childhood and marketing to them for their entire lives (McNeal, 2007). In cradle-to-grave marketing, advertisers consider what children can buy for themselves, what they can encourage parents to purchase, and what they will be able to purchase throughout adulthood. McNeal (2000, 2007) identified the following five stages of consumer behavior development in children: (a) observing (0–6 months), (b) requesting (6–24 months), (c) selecting (24–48 months), (d) co-purchasing (48–72 months), and (e) solo purchasing (72–100 months). These stages describe a behavioral progression of (a) the child's initial awareness of the products a parent provides, (b) gesturing or asking for a product when it is present, (c) independently retrieving a product, (d) performing the purchasing act with parental assistance, and (e) performing the purchasing act without parental assistance. Children even have influence over parents' purchasing of both personal items for the children themselves and larger purchases for the family, such as automobiles, home furnishings, and other brands to which youth have had media exposure ("Trillion-dollar Kids," 2006). Advertisers also target children in schools through sponsorship programs, exclusive vending agreements for popular products such as soft drinks, incentive programs, allocations of school space, sponsored educational materials, electronic marketing, and fundraising (Molnar, 2005; Molnar, Boninger, Harris, Libby, & Fogarty, 2013). Examples include Pizza Hut's "BOOK IT!" and General Mills' "Box Tops for Education," among others.

Fast-food marketers, in particular, are adept at developing consumers during childhood. From 2003 to 2009, children's exposure to fast-food advertising increased by 21.1% among 2- to 5-year-olds and 30.8% among 6- to 11-year-olds (Powell, Schermbeck, Szczypka, Chaloupka, & Braunschweig, 2011). Branding also has a powerful influence on children's perceptions. For example, when provided with identical McDonald's fast-food items in branded and unbranded packaging, preschool children, particularly those from families with low incomes, preferred the taste of the food from the branded packaging (Robinson, Borzekowski, Matheson, & Kraemer, 2007). According to a meta-analysis (Sadeghirad, Duhandy, Motaghipisheh, Campbell, & Johnston, 2016) of children's exposure to unhealthy dietary marketing, the average dietary intake increased 30.4 calories during or within 15 minutes after exposure to advertisements. Thus, marketing unhealthy food options to children through public schools certainly raises some ethical concerns.

Unfortunately, the Federal Trade Commission's (FTC) recommendation for food companies to provide healthy lifestyle countermarketing education (FTC, 2008) resulted in little more than stealth branding opportunities (Molnar & Boninger, 2015) such as Coca-Cola emphasizing exercise to combat obesity (Coca-Cola Company, 2012) and Ronald McDonald as an "ambassador for health" in schools (Corporate Accountability International, 2010, p. 11). Countermarketing is also problematic because it shifts the responsibility away from those who target children to the children themselves (Molnar & Boninger, 2015). This issue is further complicated by seemingly healthful fast-food choices that lack nutritional quality. McDonald's salads, for example, contain as much and often more fat and sodium than their burgers, while other items, such as their oatmeal and their yogurt with fruit, contain high levels of sugar comparable to a can of soda (Harris, 2016).

Furthermore, according to the most recent data available from the FTC (2012), in-school food marketing was 8.3% of overall youth-directed food marketing expenditures. However, the same FTC report cautions this is likely an underestimated amount due to local expenditures that were not included in the analysis. While these marketing efforts may seem harmless, they reinforce assumptions for students "that the path to happiness and satisfaction lies through consumption" (Molnar & Boninger, 2015, p. 8). Unfortunately, these influences are common in schools because of the need for resources beyond those provided by conventional funding (Molnar, 2005).

With regard to schools, Saltman (2000) categorizes commercialization efforts into two distinct categories: those that are intended to appear educative and those that are simply promotional. The fast-food chain McDonald's provides "McTeacher's [sic] Night" to schools in order for a school to benefit by receiving a percentage of a participating restaurant's profits. During these events, teachers work at the restaurant and serve McDonald's food to students and families who purchase it. Consequently, and consistent with Saltman's *promotional* categorization, McDonald's brands itself in the school and positions itself as a well-meaning charitable organization worthy of one's business. However, various organizations, such as the Campaign for a Commercial-Free Childhood, state and local affiliates of the American Federation of Teachers, National Education Association Healthy Futures, and Corporate Accountability International regard McTeacher's Night as a danger to children and are calling on the McDonald's Corporation to discontinue these events (Ravitch, 2015).

Extant literature addresses school commercialism and marketing efforts from outside of school without venturing inside to observe these dynamics, and corporate branding in particular, within actual classroom environments. Thus, we aim to render an understanding of how corporate branding, along with its associated commercial and market influences, operationalizes within the ecology (Eisner, 1988) of a classroom in an elementary school.

THEORETICAL FRAMEWORK

Consumerism encompasses cultural, economic, and political forces where intersections of one's agency and larger hegemonic structures are continuous; such powers may operate outside of one's conscious awareness (Kincheloe, 2002). A culture of consumption equates *more* with *better* (Molnar, 2005); therefore, consumerism itself becomes the means (albeit false) for achieving success and happiness. At its worst, consumerism produces desires that overlap with rationality whereby the consumer purchases not only a product, but a way of life and an identity formed through the rationalization of the purchase of one's desired way of life.

Eisner (1988, 2017) describes the school as an ecological environment that involves interactions among curriculum, pedagogy, the school's structure of time and space, evaluative efforts, and the school's intended aims or goals. What happens in one part influences other parts of the school's ecology (Eisner, 1988). One type of curriculum schools teach is the *implicit curriculum* (Eisner, 2002b), which consists of messages students learn at school that are not an explicit part of the school's publicized goals. For example, commercial messages are enhanced and become part of the implicit curriculum when students can intuit that their teachers and schools approve of promoted products (Molnar & Boninger, 2015). When signs of branding and consumption are embedded in the school's physical environment, these symbols become part of the school ecology as well. When conventional funding does not provide for a school's needs (Molnar, 2005), the lack of funding provides an opportunity for a business to engage in seemingly charitable efforts (Simon, 2013) that promote the business and its products in the school. Therefore, we view such efforts through Freire's (1970) lens of *false generosity*. Though providing funds and branded promotional items to underfunded schools may seem generous, these acts perpetuate injustice because the corporations do not actually empower the schools to confront the conditions that cause underfunding. Rather, this arrangement reinforces current power structures and ultimately benefits the corporation that promotes its charitable image as it deducts its contribution from the tax pool to fund federal school initiatives such as Title I (Saltman, 2010). Conversely, a critical awareness of these influences within the school ecology would provide for reflection and action to transform this reality (Freire, 1970) from the structural and systemic forces that make marketing in schools possible.

METHODOLOGY

Our research question asks, "How does corporate branding interact with the elementary school ecology?" To answer this question, we used educational connoisseurship and criticism (Eisner, 2017), a qualitative inquiry aimed at appreciating the subtle qualities of educational environments through an aesthetic lens. Uhrmacher, McConnell Moroye, and Flinders (2017) describe appreciation as it relates to educational connoisseurship, which includes complex understandings of curricular frameworks, instructional practices, learning environments, and other qualities within the educational realm. "Learning to see what we have learned not to notice remains one of the most critical and difficult tasks of educational connoisseurs" (Eisner, 2017, p.77). The second aspect, educational criticism, is a matter of disclosing what was appreciated and offering a judgment in order to improve educational circumstances. To this end, educational criticism has four dimensions: (a) description, (b) interpretation, (c) evaluation, and (d) thematics (Eisner, 2002b).

The description and interpretation dimensions work together and are commonly revealed through vignettes (Uhrmacher et al., 2017). Then a critical perspective is presented as an evaluation. "Educational criticism is an approach to educational evaluation in which the subtle qualities perceived are rendered in a form that is analogous to the writing of art critics" (Barone, 2010, p. 313). Finally, suggestive insights are revealed in the form of thematic analysis (Eisner, 2017). Through thematic analysis, we make sense of what is happening for the purpose of transferring insights to other educational situations (Eisner, 2002b) to the extent to which comparable dynamics may be occurring.

Positioning Ourselves

We are both teacher educators who came to higher education after teaching in public K–12 schools. We are both influenced by the writings of Elliot Eisner, and while working together, we delved further into the writings of Paulo Freire. This combination of Eisner's curricular insights and Freire's critical pedagogy influenced our approach to this study. Eisner (2017) tells us that educational connoisseurs must learn to see what they have learned not to notice, and Freire's work taught us to notice what we had never seen. We also know from our past experiences as public-school teachers that we took part in fund-raisers and would have likely participated in fund-raising events such as that discussed herein if it made the difference between having or not having learning materials for our students. Thus, it is not our intent to criticize schools and teachers for participating in fund-raising; rather, we aim to illuminate how corporate brands interact with other dimensions of the school ecology (Eisner, 1988; Uhrmacher et al., 2017).

Design of the Study

This research is part of a larger study where we explored commercial influences in schools (Zajdel & Conn, 2017). In selecting our participants for the study, we sought teachers highly regarded for excellence since we did not want a lack of teaching ability to influence our study. In this article, we focus on one teacher, Molly, because market forces regarding health and nutrition were specific to the learning environment in which she taught. By appreciating what is happening in Molly's classroom and offering critical insights, we aim to nurture a sense of anticipation for subsequent educational situations in which similar fund-raising efforts interact with other elementary classroom ecologies.

We interviewed Molly about her curricular and pedagogical intentions and provided her with copies of the interview transcripts to ensure accurate representation and to offer an opportunity to clarify any possible misunderstandings. Although we are focusing on one participant in one school, educational connoisseurship and criticism, which we will now refer to simply as "educational criticism," differs from case study methodology. Similar to a case study (Stake, 1995), educational criticism involves using multiple sources of data such as interviews, observations, and a collection of artifacts. However, educational criticism differs from case study because it does not simply describe a bounded unit; it also interprets, evaluates, and offers thematic understandings (Eisner, 2017).

We were both present for the interviews and classroom observations, and we recorded field notes and collected classroom materials and curricular artifacts. Immediately after each interview and observation, we discussed our collected data and compared field notes. We contacted our participant for clarification whenever we had questions based on our observations or revelations from our interview analyses. Discussions of our perceptions, interpretations, and theoretical links continued throughout the course of the 2016–2017 academic year.

We use vignettes to describe and interpret our data, and we use pseudonyms for our teacher participant and her school. In rendering our descriptions, interpretations, and criticisms, we drew from the literature as well as our own experiences to illuminate understandings of the ways in which corporate branding interacts with an elementary classroom and school ecology.

DESCRIPTIONS AND INTERPRETATIONS

Molly, who is in her 26th year of teaching, is known as a strong veteran teacher across education circles and throughout the region. Over the span of her teaching career, Molly has taught at several schools, mostly in the same district. Presently, Molly teaches third grade at McCoy Elementary. McCoy qualifies as a Title I school, and the majority of students come from low socioeconomic backgrounds. After teaching in one of the wealthiest schools in the district, Molly came to McCoy to make a positive difference.

This year is Molly's second at McCoy. Next year Molly will move to fifth grade but will remain at McCoy.

Recently, Molly was involved in a school-wide effort to participate in McTeacher's Night, whereby the McCoy teachers raised funds by working a dinner shift at the local McDonald's fast-food restaurant. The local McDonald's franchise owner agreed to give a portion of the profits from the McTeacher's Night event to McCoy. A basic online search of McTeacher's Night revealed varied percentages of the profits shared with schools by local McDonald's franchise owners. As of this writing, the percentages were around 15 to 20%. However, the local McDonald's in Molly's town shared 25% of their proceeds with McCoy. The proceeds from the fund-raiser were supposed to go toward purchasing science kits. According to Molly, it would cost around $3,000 to have enough for the whole school to use the science kits on a regular basis. As Molly told us,

> One of our moms had met with her and talked with her, the owner lady [of McDonald's], and she was very excited to provide that opportunity for our little school to raise money for different things. And the husband is really into all the STEM, and STEAM now with the art integration part of it. And so when he found out about it, he was very excited.

Interestingly, the owners of the local McDonald's franchise also own a local franchise of Curves, a fitness facility for women, and McCoy received a presentation check from McDonald's that included an additional $200 from Curves for the McTeacher's Night event. Though we appreciate the intentions of the local franchise owners and the McCoy teachers, the McDonald's brand permeated the school.

To describe and interpret the ways in which McTeacher's Night provided an opportunity for McDonald's to advertise their brand in the school, we offer the following vignette detailing the physical school environment itself. Advertising for McDonald's, and branding in particular, is present above the cafeteria entrance. Furthermore, pictures of teachers working at McDonald's during McTeacher's Night have replaced student artwork that was once displayed on the main school bulletin board. To better understand the impact of branding on the school environment, we think it necessary to describe the visual context following McTeacher's Night.

Welcome to McCoy: Would You Like to Try Our Implicit Curriculum?

Upon entering McCoy Elementary, visitors see an intersection of the building's main hall crossing with a short hall from the front entrance that leads to the school's cafeteria. A large presentation check, payable to McCoy, in the amount of $1,704.58 hangs directly above the cafeteria entrance. The large golden arches of McDonald's adorn the left corner of the check from the local franchise. "McTeacher's Night" is written in the check's memo. A bulletin board across from the office, which once displayed students' artwork, now displays photos of the school's teachers working behind the counter, the drive-thru window, and the dining area of a local McDonald's fast-food restaurant. Block letters, posted above the teachers' photos, reads, "McCOY STAFF Is More Precious Than GOLD!" followed by a color print of a rainbow leading to a pot of gold. The photos show McCoy's teachers wearing aprons with "McTeacher's Night" logos, posing with restaurant employees, and delivering trays of food to students and parents.

Reflection. The McDonald's brand permeates McCoy Elementary. This McTeacher's Night was, all things considered, a profitable night for the school. However, McTeacher's Night seems to have been a better deal for McDonald's than it was for McCoy. In the arrangement, McCoy Elementary received $1,704.58. Conversely, McDonald's received labor from professional teachers; sales from the students, parents, and community members purchasing from the menu to support the school; and the opportunity to advertise the golden arches on a giant check, as if it were a donation, over the cafeteria—in plain sight from the front doors of the school. As a bonus, McDonald's gave the students red rubber bracelets with the McDonald's logo. In return, the McDonald's brand is potentially on every student in the school. Based on our prior discussion with Molly about McTeacher's Night and noting the large check from McDonald's for $1,704.58 above the school cafeteria, we noted the amount is short of the $3,000 price for the science kits. Nevertheless, the school's teachers and the franchise were eager to schedule another McTeacher's Night for the following month with the school hoping to raise enough money to purchase the science kits.

The following vignette details the beginning of a school day in Molly's third-grade classroom. We will describe and interpret classroom routines, as well as the cost associated with Molly purchasing learning materials for her students. In this vignette, we illuminate why fund-raising for science kits is a big deal to Molly.

Ba Da Ba Ba Bah…. A False Generosity

As the students come into the classroom, we notice the vast majority wearing red rubber McDonald's bracelets around their wrists. Molly walks to her desk and starts calling for the lunch count. "Chicken patties for lunch. Did you bring your own lunch or are you having a chicken patty?" Even the way the students give their morning lunch orders in the classroom takes on the shape of an embedded fast-food pedagogy. As Molly calls each student by number (not name), a rhythm of call and response ensues.

  Molly: One?
 Student 1: Brought my own.
  Molly: *Two?*
 Student 2: Chicken patty.
  Molly: Three?
 Student 3: Chicken patty.

The routine continues, with 12 out of 14 students selecting the chicken patty option. Molly finishes submitting the lunch order and transitions to math.

 The math lesson lasts about 45 minutes. The students review math vocabulary, solve problems on the class whiteboard, review more vocabulary using a website from the My Math curriculum (produced by McGraw-Hill), and then they take a math test. While taking the math test, all of the students guard their tests with thin, blue, cardboard privacy shields branded with the label "Lakeshore" in glossy white font. We ask what "Lakeshore" refers to, and Molly hands us a Lakeshore catalog. Molly confesses to us in a soft whisper that she orders classroom supplies such as privacy shields and standardized mathematical practice activity cards (i.e., flash cards with puzzle boarders that lock with corresponding pieces) often with her own money.

 Molly also uses her own money to pay for a subscription to H3TV, a video series designed to motivate students to exercise by dancing to music. Molly refers to this practice as "brain breaks." Suddenly, Molly announces, "Okay, everyone, let's take a quick brain break." The class seems to be excited for the brain break as they move to the front of the room and in front of the interactive whiteboard screen. Today's video features Rapping Roy and Reggie Regg. The company, H3TV, orchestrates hip-hop beats to share uplifting messages about education, as well as health and wellness. The students sing along and dance, following the words projected across the screen. Every student participates. Even the more reluctant students sway back and forth to the beat. Although Molly does not dance with the class, we do see a playful side of her as she encourages the class to dance and sing along.

 After about four minutes of dancing, the video comes to an end, and the students go back to their tables without Molly having to tell them. Sensing a break in the action, Molly sits by us and begins talking about some of her favorite products in the Lakeshore Catalog she provided to us earlier.

Suddenly, an adult (from the cafeteria) places a box of apples on a table near the classroom door, and the students say "thank you" without being prompted. We ask Molly about the apples, and she explains that, due to an agricultural grant, the students receive fruit as a daily snack in order to promote nutritious eating. Molly continues pointing out her favorite items in the catalog and admits some of the products are quite expensive. "It's 90 bucks for the leveled social studies readers." We can see why Molly likes McTeacher's Night. It costs Molly a great deal of her own money to purchase the educational products used in her classroom. While there is no doubt Molly is an effective and caring teacher, we came to realize that keeping the school and her class equipped with the latest educational materials is a challenge. We saw, first-hand, that McDonald's and other companies can advertise their brand throughout schools in the name of fund-raising.

Reflection. To understand what is happening, we turn again to Saltman (2000) who stresses that such corporate partnerships with public schools constitute a self-interested behavior where a corporation's primary concern is its own profit margin. Likewise, the rationale for these partnerships and philanthropic efforts is often grounded in branding and conditioning students and teachers to consume products (Saltman, 2000). Although students receive fruit to encourage nutritious eating, we now see the McDonald's brand throughout McCoy, and the McCoy teachers are already planning for the next McTeacher's Night when they will, once again, encourage students and their families to eat at McDonald's in order to support the school.

In trying to make sense of what was happening at McCoy, we learned that McDonald's has refocused its efforts toward marketing to children and their families in schools in order to curb their declining profits in the United States. According to Picchi (2014), the president of the U.S. McDonald's chain detailed a plan to investors to "start with mom and we will be helping her to feel great about McDonald's—whether it's McTeacher's Nights, sponsoring kids [sic] sports, or being a visible partner in local initiatives" (para. 3). Even though the teachers were certainly generous with their time in volunteering for McTeacher's Night, and the local franchise owner was comparatively generous with the percentage of the profits given to the school, we found what Freire (1970) refers to as "false generosity." McDonald's seems generous, and its brand throughout the school implies generosity, but McTeacher's Night allows McDonald's to advertise their corporate brand throughout the school. McTeacher's Night is ultimately about helping the school community to feel great about McDonald's.

EVALUATION: IS IT WORTH THE COST FOR SCHOOLS TO DO BUSINESS WITH CORPORATIONS?

Corporate branding and marketing at McCoy influenced the community the school serves. In turn, support for the McTeacher's Night event was an evaluation in itself from the community (Uhrmacher & Matthews, 2005). The community supported McCoy by buying dinner at McDonald's, and the giant check above the cafeteria entrance validates this support. Yet, we also saw the McDonald's brand interacting with the ecology of the school (Eisner, 1988). An assembly, to present the check from McDonald's, altered the structure of the school day, and space was provided to display McTeacher's Night photos and the presentation check. Even the way Molly took the lunch count resembled ordering from the dollar menu.

With regard to how corporate branding acts upon the ecology of a school, we found notable insights among interactions of the curricular and pedagogical dimensions. Throughout our observations in the classroom, we noticed marketing brands manifest as explicit and implicit curricula. While these subtle advertising messages might seem harmless, Molnar, Boninger, and Fogarty (2011) warn that these messages present a less obvious but more serious threat to children because such messages can undermine a school's intended curriculum. For example, promoting fast food to the students undermined the curricular message of eating healthfully and the nutritious daily snacks to reinforce this message.

THEMATICS

We witnessed two themes based upon the presence of corporate branding as part of the school ecology: commercial normativity and modeling consumption. We discuss these themes and provide examples below. We also ground our discussion in the literature to help make sense of these themes and establish referential adequacy regarding the larger implications of corporate branding in schools (Eisner, 2017).

Commercial Normativity

The presence of commercial normativity in school sets the foundation for corporate-inspired school reforms, advertising, and branding, in particular, to build upon. The presence of these symbols is often overlooked, but the influence is there nonetheless as a part of the school environment. While we prefer Eisner's (2002a) notion of the implicit curriculum, which is present by teachers' implicit endorsement of brands and products, we also find ourselves embracing the notion that these unquestioned symbols are literally hidden in plain sight. Seeing brand names and logos in the school creates an environmental norm for commercialism within the school. The examples that follow are related to Eisner's (1988) "modes of thinking and forms," as well as "the means through which curriculum is mediated" (p. 26).

McDonald's tends to market itself to children and families as a joyful place, complete with a cast of characters that appeal to children. Often McDonald's provides a playground for children at its restaurants. Seeing the McDonald's logo in school and wearing bracelets containing the logo serve as branding. When this fast food is promoted to students, it promotes the illusion that happiness and fun are attainable by consuming the brand. However, it is unlikely that consuming the brand will really help to alleviate a child's problems, and such consumption could lead to health problems as well (Molnar et al., 2013). Lastly, there is the issue of curricular materials marketed to and purchased by school personnel. In this instance, McCoy participated in McTeacher's Night to get money to buy science kits.

Modeling Consumption: I Buy, We Buy, You Buy

Modeling consumption serves to condition students as consumers for the market instead of educating them as citizens for democracy (Giroux, 2015). We observed a conspicuous juxtaposition at McCoy Elementary: the promotion of eating healthfully and exercising as a "brain break" with the simultaneous promotion of fast food containing large amounts of salt, sugar, and fat. Nonetheless, to obtain funding, the school participated in McTeacher's Night. Thus, juxtaposition exists whereby the school serves fruit as a daily snack to promote nutrition while the students and the building are branded with the McDonald's logo. It is unfortunate that any public school, and a Title I school in particular, should have to engage in the promotion of fast food just to obtain funding. While a further inquiry and discussion of tax breaks and philanthropic tax deductions for corporations is beyond the scope of this research, we cannot help but wonder how the circumstances might be if schools were not in need of additional funding.

RECOMMENDATIONS

Due to the benefits provided to schools, people may believe corporate philanthropy is good and altruistic. However, we would disagree, and we submit that if it were not for inadequate school funding, these philanthropic contributions would be neither possible nor even necessary. These contributions serve to create goodwill images of the corporations for the public, which also places the corporations above criticism due to the good work they do with schools (Kincheloe, 2002; Simon, 2013). But if these contributions are merely altruistic and serve no promotional business purpose, why are the contributions not anonymous? Economist Milton Friedman (2002) believed the only social responsibility of business is to serve the interest of stockholders by increasing profit and reasoned it as irresponsible to donate money for socially responsible purposes unless it serves to maximize the bottom line (Bakan, 2004). The mission of a corporation, such as McDonald's, is not to educate children but to generate profit as they place the interests of their shareholders first (Molnar & Bolinger, 2015). We do not fault any company for having this mission, but we do take issue with any company that exploits public schools and children in order to accomplish it.

We offer the following recommendations to begin to address the issues described:

1. Advocate for adequate public-school funding so that students, teachers, and schools are not in a position in which commercial exploitation is possible.
2. Call for an end to the school fund-raising industry, which often profits from child labor to sell items and would ultimately not exist if schools were adequately funded.
3. If a school must engage in fund-raising, there should be transparency for all stakeholders in the community with regard to the monetary split between the school and the vendor and a cost accounting of employee, parent, and student time spent during implementation.
4. If a school must engage in fund-raising, it should refrain from all vending contracts, business partnerships, and so forth where the product is detrimental to students' health and well-being. For example, due to advocacy, the Los Angeles Unified School District has prohibited participation in McTeacher's Night events (Molnar & Boninger, 2015).
5. Since corporate branding is rampant in the schools (Molnar, 2005), teachers can engage with it critically to underscore the represented values, ideologies, and interests, as well as the structural and systemic realities that make it so (Saltman, 2010).

CONCLUSION

As we reflect upon the larger implications of corporate branding in schools, we look beyond the example of McDonald's advertising its corporate brand through McTeacher's Night and ask, "What does it all add up to?" (Eisner, 2002b, p. 233). McDonald's is simply one corporation among many to offer programs of support to public schools, and this support comes with a cost. Such arrangements become normative to the extent to which hegemonic power eludes conscious awareness as corporate power agents produce discourse and signifiers to construct experiences, perceptions, and feelings to position the corporation positively (Kincheloe, 2002). Although the implications of McDonald's capitalizing on McTeacher's Nights may seem benign, this practice normalizes corporate branding in schools and sets precedence for other hegemonic forces to buy their way into classrooms. When we asked Molly a question regarding conditions in education that she may find bothersome, she responded, "Well, it just depends on whether you want to have a job or not." Given that she was completing a master's degree and preparing to defend her thesis, we did not suspect that such a response was due to a lack of critical thinking on her part. Yet, when asked about the number of science kits she hoped to purchase, her response was, "I'm not in charge of that; I just deliver the fries. I'm just the fry delivery lady."

REFERENCES

Bakan, J. (2004). *The corporation: The pathological pursuit of profit and power.* New York, NY: Free Press.

Barone, T. (2010). Educational connoisseurship. In C. Kridel (Ed.), *Encyclopedia of curriculum studies* (pp. 313–314). Thousand Oaks, CA: SAGE.

Coca-Cola Company. (2012). *Our position on obesity: Including well-being facts.* Retrieved from http://assets.coca-colacompany.com/9b/62/c661da674cc690db3ccad9195639/obesity-position-statement.pdf

Corporate Accountability International. (2010). *Clowning with kids' health: The case for Ronald McDonald's retirement.* Boston, MA: Author.

Eisner, E. W. (1988). The ecology of school improvement. *Educational Leadership, 45*(5), 24–29.

Eisner, E. W. (2002a). *The arts and the creation of mind.* Harrisonburg, VA: Yale University Press.

Eisner, E. W. (2002b). *The educational imagination: On the design and evaluation of educational programs* (3rd ed.). Upper Saddle River, NJ: Prentice-Hall.

Eisner, E. W. (2017). *The enlightened eye: Qualitative inquiry and the enhancement of educational practice.* New York, NY: Teachers College Press.

Federal Trade Commission. (2008). *Marketing food to children and adolescents: A review of industry expenditures, activities, and self-regulation.* Washington, DC: Author. Retrieved from https://www.ftc.gov/sites/default/files/documents/reports/marketing-food-children-and-adolescents-review-industry-expenditures-activities-and-self-regulation/p064504foodmktingreport.pdf

Federal Trade Commission. (2012). *A review of food marketing to children and adolescents: Follow-up report.* Washington, DC: Author. Retrieved from https://www.

ftc.gov/sites/default/files/documents/reports/review-food-marketing-children-and-adolescents-follow-report/121221foodmarketingreport.pdf

Freire, P. (1970). *Pedagogy of the oppressed*. New York, NY: Continuum.

Friedman, M. (2002). *Capitalism and freedom* (40th anniversary ed.). Chicago, IL: University of Chicago Press.

Giroux, H. A. (2015). *Education and the crisis of public values: Challenging the assault on teachers, students, and public education* (2nd ed.). New York, NY: Peter Lang.

Harris, S. (2016, February 3). Healthy fast food? McDonald's kale salad has more calories than a Double Big Mac. *CBC News*. Retrieved from http://www.cbc.ca/news/business/mcdonalds-kale-calorie-questions-1.3423938

Kincheloe, J. L. (2002). *The sign of the burger: McDonald's and the culture of power*. Philadelphia, PA: Temple University Press.

McNeal, J. U. (2000). *Children as consumers of commercial and social products*. Washington, DC: Pan American Health Organization. Retrieved from http://www1.paho.org/hq/dmdocuments/2010/Los-ninos-como-consumidores-productos-sociales-y-comerciales.pdf

McNeal, J. U. (2007). *On becoming a consumer: Development of consumer behavior patterns in childhood*. Burlington, MA: Elsevier.

Molnar, A. (2005). *School commercialism: From democratic ideal to market commodity*. New York, NY: Routledge.

Molnar, A., & Boninger, F. (2015). *Sold out: How marketing in school threatens children's well-being and undermines their education*. Lanham, MD: Rowman & Littlefield.

Molnar, A., Boninger, F., & Fogarty, J. (2011). *The educational cost of schoolhouse commercialism—the fourteenth annual report on schoolhouse commercializing trends: 2010–2011*. Boulder, CO: National Education Policy Center.

Molnar, A., Boninger, F., Harris, M. D., Libby, K. M., & Fogarty, J. (2013). *Promoting consumption at school: Health threats associated with schoolhouse commercialism—the fifteenth annual report on schoolhouse commercializing trends: 2011–2012*. Boulder, CO: National Education Policy Center.

Picchi. A. (2014). Why McDonald's says it wants "to be in the schools." *CBS News*. Retrieved from: https://www.cbsnews.com/news/why-mcdonalds-says-it-wants-to-be-in-the-schools/

Powell, L. M., Schermbeck, R. M., Szczypka, G., Chaloupka, F. J., & Braunschweig, C. L. (2011). Trends in the nutritional content of television food advertisements seen by children in the United States: Analyses by age, food categories, and companies. *Archives of Pediatrics and Adolescent Medicine, 165*, 1078–1086. doi:10.1001/archpediatrics.2011.131

Ravitch, D. (2015, October 14). Tell McDonald's "no" to McTeacher Nights [Blog post]. Retrieved from https://dianeravitch.net/2015/10/14/tell-mcdonalds-no-to-mcteacher-nights/

Robinson, T. N., Borzekowski, D. L. G., Matheson, D. M., & Kraemer, H. C. (2007). Effects of fast food branding on young children's taste preferences. *Archives of Pediatrics and Adolescent Medicine, 161*, 792–797. doi:10.1001/archpedi.161.8.792

Sadeghirad, B., Duhandy, T., Motaghipisheh, S., Campbell, N. R. C., & Johnston, B. C. (2016). Influence of unhealthy food and beverage marketing on children's dietary intake and preference: A systematic review and meta-analysis of randomized trials. *Obesity Reviews, 17,* 945–959. doi:10.1111/obr.12445

Saltman, K. J. (2000). *Collateral damage: Corporatizing public schools—a threat to democracy.* Lanham, MD: Rowman & Littlefield.

Saltman, K. J. (2010). *The gift of education: Public education and venture philanthropy.* New York, NY: Palgrave Macmillan.

Simon, M. (2013). *How McDonald's exploits philanthropy and targets children.* Boston, MA: Corporate Accountability.

Stake, R. (1995). *The art of case study research.* Thousand Oaks, CA: SAGE.

Trillion-dollar kids. (2006, November). *The Economist.* Retrieved from https://www.economist.com/node/8355035

Uhrmacher, P. B., & Matthews, J. (Eds.). (2005). *Intricate palette: Working the ideas of Elliot Eisner.* Columbus, OH: Prentice-Hall.

Uhrmacher, P. B., McConnell Moroye, C., & Flinders, D. J. (2017). *Using educational criticism and connoisseurship for qualitative research.* New York, NY: Taylor & Francis.

Zajdel, J., & Conn, D. R. (2017, April). *Market influences in classrooms: Hidden in plain sight.* Paper presented at the American Educational Research Association Conference, San Antonio, TX.

CHAPTER 6

AAA+ PROFESSIONAL DEVELOPMENT FOR TEACHER EDUCATORS WHO PREPARE CULTURALLY AND LINGUISTICALLY RESPONSIVE TEACHERS

Carla Lynn Tanguay, Ruchi Bhatnagar,
Kim Stevens Barker, and Joyce E. Many

ABSTRACT

Professional learning that supports teacher educators, supervisors, and school partners is critical in teacher education where candidates are prepared to teach culturally and linguistically diverse populations. This article focuses on a professional development framework for teacher educators working with prospective elementary teachers of English language learners. The model incorporates the following components: (a) developing *Awareness* of faculty members' biases/attitudes, (b) taking *Action* to develop faculty members' pedagogical knowledge/skills, and (c) facilitating the *Alignment* of program goals during clinical experiences with culturally responsive P–12 cooperating teachers.

While the demographics of the student population in public schools in the United States are becoming increasingly diverse, the teaching force and a large proportion of our candidates remain racially, culturally, ethnically, linguistically, and socioeconomically different from their students (Gay, 2010; Johnson, 2008; Ukpokodu, 2011). Teacher educators are charged with the important task of preparing teachers who are culturally competent and can teach effectively in a multicultural democracy (Ukpokodu, 2011). At our institution, faculty have endeavored to make changes to program design and curriculum in an effort to better prepare elementary school teacher candidates to teach culturally and linguistically diverse learners in culturally responsive ways (Ladson-Billings, 1999; Lucas & Villegas, 2013; Sleeter, 2001). Faculty have embraced the notion that preparing teachers to make a difference in classrooms of learners from varied ethnic, cultural, and socioeconomic backgrounds requires not only academic knowledge but also deep understanding and dispositions about diversity and its integral relationship with teaching and learning (Milner, 2010). To be effective, we also realize faculty need to consider the complexity of issues encompassed within approaches to multicultural education, such as social justice, equity, teacher learning, social change, and the need to prepare highly qualified teachers for all students (Cochran-Smith, 2003). In order to address these needs, faculty from our two initial licensure elementary education programs (i.e., at the undergraduate and master's levels) at a large, urban southeastern research university in a linguistically diverse area responded by (a) embedding an English for speakers of other languages (ESOL) endorsement in programs of study and (b) carefully integrating coursework and field experiences to prepare candidates to teach English language learners (ELLs).

As we began to make changes to enhance the focus of our programs on the needs of culturally and ethnically diverse learners, we also acknowledged the differences between our diverse candidate population and our program faculty. Seventy percent of candidates mirror underrepresented populations, while 30% of the candidates are White and female, much like the U.S. teaching force. Thirty-four percent of program faculty are from underrepresented populations and 66% are White and female. We realized that changes to curricular and program design would only be effective if accompanied by an exemplary model of professional development for all educators working with our candidates. Therefore, faculty in both programs turned to the literature as they considered what types of professional development might be most effective to help educators working with the candidates. As we have increased the professional learning opportunities for program faculty, part-time supervisors, and school partners and studied the literature, we have created a repertoire of approaches that provide an overall strong model of professional development for all stakeholders.

The purpose of this conceptual article is (a) to provide an overview of the research base for the model for professional development that has evolved for teacher educators working in programs designed to prepare effective teachers for ELL students, and (b) to provide illustrative descriptions of how we used this model to guide the professional development of faculty who work in our undergraduate and master's (MAT) elementary education programs.

CREATING AN AAA+ PROFESSIONAL DEVELOPMENT MODEL FOR TEACHER EDUCATORS

We drew on Lucas and Villegas's (2013) "orientations and pedagogical knowledge and skills for preparing linguistically responsive teachers" (p. 98) to create the framework for our professional development approach. Our model approaches faculty development in three main areas: (a) *Awareness*, (b) *Action*, and (c) *Alignment*. This framework emerged as we turned to the research focusing on preparing teachers to work with culturally and linguistically diverse learners and studies focusing on the needs of teacher educators who work in such preparation programs to substantiate the value of each component. The framework and the literature review informed our faculty's plans for their own development in a recursive and generative process. An overview of the key elements from the literature associated with each component of our framework can be seen in Table 6.1. In the sections that follow, we outline each of the AAA+ components and the associated literature.

Awareness: Teacher Educators Need to Develop Self-Awareness

The first component of our AAA+ Model of Professional Development is *Awareness*. Having awareness is defined as having the ability to acknowledge and value one's own cultural, linguistic, and racial background, as well as biases and attitudes toward others from diverse populations (Jennings, 2007; Pennington et al., 2012; Ukpokodu, 2011). Jennings (2007) highlights the need for teacher educators to develop an awareness of ways that their own biases and attitudes influence their curricular decisions in developing culturally responsive or nonresponsive teacher candidates. Faculty beliefs can influence program emphases resulting in differential attention spent on topics related to diversity with more attention given to issues such as race/ethnicity, special needs, and language and less time focused on social class, gender, and sexual orientation.

Table 6.1.
Three Main Areas of Focus for AAA+ Professional Development

Awareness: Teacher Educators Need to Develop Self-Awareness	• Develop cultural and sociolinguistic consciousness
	• Assess Funds of Knowledge: self-awareness and others' assets
	• Uncover biases, attitudes
	• Understand policies affecting ESOL instruction and English Language Learners (ELLs)
	• Include specific topics on cultural, linguistic, and racial diversity
Action: Teacher Educators Need to Serve as Models of Change in Attitude and Practice	• Model through differentiation: content, process, product, learning environment, social and academic language
	• Scaffold preservice teachers' effectiveness as ELL educators by drawing on their understanding of candidates' culture, background knowledge, and experiences
	• Demonstrate knowledge of principles of first and second language acquisition
	• Understand language proficiency levels and developmental needs
	• Plan for instruction and assessment of ELLs
	• Use strategies for supporting academic language in the content areas and language demands
	• Collaborate in classroom and in communities
Alignment: Teacher Educators, Supervisors, and Cooperating Teachers Need to Align Goals	• Acknowledge and respect program goals
	• Model instruction and assessment aligned with coursework
	• Construct knowledge through mutual interactions
	• Expect advocacy and change agency for ELLs and their families

Assaf, Garza, and Battle (2010) examined teacher educators' perceptions, beliefs, and practices in order to assess the coherence of their multicultural teacher education program. The authors found that the instructors seemed to reflect the "happy talk" perspective about multiculturalism (p. 123). Instructors expressed an uncertainty about addressing issues of diversity in courses, and their own White, middle-class, and monolingual backgrounds fed their insecurity about having open discussions on multiculturalism and diversity. The instructors felt a responsibility to foster optimism about the teaching profession with candidates and feared that too much discussion around teaching challenges in a multicultural, diverse classroom would dampen their spirits (Assaf, Garza, & Battle, 2010). Abt-Perkins, Hauschildt, and Dale (2000) confirm this problem. They examined their preservice teacher supervisor practices and biases as White women. The researchers reflected on their attention to racial, social class, and gender equity in their interactions with preservice teachers. Abt-Perkins et al. (2000) documented and critiqued their supervisory work in three separate contexts: rural, urban, and suburban, and the opportunities that each context offered for discussions about multiculturalism. They experienced tensions advocating for change and challenging established teaching practices, because the supervisory role has traditionally been limited to facilitating a student teacher's assimilation into the school culture. The authors gradually changed their approach from being "spoilers" to "positive irritants" (Abt-Perkins et al., 2000, p. 39). They felt that the most productive discussions about stereotyping and bias occurred when they talked about issues of authority and relationships with particular students (Abt-Perkins et al., 2000)

Understanding the beliefs of those working with our preservice teachers extends also to the importance of considering the awareness of the cooperating teachers with whom our candidates work. Ukpokodu (2011) used "reflectivity and reflexivity" to inquire into the phenomenon of teaching and learning (p. 438) with attention to views of both cooperating teachers and candidates. Ukpokodu conducted a self-study that revealed that candidates in the program and cooperating teachers in the school lacked cultural awareness and had limited cross–cultural interaction and relationships. Candidates and teachers harbored a false sense of cultural competence and believed that they did not have any biases or racist dispositions, limiting their ability to engage in deep reflection.

To understand how faculty might develop greater self-awareness, we turned to Hyland and Noffke's (2005) work with their preservice teachers. Hyland and Noffke conducted a long-term action research study in two universities where a majority of students were White and where minority communities were not in immediate proximity to the campuses. Hyland and Noffke reflected upon the challenges involved in providing authentic opportunities for candidates to engage in cross-cultural interactions and to develop a deep understanding of issues of diversity and social justice. Their faculty aimed to foster candidate inquiry in their quest to understand and to move beyond cultural boundaries rather than develop sympathy toward oppressed groups. In these cross-cultural inquiries, candidates were asked to: attend a religious/cultural event, interview and interact with people unlike them, spend time within a community where they were underrepresented, and/or watch movies/read texts about this ethnic/cultural group. Instructors assessed the effectiveness of the assignments to see if candidates engaged in authentic experiences and had opportunities to reflect on White privilege and its contribution to the oppression of others. Hyland and Noffke concluded that to prepare effective teachers for low-income, ethnically diverse students, authentic assignments and opportunities to interact with the community are crucial in challenging deficit notions. Additionally, the researchers found that service learning experiences helped educators develop a critical lens for understanding issues facing communities that have been historically marginalized (Hyland & Noffke, 2005).

Our review revealed that more attention is needed in supporting faculty and cooperating teacher awareness of beliefs/attitudes that may hinder their engagement in topics of diversity. Research examining effective experiences that have been used with teacher candidates helped guide us to potentially promising initiatives that faculty might undertake to understand and value their own and others' culture and to help them uncover and work through their own biases.

Action: Teacher Educators Need to Serve as Models of Change in Attitude and Practice

The second component of our AAA+ model is *Action*. Taking action is using pedagogical knowledge and skills to take a stance and to move toward issues of diversity, including addressing linguistic differences (Achinstein & Athanases, 2005; Hyland & Noffke, 2005; Nadeem, 2012). Studies focused on the importance of teacher educators' actions as models of change within and outside the classroom emphasize the need for educators to move beyond tolerance and toward change in attitude and practice (Achinstein & Athanases, 2005; Santangelo & Tomlinson, 2012). Beyond a level of awareness of personal background and biases, teacher educators needed to possess not only dispositions but also knowledge and skills to effectively teach and model practices for teaching diverse learners.

Santangelo and Tomlinson (2012) examined self-reported data from 70 teacher educators who completed questionnaires on their programs. Their study summarized the need for teacher educators to provide access and support for a diverse pool of teacher candidates by modeling effective practices through differentiation so that their candidates would translate coursework to teaching practices. Findings revealed that teacher educators who taught an academically diverse group of candidates recognized their range in readiness and the importance of modeling how to differentiate; however, educators needed development in assessment of candidates' readiness, interests, and learning profiles. They needed development in planning for differentiated instruction, considering purposeful grouping formats, and providing equitable attention. Thus, teacher educators need professional learning to appropriately model ways to differentiate content, process, product, and learning environment to increase equitable instruction time (Santangelo & Tomlinson, 2012). By increasing their knowledge and pedagogical base, teacher educators become equipped to work effectively with a diverse pool of teacher candidates while maintaining focus on the pupils their candidates will serve.

Research is needed to verify whether teacher educators' practices modeling differentiation are effectively used by their candidates and impact pupil learning (Santangelo & Tomlinson, 2012). Many and Aoulou's (2014) inquiry analyzed four teacher educators' attempts to scaffold their preservice teachers' effectiveness as ELL educators by drawing on their understanding of candidates' culture, background knowledge, and experiences. The case study illustrated how teacher educators from diverse cultural, linguistic, and experiential backgrounds supported ELL preservice teachers' dispositions, strategies, and conceptual understandings through modeling, feedback, structured assignments, and reflection. Faculty members' use of scaffolding varied, however. In fact, the participant with more years of experience in teacher education drew on a wider repertoire of strategies to tap into candidates' unique cultural and linguist backgrounds and used that information to support their own learning or to involve the candidates in conveying content to others in the program. These educators worked to model in their classrooms the approach to working with diverse learners they hoped to develop in their teacher candidates.

Achinstein and Athanases (2005) developed a knowledge base framework for mentors who prepare teachers for equity-oriented teaching. They conducted a multistage study beginning with an analysis of two open-ended survey question responses of 37 Leadership Network for Teacher Induction members. Part two of their study, a mentor-mentee case study (Achinstein & Barrett, 2004), included participants' audio recordings of collaborative planning and reflections and follow-up interviews across two years. Survey data analyses revealed that participants chose pedagogical knowledge nearly unanimously as the most important tool mentors needed to lead student teachers toward proficiency with diverse students; however, mentors needed pedagogical knowledge that extended beyond the classroom. While mentors need knowledge of effective strategies for teaching diverse students, they must also be able to guide their beginning teachers as they develop awareness and an active stance toward equity through a bilevel pedagogical knowledge. Mentors must have a bifocal perspective in understanding their mentees and their pupils and the assets that they both bring to the learning experiences. While the novices must move beyond their own performance and shift their focus toward their pupils' needs, the mentor must be equipped to help the mentee assess and meet individual needs, supporting their learning in ways to adjust differentiated instructional strategies (Achinstein & Athanases, 2005). In addition to pedagogical knowledge, mentors emphasized the importance of instilling within new teachers an awareness of the nested contexts that are inherently influential when teaching diverse children (Achinstein & Athanases, 2005).

For example, mentors identified family culture and influence from local communities and influence from the broader culture, national and international contexts as necessary components of the mentor knowledge base. Mentors have to expand their work beyond acting as local guides to becoming agents of change in order to lead new teachers to think beyond their classroom environments into neighborhoods and on to larger contexts (Feiman-Nemser, 2001). In doing so, mentors demonstrate for teacher candidates the possibilities, if not the requirements, for effectively educating diverse students (Achinstein & Athanases, 2005).

Alignment: Teacher Educators, Supervisors, and Cooperating Teachers Need to Align Goals

The third component of our AAA+ model is *Alignment*. Alignment occurs when teacher educators, cooperating/mentor teachers, and supervisors have the same goal: to prepare culturally and linguistically responsive teachers (Keehn & Martinez, 2006; Tellez, 2008). Rather than disparately addressing issues of diversity in teacher preparation programs focusing on multicultural education courses or methods for teaching ELLs and/or diverse field experiences, some educators advocate for addressing multicultural education as a systemic topic that weaves throughout the program (Villegas & Lucas, 2002). Keehn and Martinez (2006) offer a third approach focusing on professional development, the Diversity Initiative, not only for faculty but also adjuncts. Part-time instructors and/or adjunct professors are stakeholders often left out of the immediate arena of conversations and professional learning held at faculty meetings, retreats, and conferences. This study took place at a large public university designated by the federal government as a Latino-serving institution, where the Interdisciplinary Studies Department relied on adjunct faculty to teach 75% of the undergraduate courses. The Diversity Initiative offered two phases, one for faculty and the other for adjuncts, focusing on knowledge and skills needed to prepare teacher candidates to work with culturally and linguistically diverse populations. Findings indicated that an increased level of stakeholder participation led to greater impact on the amount of attention shown to diversity, the infusion of diversity issues in coursework, and stakeholders' competency in multicultural pedagogical knowledge and skills (Keehn & Martinez, 2006).

While professional development for faculty and adjuncts may increase their knowledge base and skills to promote equity in education, teacher educators need to provide professional learning, in alignment with university priorities, for cooperating teachers who will work with their teacher candidates. Tellez (2008) conducted a study of five cooperating teachers recognized for their work with Latino students and families. Through multiple interviews, the teachers recommended that teacher educators continually evaluate, analyze, and adjust professional learning to facilitate the roles of mentor teachers. They suggested that attention should be focused in three different potentially challenging areas in order to better align their work with teacher candidates and university priorities: (a) high standards/caring paradox, (b) instructional conversations, and (c) relationship to student culture. While maintaining high academic standards for all learners, cooperating teachers stressed the importance of striking a balance between understanding and acknowledging challenges from different student populations. They also explained that developing teacher candidates' shallow understandings of their students' lives hindered them from engaging in beneficial instructional conversations, and their lack of understanding of the wider cultural context minimized opportunities for them to develop authentic relationships with their students' parents (Tellez, 2008). Tellez suggests that when cooperating teachers' beliefs and practices are aligned with university philosophies on teaching diverse student populations, the likelihood of emerging contradictions between coursework and fieldwork is minimized for developing teachers, and the influence that cooperating teachers have on developing teacher candidates is maximized.

Thus, our review of literature showed that teacher educators and cooperating teachers frequently face the complicated task of preparing teacher candidates from White, middle-class backgrounds for work in diverse classrooms. Research focused on the knowledge and effective practices of teacher educators indicates that, ultimately, awareness and understanding of the many faces of diversity influence the presentation and preparation of new teachers. Additionally, teacher educators must be proficient in a wide range of pedagogical practices appropriate for use with diverse pupils and adult learners preparing to be teachers. By providing ongoing professional development through recursive reflection and adjustment, teacher educators will assist cooperating teachers in maintaining congruence between field experiences and university coursework.

USING THE AAA+ PROFESSIONAL DEVELOPMENT MODEL IN OUR PROGRAMS

To illustrate the application of the AAA+ Model, we will share how two different elementary teacher preparation programs draw on the three components of support (i.e., Awareness, Action, Alignment) to sustain the growth and development of teacher educators, part-time supervisors/doctoral fellows, and cooperating/mentor teachers. Both programs are grounded in a commitment to prepare candidates who will value social justice aims and meet the needs of linguistically and culturally diverse students in high-need urban schools. Theory and action related to this vision are embedded throughout the design of the programs. Educators believe the effectiveness of this integration hinges on the knowledge, ability, and intentionality of each faculty member and cooperating teacher to make explicit connections with the teacher candidates.

Faculty created three goals to guide the content and process of the AAA+ professional development: (a) to develop stakeholders' awareness of their cultural, linguistic, and racial backgrounds, and their biases and attitudes toward others from diverse populations; (b) to take action by developing stakeholders' pedagogical knowledge and skills to teach diverse learners; and (c) to align program goals in professional learning experiences for stakeholders to ensure coordinated preparation of culturally and linguistically responsive teachers who are advocates for all learners. In the examples that follow, we show how the undergraduate program faculty has afforded professional development for their teacher educators and part-time supervisors/adjuncts, while the graduate program faculty offered additional opportunities for their school partners. Both programs provide a strong array of initiatives for all stakeholders in the three goals of our model (see Figure 6.1).

Figure 6.1. AAA+ Professional Development Goals for Embedding Awareness, Action, and Alignment Initiatives.

Developing Stakeholders' Awareness of Their Identities, Biases, and Attitudes

The undergraduate program provides a strong model for developing teacher educators' awareness of their cultural, linguistic, and racial backgrounds and their own biases and attitudes. Members from the diverse program faculty created a Diversity Exchange, an opportunity provided for faculty to engage in conversations on specific topics focusing on diversity and to participate in professional development sessions centered on building community. The Diversity Exchange is enacted in multiple ways. Often, faculty arrive at topics for discussion resulting from books that they are reading in their book clubs. At book club meetings, faculty engage in a response to their reading following time for reflection and discussion. Meeting at faculty members' homes or at the university campus, faculty understand that these book clubs and Diversity Exchange sessions are completely optional but provide an invaluable opportunity to get to know their colleagues and to reflect upon their own identities and potential biases. Additionally, at program meetings, faculty share how they embed topics around diversity in their coursework. Often, books chosen at faculty book clubs are added as supplemental texts for discussions with teacher candidates as part of their course assignments. Some of the suggested book topics used in coursework with candidates are as follows: *Bad Boys: Public Schools in the Making of Black Masculinity* (Ferguson, 2001); *Subtractive Schooling: U.S.-Mexican Youth and the Politics of Caring* (Valenzuela, 1999); *Savage Inequalities: Children in America's Schools* (Kozol, 1991); and *White Teacher* (Paley, 1989). One of our faculty explained that it was through the book clubs with undergraduates that she became more comfortable having conversations with students about a range of topics regarding diversity.

Taking Action by Developing Stakeholders' Pedagogical Knowledge and Skills to Teach Diverse Learners

Our teacher educators took action to develop knowledge and skills of stakeholders in several ways. First, by providing opportunities with their colleagues to reflect on their own identities considering family history, their cultural self in relation to others, their cultural self as personal, and their cultural self as a professional, we identified experiences where instructors offered similar experiences in their courses for their teacher candidates. For instance, by modeling how to create a *Culture Quilt*, instructors provide opportunities for candidates to respond to questions and to engage in discussions within their class community. All members of the community reflect on their family origins, traditions, and values; cultures that are familiar and unfamiliar to them; and opportunities and challenges with diversity. They explore their personal interests and modes of learning and their reasons for becoming a teacher. Learning from one another, both the teacher educator and teacher candidates uncover personal biases and develop mutual respect and rapport with each other. Also, participants have opportunities to initiate dialogue through the use of children's literature and blog posts. The candidates use literature, much like the faculty who teach them, to explore critical issues related to diversity.

Faculty also benefit in learning from their colleagues and from those who have expertise in specific areas (e.g., ESOL and cultural foundations). Faculty have opportunities to share related research with each other and part-time supervisors and doctoral fellows at Supporting Our Supervisor (SOS) meetings. Faculty and P–12 partners provide professional learning across content areas for part-time faculty making connections between coursework and field experiences supporting their supervisory practices (Dangel & Tanguay, 2014). For example, in support of developing faculty knowledge base in teaching diverse learners, we invited guest speakers from local school systems to share their expertise on topics such as using WIDA English Language Development Standards (2012, 2015) for instruction, the assessment of ELLs, and ACCESS for ELLs 2.0 Summative Assessment, an English language proficiency assessment administered to students identified as ELLs in grades K–12. Furthermore, course instructors provided additional support for supervisors on the use of our observation instrument specifically noting areas where supervisors had difficulty rating our candidates' competencies in making connections to their learners' cultural and community assets.

Teacher educators have also taken action to ensure teacher candidates benefit (a) from experiences in ESOL methods courses and (b) from a faculty coteaching ESOL input model. The ESOL curriculum and instruction methods course emphasizes literacy instruction that supports ELLs, incorporating strategies for teaching and learning and assessing language development proficiency. The ESOL input model is an innovative approach designed by faculty to infuse methods for working with diverse learners throughout the program. The university hires faculty with expertise in linguistic diversity and ESOL to coteach with methods instructors across content areas (i.e., literacy, mathematics, science, and social studies), assessment, child development, and classroom management/field courses. In this unusual collaborative effort across disciplines, teacher educators demonstrate multiple ways of coteaching for teacher candidates and model strategies for differentiating instruction and assessment for diverse learners. For a list of topics addressed through the ESOL input model, refer to Appendix A. In these ways, teacher educators and teacher candidates have opportunities to construct knowledge, develop dispositions that are respectful of diverse learners, and respect multiple perspectives in their interactions with one another.

A final way our faculty members have taken action can be seen in another example from our master's program. Faculty provide an example of the program's vision, *a commitment to activism*, by supporting their candidates in the implementation of the Problem Solution Project (Stenhouse & Jarrett, 2012). This project involves service learning and critical pedagogy, and an experience of community engagement "not as charity, but as a vehicle for social change" (Stenhouse & Jarrett, 2012, p. 52). Candidates are continuously challenged throughout their program to cross-cultural boundaries and have authentic interactions with communities *different* than their own: racially, culturally, and economically, with the goal of examining their own biases and dispositions about various populations (Assaf, Garza, & Battle, 2010; Ukpokodu, 2011). The candidates, who are placed in urban, high-need public schools, participate in a democratic process with their faculty to identify a service learning project to serve their school community (Stenhouse & Jarrett, 2012).

Aligning Program Goals Defined in Professional Learning Experiences for Stakeholders

Similar to undergraduate program initiatives, the master's initial certification program faculty invite cooperating teachers and supervisors to campus for professional learning to (a) model coteaching, (b) advocate for ELLs via conversations with one another, and (c) review program goals. Supervisors are prepared by the program coordinator to provide weekly on-site consultation for the teachers. Faculty model or coteach lessons on site at partner schools, and candidates have opportunities for practice. Teacher educators also work with cooperating teachers and candidates to prepare and implement family nights around specific content areas. P-12 children, their parents, and siblings are invited to these school-wide events to participate in various educational activities (Keehn & Martinez, 2006; Tellez, 2008). Finally, faculty facilitate school-wide inquiry groups with teachers on site at partner schools. Research on our Professional Development School (PDS) partnerships has shown that a congruency between program goals and teachers' beliefs creates engagement, ownership, and positive work climate, which enables teachers and candidates to work as advocates for children in addition to having a positive impact on teacher retention in schools (Swars, Meyers, Mays, & Lack, 2009). Instructors model ways of navigating shared power and democratic processes for teacher candidates working in partner schools (Stenhouse & Jarrett, 2012). For example, the instructor challenges the authoritarian position of the instructor by modeling the role of a facilitator during the Problem and Solution Project described in the earlier section. As a result, the students are given opportunities to reach decisions through open dialogue and mutual consensus, which enables a feeling of empowerment and ownership of the project.

CHALLENGES AND OPPORTUNITIES IN OUR WORK

We recognize that sustaining professional development for all stakeholders who are preparing teacher candidates for teaching diverse learners in diverse contexts is challenging work; however, the benefits are worth it. We recommend that opportunities provided for teacher educators are offered frequently. Building a community is an important first step in obtaining faculty interest. Professional learning communities (Doolittle, Sudeck, & Rattigan, 2008; Lave & Wenger, 1991; Stoll, Bolam, McMahon, Wallace, & Thomas, 2006) provide an avenue for stakeholders to participate in a safe space where open communication is welcomed and respected. Taking faculty suggestions on topic discussions, book club ideas, and guest speaker expertise are strategies to facilitate engagement. Through coteaching, faculty have opportunities to expand their knowledge/skills and to prepare part-time instructors and doctoral fellows. By providing a lead faculty coordinator to plan and coteach sessions with other program faculty, scheduling becomes more manageable. Finally, creating a warm, nonhostile learning environment, where people mutually respect one another, creates a strong model for teacher candidates. It is critical that candidates observe teacher educators and cooperating teachers as strong models so that they will develop the necessary knowledge base, skills, and dispositions to embrace teaching and learning in diverse contexts.

RECOMMENDATIONS FOR RESEARCHERS AND PRACTITIONERS

Teacher educators are responsible for preparing teacher candidates for diverse classrooms, yet sometimes the racism and ethnocentrism educators warn against manifests in their own classrooms. We recommend that faculty begin with awareness and then expand gradually to incorporate steps to take action and finally align their programs to school and community partnerships. Our professional development model has been sustainable, varying in topic coverage across time. Faculty, supervisors, and cooperating teachers have maintained interest and participation. Although we have not conducted a self-study, we continuously seek feedback from supervisors and faculty regarding how we can meet their professional learning needs and improve our work.

Racial introspection through self-study is one way that teacher educators can address this delicate teaching terrain (Adler, 2011; Galman, Pica-Smith, & Rosenberger, 2010; Writer & Chávez, 2001). Some researchers have also examined racial and cultural tensions that have emerged in the instructional experiences of graduate teaching assistants (Gomez, Khurshid, Freitag, & Lachuk, 2011). Using a theoretical framework such as critical race theory can be helpful for researching social justice among teacher educators, as it allows scholars to examine existing political and institutional structures of racism and question racial power in the academy.

Previous research has called for a change in policy to combat racism and racist acts in the academy. There is also a call for more diversity within the teacher educator workforce (Fitts & Weisman, 2010; Gomez et al., 2011). Galman et al. (2010) recommended a change in job descriptions and a shift in outlined priorities for teacher educators. Teacher educators cannot have social justice and equity as a topic for the backburner, apart from the specific content they are paid to teach. Teaching for social justice, and the skills and dispositions it requires, needs to be part of the institutionalized employment descriptions for teacher educators. As the workforce continually changes, the learning communities that we recommend for teacher education faculty, supervisors, and adjuncts will also grow and change. Current and new members will need support to continue reflecting on their personal biases and attitudes, to continue new ways to take action, and to align program goals to better meet the needs of increasingly diverse P–12 students.

REFERENCES

Abt-Perkins, D., Hauschildt, P., & Dale, H. (2000). Becoming multicultural supervisors: Lessons from a collaborative field study. *Journal of Curriculum and Supervision 16*(1), 28–47.

Achinstein, B., & Athanases, S. (2005). Focusing new teachers on diversity and equity: Toward a knowledge base for mentors. *Teaching and Teacher Education, 21*(7), 843–862.

Achinstein, B., & Barrett, A. (2004). (Re)Framing classroom contexts: How new teachers and mentors view diverse learners and challenges of practice. *Teachers College Record, 106*(4), 716–746.

Adler, S. M. (2011). Teacher epistemology and collective narratives: Interrogating teaching and diversity. *Teaching and Teacher Education, 27*(3), 609–618.

Assaf, L. C., Garza, R., & Battle, J. (2010). Multicultural teacher education: Examining the perceptions, practices, and coherence in one teacher preparation program. *Teacher Education Quarterly, 37*(2), 115–135.

Cochran-Smith, M. (2003). The multiple meanings of multicultural teacher education. A conceptual framework. *Teacher Education Quarterly, 30*(2), 7–26.

Dangel, J., & Tanguay, C. (2014). Don't leave me out there alone: A practical guide for supporting supervisors. *Action in Teacher Education, 36*(1), 3–19.

Doolittle, G., Sudeck, M., & Rattigan, P. (2008). Creating professional learning communities: The work of professional development schools. *Theory into Practice, 47*(4), 303–310. doi:10.1080/00405840802329276

Feiman-Nemser, S. (2001). From preparation to practice: Designing a continuum to strengthen and sustain teaching. *Teachers College Record, 103*(6), 1013–1055.

Fitts, S., & Weisman, E. M. (2010). Exploring questions of social justice in bilingual/bicultural teacher education: Towards a parity of participation. *Urban Review: Issues and Ideas in Public Education, 42*(5), 373–393.

Ferguson, A. A. (2001). *Bad boys: Public schools in the making of black masculinity.* Ann Arbor, MI: University of Michigan Press.

Galman, S., Pica-Smith, C., & Rosenberger, C. (2010). Aggressive and tender navigations: Teacher educators confront whiteness in their practice. *Journal of Teacher Education, 6*(3), 225–236. doi:10.1177/0022487109359776

Gay, G. (2010). *Culturally responsive teaching: Theory, research, and practice* (2nd ed.). New York, NY: Teachers College.

Gomez, M. L., Khurshid, A., Freitag, M. B., & Lachuk, A. J. (2011). Microaggressions in graduate students' lives: How they are encountered and their consequences. *Teaching and Teacher Education: An International Journal of Research and Studies, 27*(8), 1189–1199.

Hyland, N. E., & Noffke, S. E. (2005). Understanding diversity through social and community inquiry: An action-research study. *Journal of Teacher Education, 56*(4), 367–381.

Jennings, T. (2007). Addressing diversity in US teacher preparation programs: A survey of elementary and secondary programs' priorities and challenges from across the United States of America. *Teaching and Teacher Education: An International Journal of Research and Studies, 23*(8), 1258–1271.

Johnson, C. (2008). Meeting the challenges in US education. Striving for success in a diverse society. In W. Guofang (Ed.). *The education of diverse student populations: A global perspective* (pp. 79–95). London, England: Springer.

Keehn, S., & Martinez, M. G. (2006). A study of the impact of professional development in diversity on adjunct faculty. *Action in Teacher Education, 28*(3), 11–28.

Kozol, J. (1991). *Savage inequalities: Children in America's schools.* New York, NY: Random House.

Ladson-Billings, G. J. (1999). Preparing teachers for diverse student populations: A critical race theory perspective. *Review of Research in Education, 24*, 211–247.

Lave, J., & Wenger, E. (1991). *Situated learning: Legitimate peripheral participation.* New York, NY: Cambridge University Press.

Lucas, T., & Villegas, A. M. (2013). Preparing linguistically responsive teachers: Laying the foundation in preservice teacher education. *Theory into Practice, 52*(2), 98–109. doi: 0.1080/00405841.2013.770327

Many, J. E., & Aoulou, E. (2014). Understanding literacy teacher educators' use of scaffolding. *Reading Horizons, 53*(3). Retrieved from http://scholarworks.wmich.edu/reading_horizons/vol53/iss3/4

Milner, H. R. (2010). What does teacher education have to do with teaching? Implications for diversity studies. *Journal of Teacher Education, 61*(1–2), 118–131. doi:10.1177/0022487109347670

Nadeem, M. (2012). Urlish: A code switching/code mixing pedagogical approach in teacher education. *Journal of Research and Reflections in Education*, *6*(2), 154–162.

Paley, V. G. (1989). *White teacher*. Cambridge, MA: Harvard University Press.

Pennington, J. L., Brock, C. H., Abernathy, T. V., Bingham, A., Major, E. M., Wiest, L. R., & Ndura, E. (2012). Teacher educators' dispositions: Footnoting the present with stories from our pasts. *Studying Teacher Education*, *8*(1), 69–85.

Santangelo, T., & Tomlinson, C. A. (2012). Teacher educators' perceptions and use of differentiated instruction practices: An exploratory investigation. *Action in Teacher Education*, *34*(4), 309–327.

Sleeter, C. E. (2001). Preparing teachers for culturally diverse schools: Research and the overwhelming presence of whiteness. *Journal of Teacher Education*, *52*(2), 94–106. doi:10.1177/0022487101052002002

Stenhouse, V. L., & Jarrett, O. S. (2012). In the service of learning and activism: Service learning, critical pedagogy, and the problem solution project. *Teacher Education Quarterly*, *39*(1), 51–76.

Stoll, L., Bolam, R., McMahon, A., Wallace, M., & Thomas, S. (2006). Professional learning communities: A review of the literature. *Journal of Educational Change*, *7*, 221–258.

Swars, S., Meyers, B., Mays, L., & Lack, B. (2009). A two-dimensional model of teacher retention and mobility: Classroom teachers and their university partners take a closer look at a vexing problem. *Journal of Teacher Education*, *60*(2), 168–183.

Tellez, K. (2008). What student teachers learn about multicultural education from their cooperating teachers. *Teaching and Teacher Education*, *24*(1), 43–58.

Ukpokodu, O. (2011). Developing teachers' cultural competence: One teacher educator's practice of unpacking student culturelessness. *Action in Teacher Education*, *33*(5–6), 432–454.

Valenzuela, A. (1999). *Subtractive schooling: U.S.-Mexican youth and the politics of caring*. Albany, NY: State University of New York Press.

Villegas, A. M., & Lucas, T. (2002). Preparing culturally responsive teachers: Rethinking the curriculum. *Journal of Teacher Education*, *53*(1), 20–32.

WIDA. (2012). The 2012 amplification of the English language development standards, Kindergarten-grade 12. Board of Regents of the University of Wisconsin System, on behalf of the WIDA Consortium. Retrieved from file:///C:/Users/ctanguay/Desktop/WIDA_booklet_2012%20Standards_web.pdf

WIDA. (2015). ACCESS for ELLs 2.0 2015-2016 Implementation. Retrieved from https://www.wida.us/assessment/ACCESS20.aspx

Writer, J. H., & Chavez, R. C. (2001). Storied lives, dialog→ retro-reflections: Melding critical multicultural education and critical race theory for pedagogical transformation. *Studies in Media & Information Literacy Education*, *1*(4), 1–14. Retrieved from http://ci.education.nmsu.edu/files/2013/07/storiedlives_jhwrcc.pdf

APPENDIX A

- ESOL Input Model—Topics for Infusion across Coursework
- Who are English language learners?
- Linguistic diversity/variation
- Models of bilingualism/biliteracy and myths about both
- Language policy and planning pertaining to ELLs
- Legal obligations to ELLs
- Identifying ELLs (legal process)
- ESOL program models
- Theories of first language acquisition
- Theories of second language acquisition
- L2 teaching methods
- ELL standards (WIDA)
- Materials (books, technology, etc.) that support the language and content learning of ELLs
- Assessing ELLs: English language proficiency (ACCESS and teacher-created assessments)
- Assessing ELLs: Content
- Literacy instruction that supports ELLs (ELA)
- Content instruction that supports ELLs (math, science, social studies)
- Creating meaningful home/school/community connections
- Classroom management and ELLs
- Professional development and collaboration

CHAPTER 7

HELPING EARLY-CAREER TEACHERS TO SEE THE AESTHETIC DIMENSION OF MATHEMATICS WITHIN STANDARDS-BASED CURRICULA

Aaron Samuel Zimmerman

ABSTRACT

In this conceptual essay, I argue that there is an aesthetic dimension to all mathematical inquiry and that it is possible for teachers to highlight this aesthetic dimension, even within the context of standards-based mathematics curricula. This curricular approach, however, presents unique challenges to early-career teachers. I highlight those challenges and discuss how an appreciation for the aesthetic dimension of mathematics can inform the endeavors of teaching and teacher education.

Mathematician Benoit Mandelbrot (1982) described his work as the attempt to "investigate the morphology of the amorphous" (p. 1). This desire to perceive and appreciate the deep, hidden (and, oftentimes, beautiful) features of reality falls not only within the realm of rational thought but also within the aesthetic dimension of human experience.

Consider the following historical example: Mathematician Georg Cantor (1845–1918) put forth the radical idea that there exist infinities of different sizes; specifically, some infinite sets are countable, while some infinite sets are uncountable. Furthermore, Cantor proposed that there exists one particular infinite set—labeled by Cantor as "absolute infinity"—that transcends all other infinite sets (Gamwell, 2016).

Members of the artistic avant-garde in Russia became familiar with Cantor's writings and were transfixed by the concept of an infinity that transcends all other infinities (Gamwell, 2016). Poet Aleksei Kruchenykh, for example, attempted to depict this transcendent infinity by composing poems comprised solely of nonsense words and devoid of any perceivable syntax. Kruchenykh believed that by depicting that which eluded sensible discernment, the artist and the reader would be forced to rely on their intuition alone, an intuition that Kruchenykh believed would lead to the experience of the "absolute infinity" that Cantor had defined. The painter Cantor influenced the writings of Kazimir Malevich as well as that of Kruchenykh. As his art evolved, Malevich moved away from depicting natural objects and toward crafting abstract representations of the infinite. Malevich (2003) wrote, "a blissful sense of non-objectivity drew me forth … where nothing is real except feeling" (p. 68).

It is notable that Cantor's radical mathematical ideas (which now serve as the foundational axioms of the well-established branch of mathematics known as "set theory") were able to ignite the imaginations of poets and painters. Cantor himself believed that his mathematical work had religious significance (Dauben, 1990). What Cantor, Kruchenykh, and Malevich all had in common was a desire to apprehend an infinity above all other infinities. Thus, the mathematical concept of "absolute infinity" can be understood and appreciated in both logical and affective terms.

Cantor's ideas are only one example of the intersection between mathematics and art. Given that mathematics contains an aesthetic dimension, this chapter will argue that aesthetic experiences serve a critical function in the teaching and learning of mathematics. Some scholars (Dreyfus & Eisenberg, 1986; Silver & Metzger, 1989) have argued that the aesthetic dimension of mathematics should be the exclusive purview of experts; that is to say, only after acquiring an understanding of the more advanced and sophisticated aspects of mathematics can students be expected to appreciate mathematical beauty. Other scholars (Eberle, 2014; Sinclair, 2009), however, have argued that even though expert and novice mathematicians may not arrive at the same aesthetic judgments, students (including children) can still appreciate the beauty of mathematics. This paper adopts the latter perspective and argues that teachers can always provide opportunities for students to explore the aesthetic dimension of mathematics.

Creating opportunities for aesthetic exploration depends, in large part, on how teachers interpret curriculum. In fact, the manner in which a mathematics teacher interprets a given curriculum is one of the most significant factors contributing to student motivation and achievement (Crespo & Sinclair, 2008; Remillard & Kim, 2017). Teachers translate curriculum into instruction by filtering curricular materials through their knowledge, beliefs, intentions, practical resources, and contextual limitations (Nicol & Crespo, 2006; Schoenfeld, 1988; Sherin & Drake, 2009). All teachers, therefore, are faced with the challenge of devising ways to design and interpret curriculum so that multiple (and sometimes conflicting) educational goals are accomplished (Labaree, 2011; Schiro, 2013).

This essay argues that it is the responsibility of teacher educators to help preservice and early-career teachers see opportunities for students to experience the aesthetic dimension of mathematics even within standards-based curricula. I will begin by presenting the advantages and disadvantages of standards-based curricula, including why standards-based curricula possess a unique valence for early-career teachers. I will then argue that mathematical inquiry always contains both a logical and an aesthetic dimension and that teachers should be encouraged to see the aesthetic potential within all mathematical content. I will conclude by discussing the implications that the aesthetic dimension of mathematical inquiry has for the endeavor of teacher education. Specifically, I will argue that mathematical inquiry requires both thinking and feeling and that teachers and teacher educators should incorporate both of these dimensions into their curricular practices.

EARLY-CAREER TEACHERS AND STANDARDS-BASED MATHEMATICS CURRICULA

Within a standards-based curriculum, students are expected to develop an understanding of specific knowledge and a mastery of specific skills (Graham & Fennell, 2001; Trafton, Reys, & Wasman, 2001), and the responsibility of the teacher within this curricular framework is to ensure that students learn and demonstrate their achievement of the outlined standards. This curricular approach has dangers. Most notably, when a school adopts a standards-based curriculum, teachers, under pressure to ensure that students achieve mastery of all the standards outlined by the curriculum, may intentionally design and enact lessons that are narrow in intellectual scope. This curricular approach tends to limit students to only surface-level exposure to mathematical concepts, preventing students from engaging in authentic mathematical inquiry (Bengtson & Connors, 2014; Brown & Weber, 2016; Ede, 2006; Ogawa, Sandholtz, Martinez-Flores, & Scribner, 2003; Timberlake, Thomas, & Barrett, 2017).

Despite these negative effects, there are several reasons why early-career elementary teachers might be inclined to narrow their instruction in accordance with a high-stakes, standards-based curriculum. First, many preservice teachers possess an educational history within which they themselves experienced traditional, teacher-centered mathematics education (Holt-Reynolds, 1992; Smith, 1996). As a result, many preservice teachers may believe that teaching is synonymous with direct instruction and that quality mathematics teaching simply requires the teacher to model mathematical procedures. Unless these beliefs are challenged within the context of teacher education, early-career teachers may mimic the mathematics instruction they themselves received as students.

Second, many preservice and early-career teachers experience mathematics anxiety, an insecurity related to their self-perceived lack of expertise in the subject (Bekdemir, 2010; Bursal & Paznokas, 2006; Gresham, 2007, 2017). As a result of this anxiety, early-career teachers may gravitate toward curricula that outline specific learning outcomes and specific learning activities (McDuffie, Choppin, Drake, Davis, & Brown, 2017). Furthermore, early-career teachers often lack the expertise and time necessary to create rich curricular resources from scratch; thus, being provided with a curriculum with explicit standards (and even explicit scripts) can help mitigate early-career teachers' anxiety related to the daunting task of planning for and enacting mathematics lessons (Grossman & Thompson, 2008; Wood, Jilk, & Paine, 2012).

Third, given the multidimensionality of the classroom (Kennedy, 2005), early-career teachers tend to be cognitively overloaded while teaching (Moos & Pitton, 2014; Saariaho, Pyhältö, Toom, Pietarinen, & Soini, 2016). A curriculum that delineates explicit learning standards and activities can mitigate early-career teachers' cognitive load. For example, if a mathematics curriculum provides teachers with a predetermined learning objective for any given day, early-career teachers can use this specified learning objective to funnel students' thinking toward specific facts or computational fluencies (Herbel-Eisenmann & Breyfogle, 2005; Schoenfeld, 1988; Webel & Conner, 2017). Although this approach significantly narrows the intellectual scope of the lesson and dilutes the authenticity of mathematical inquiry, this approach may succeed in reducing complexity and uncertainty as the lesson unfolds.

Finally, early-career teachers are entering into a profession where, increasingly, mathematics curricula are being designed to align with high-stakes accountability measures (Bhola, Impara, & Buckendahl, 2003;

Cuban, 2007; Martone & Sireci, 2009; Porter, Fusarelli, & Fusarelli, 2015; Schiller & Muller, 2003). As a result, school districts and individual teachers are becoming increasingly inclined to narrow the scope of curricula with the intention of better preparing students for high-stakes assessments (Burkhauser & Lesaux, 2017; Schoenfeld, 2002, 2006). When early-career teachers join a school that experiences the pressures associated with high-stakes accountability, these teachers will likely conform to the narrowed curricular practices of their organization (Frank, Penuel, Sun, Kim, & Singleton, 2013; Penuel, Fishman, Yamaguchi, & Gallagher, 2007).

Standards-based curricula, despite their limitations, provide teachers with some affordances. For example, a standards-based curriculum provides teachers with an outlined sequence of standards that can help early-career teachers to connect big curricular ideas across lessons and units (Clements & Sarama, 2004; Purpura, Baroody, & Lonigan, 2013). Furthermore, emphasizing specific learning objectives and making explicit connections between these objectives has been shown to increase student achievement, albeit on standardized measures (McCaffrey et al., 2001; Riordan & Noyce, 2001). Above all else, standards-based curricula (especially curricula tied to high-stakes accountability measures) are likely to be a permanent feature of the educational policy landscape in the foreseeable future. Therefore, in this chapter, I do not wish to reject standards-based mathematics curricula; rather, I will attempt to illuminate the ways in which the practice of mathematical inquiry—even in the context of standards-based mathematics curricula—always presents an opening for aesthetic exploration.

THE AESTHETIC DIMENSION OF MATHEMATICAL INQUIRY

John Dewey (1938) argued that every experience has a particular *quality*, and it is this quality that determines whether the experience is educative, cultivating growth, or stultifying to growth and motivation. In the context of education, when curricular experiences are disconnected from students' lives and lived experience, students are being asked to serve the curriculum as opposed to positioning the curriculum to serve the students (Barrow, 2006; Toraman & Demir, 2016). For a curriculum to motivate students toward genuine inquiry, the literature demonstrates that the curriculum present students with a meaningful experience (Hadzigeorgiou & Schulz, 2017; Stuckey, Hofstein, Mamlok-Naaman, & Eilks, 2013). That is to say, genuinely educative experiences possess meaningful qualities, and the discernment of these qualities, according to Dewey, is primarily a function of aesthetic perception.

While Dewey (1933) posited that thinking is a function of rationality, he (1934) also argued that everyday human experience always possesses an aesthetic dimension. As Sinclair (2009) writes,

> In Dewey's conception, the aesthetic does not describe the qualities of perceptual artifacts; rather, it characterizes experiences that are satisfactory.... Aesthetic experiences can be had while appreciating art, while fixing a car, while having dinner, or while solving a mathematics problem. They are aesthetic in that they combine emotion, satisfaction and understanding. (p. 50)

One can argue, therefore, that mathematical inquiry is not only a function of logic and rationality but also a function of aesthetic perception. Certainly, one might argue that aesthetic experience is an essential component of (and not simply an upshot of) mathematical inquiry (Eberle, 2014; Griffiths, 2010; Koichu, Katz, & Berman, 2017; Satyam, 2016; Sinclair, 2004). As in the case of Cantor, mathematicians must employ their imaginations to identify problems worth solving and must devise clever and elegant solutions to these invented problems.

Mathematical inquiry, therefore, is not about getting a correct answer to a predetermined problem but, rather, about crafting a satisfying solution to an interesting question. Determining what counts as a satisfying solution requires assessing the goodness of fit of a particular solution to a given problem. Eisner (2002) wrote, "[p]roblems of fit must be addressed ... through being tuned in to the work and being able to make adjustments ... on the basis of what is felt emotionally" (p. 76). Another way of phrasing Eisner's insight is that effective mathematical inquiry requires a particular "tuning," and the relationship between a mathematical problem and its satisfying solution must be equally *felt* as well as *thought* (An, Capraro, & Tillman, 2013; Quigley & Herro, 2016). In sum, while mathematical solutions are partly rooted in rationality, there is also an aesthetic dimension to inquiry that guides the mathematician's craft.

If, indeed, mathematics can be both felt and thought, and if both rationality and aesthetic discernment are essential to authentic mathematical inquiry, then early-career teachers should be encouraged to see both the rational and aesthetic dimensions inherent within standards-based mathematical curricula. Furthermore, early-career teachers should recognize that mathematical inquiry may not always lead to correct answers or predetermined learning objectives. Eisner (2008) suggested that authentic "[i]nquiry always yields tentative conclusions rather than permanently nailed down facts" (p. 4). The challenge for early-career teachers, therefore, is to develop ways to frame curriculum as an opportunity to explore the aesthetic dimension of mathematics. I will now suggest two such approaches.

THE AESTHETICS OF MULTIPLE REPRESENTATIONS

One curricular strategy that teachers can use to highlight both the rational and the aesthetic dimensions inherent in any given mathematical concept is to invite students to generate and justify multiple representations of the given concept. Number talks (Humphreys & Parker, 2015; Parrish, 2010), for example, are a simple yet remarkably effective curricular component of elementary mathematics education. Within a number talk, students are asked to construct and compare mental strategies to solve arithmetic problems, such as 19 + 14 and 31 − 16. These problems can be solved algorithmically; however, by encouraging students to invent and justify as many approaches as possible, students are invited to exercise their mathematical imagination and to examine the same arithmetic expression from a variety of perspectives. This compels students to compare and contrast a variety of mathematical representations, a process that, in turn, deepens students' conceptual understanding (Ainsworth, 2006; Dreher & Kuntze, 2015; Große & Renkl, 2006; Kazemi, Gibbons, Lomax, & Franke, 2016). Research has shown that when students invent and compare multiple representations and multiple strategies, they develop more sophisticated and enduring conceptual understandings as opposed to when they simply memorize facts and practice standardized algorithms (Brenner et al., 1997; Bulgar, 2003; Sleep & Eskelson, 2012; Stein, Engle, Smith, & Hughes, 2008; Tirosh, 2000).

For example, consider something as deceptively simple as the number ½. This number can be represented as a fraction (½), as a decimal (0.50), as a percentage (50%), on a number line (somewhere between 0 and 1), or pictorially (1 out of 2 circles shaded). Students might also represent and explore the concept of this number in terms of a story: e.g., "Gina and Robert each ordered a sandwich, and they each ate half of the sandwich. Did they eat the same amount?" Of course, no one representation is *correct*. Rather, each new representation provides a new perspective through which to appreciate the concept, and exploring the concept from different angles is akin to the manner in which one would explore and appreciate any given work of art (Hofstadter, 1999; Peterson, 2001).

To continue this analogy, I invite the reader to listen to J. S. Bach's fugue in the key of B-flat minor from *The Well-Tempered Clavier: Book II*. Traditionally, fugues are musical pieces that begin with the presentation of an unaccompanied musical theme (or subject). As the fugue develops, additional voices present the subject as the music grows in complexity. This particular Bach fugue opens with a subject that is quite jagged and aggressive. He explores the musical subject by presenting it to the listener multiple times before developing and transforming the subject through canon (having it played in overlapping voices) and inversion (playing the theme upside-down). While doing this, Bach also modulates through a variety of harmonies, each illuminating a new quality of the subject: As the harmonies become more chromatic, the jagged subject becomes more slippery and devious; as the harmonies modulate into major keys, the assertive nature of the subject comes to sound almost triumphant. Sometimes the music sounds calm and serene; other times, it sounds combustible and unstable. Throughout the short piece, Bach examines a theme of only a few notes from a seemingly inexhaustible series of kaleidoscopic angles, each variation making a case for its own goodness of fit in the listener's ears. He portrays the fugue subject, although simple on its own, in so many distinct ways, with each new perspective being uniquely illuminating. Thus, through this musical inquiry, the listener deepens his or her appreciation for the art of fugue. The same statement, of course, could be said of a number talk; that is, by exploring relatively simple arithmetic combinations from a multitude of angles, students and teachers can deepen their appreciation for the richness of numbers.

THE AESTHETICS OF INCOMPLETENESS

The National Council of Teachers of Mathematics recommends that all students become proficient in a variety of sophisticated mathematical practices, including being able to construct viable arguments, being able to critique the reasoning of others, being able to construct mathematical models, and being able to identify mathematical structure (Committee on Science and Mathematics Teacher Preparation & National Research Council, 2000; Lester, 2007). Although these practices require the exercise of rationality, making mathematical arguments and discerning mathematical structure often rely on imagination (as noted earlier in relation to the radical ideas of Georg Cantor). While mathematics is a language of logic, mathematical argumentation can often lead to paradoxical results. Thus, another curricular strategy teachers can use to highlight the aesthetic dimension of mathematics is to highlight mathematics' inherent incompleteness.

Kurt Gödel (1906–1978) powerfully demonstrated the paradoxically incomplete mathematics by ingeniously constructing a metamathematical argument about arithmetic (Gamwell, 2016). Through his invented method, Gödel was able to show that systems of mathematical logic are inherently self-referential. In other words, Gödel was able to show that some mathematically true statements can never be proven from outside the system itself and that, therefore, the entire axiomatic system of arithmetic is, forever, by its very nature, incomplete.

Notably, Gödel's fascination with intrinsic incompleteness has been mirrored in artwork. For example, the artwork of M. C. Escher (2016/1948), such as the perpetually self-referential *Drawing Hands* (see Figure 7.1), produces images that forever remain incomplete. A similarly inscrutable work of art is René Magritte's painting *The Treachery of Images* (see Figure 7.2), where the viewer is presented with an image of a pipe while simultaneously being told "This is not a pipe." The paradoxically self-referential nature encountered within Gödel's mathematics, Escher's drawings, and Magritte's paintings are aesthetic properties that have inspired philosophers to reconsider the limits of representation (Foucault, 1983; Gamwell, 2016; Hofstadter, 1999; Wittgenstein, 2009).

Given the fascinating nature of mathematics' incompleteness, I argue that while mathematics teachers should cultivate their students' abilities to formulate and critique mathematical arguments and to construct robust and comprehensive mathematical models, they should also seize upon opportunities to point out the limits of mathematical representation. Just as Magritte and Escher created works of art *about* art, perhaps teachers and students can engage in meta-mathematical conversations, thinking critically about what mathematics, by its very nature, can and cannot do. Just as Magritte's paintings and Escher's drawings create aesthetic experiences by confronting the viewer with self-referential paradoxes, calling attention to the incompleteness of mathematical systems of logic may serve as effective invitations to explore the aesthetic (and affective) dimension of mathematics.

IMPLICATIONS FOR TEACHER EDUCATION

Number talks and the mathematical practices suggested by the National Council of Teachers of Mathematics are instructional strategies that mathematics teacher educators already endorsed. Thus, the novel argument within this conceptual essay is that teacher educators should frame these existing instructional strategies as opportunities not only for building conceptual understanding (i.e., the cognitive dimension of mathematics) but also as opportunities to explore the aesthetic dimensions of mathematics. This would require teacher educators to orient preservice teachers' attention to the mathematical content discussed within a number talk and to the quality of the experience, that is, the affective dimensions of the classroom encounter. Many scholars (Dixon & Senior, 2011; Garcia & Lewis, 2014; McPherson & Saltmarsh, 2017; Mulcahy, 2012; Zembylas, 2005, 2007) have highlighted how discourses around teacher practice, identity, and development tend to overemphasize the cognitive components of teaching (e.g., knowledge, theories, prescribed instructional strategies). These scholars,

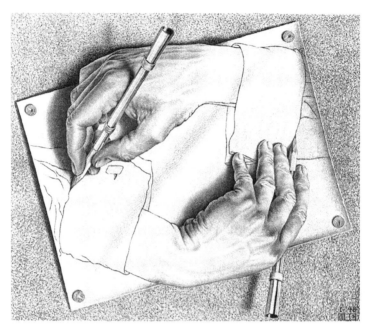

Figure 7.1. *Drawing hands* (1948) by M. C. Escher.

Figure 7.2. *La trahison des images* (The treachery of images) (2016/1929) by René Magritte.

however, encourage teacher educators to help preservice teachers tend to the more holistic dimensions of teaching, including the teacher's subjective experience of body, emotion, space, time, affect, and mood.

For example, teacher educators might call preservice teachers' attention to what a particular number talk *feels* like. When the teacher facilitates a number talk, what is the mood in the classroom? What are the emotions experienced by the teacher and students? Does the number talk ignite imagination and curiosity? These questions are just as essential as questions about student understanding; as Zembylas (2007) writes, "without desire, there is no pedagogy" (p. 338). Hence, the teacher must ask, does the number talk effectively call forth desire, curiosity, imagination, excitement, and wonder? What are the aesthetic qualities of the mathematical ideas brought forth through the number talk?

These questions, aesthetic in nature, should be just as prominent as questions about learning outcomes, content knowledge, and procedural fluency; however, as discussed earlier in this essay, there are multiple reasons why early-career teachers may be reluctant to turn their attention away from concerns about measurable learning outcomes and high-stakes testing. It is, therefore, in part, the teacher educator's responsibility to encourage preservice teachers to attend to aesthetic questions in the mathematics classroom.

If teacher educators are to support preservice and early-career teachers toward this aim, there are at least four concrete strategies that they can employ. First, teacher educators should help preservice teachers practice the professional skill of interpreting standards-based curriculum materials (Beyer & Davis, 2009; Land, Tyminski, & Drake, 2015; Nicol & Crespo, 2006; Remillard & Bryans, 2004; Remillard & Kim, 2017). Given that early-career teachers lack the expertise and time to design their own curricular materials (Grossman & Thompson, 2008; Wood et al., 2012), teacher educators should encourage preservice teachers to utilize the standards-based curricula provided to them by their school; teacher educators should also, however, cultivate within preservice teachers the disposition to supplement these curricular materials with instructional approaches (e.g., number talks) that bring to light the aesthetic dimension of mathematics.

Second, teacher educators should provide preservice teachers with aesthetic mathematical experiences within the teacher education classroom. Such authentic experiences of mathematical inquiry, specifically highlighting the aesthetic dimension, may challenge preservice teachers' preexisting (traditional, teacher-centered) beliefs about the teaching of mathematics (Hourigan, Leavy, & Carroll, 2016). Consistent with Dewey's (1938) educational philosophy, it is important to note that it is only by *experiencing* this new approach to mathematical instruction (i.e., mathematical inquiry as aesthetic experience) that preservice teachers will begin to expand their conceptualization of what mathematics education—and, more fundamentally, what mathematics itself—can be (see Richardson & Liang, 2008; Windschitl, 2003). It is also worth noting that the experience of authentic mathematical inquiry in the teacher education classroom may serve to reduce preservice teachers' mathematics anxiety. As preservice teachers begin to realize that the practice of mathematical inquiry (as practiced by mathematicians) is more about intuiting and articulating goodness of fit than it is about arriving at one correct answer, preservice teachers may begin to feel more capable of facilitating mathematical inquiry and mathematical discussions in their own classrooms (Bates, Latham, & Kim, 2011; Gresham, 2017).

Third, in order to ensure that early-career teachers stay committed to highlighting the aesthetic dimension of mathematical inquiry for their students, teacher educators should actively partner with local schools (Ryan et al., 2014; Zeichner, 2010). The ambitious instructional beliefs and practices of early-career teachers can easily be diluted by organizational norms present within a given school (Frank et al., 2013; Penuel et al., 2007), especially when these schools are facing accountability pressures. While teacher educators cannot erase the accountability pressures and high-stakes testing mandates that exist, they can serve local schools by supporting and encouraging both early-career and experienced teachers to find ways to integrate aesthetic experiences into their mathematics curriculum.

Finally, teacher educators must prepare preservice teachers for uncertainty (Floden & Clark, 1988; Reeve, 2009). Early-career teachers must learn to be comfortable with uncertainty and complexity if they are to encourage their students to exercise agency in exploring the aesthetic dimensions of mathematics. The products of genuine inquiry "are closer in function to deep conversation and insightful dialogue than they are to error-free conclusions" (Eisner, 2008, p. 7). Both teacher educators and early-career teachers must recognize that the act of inviting students to become authentic mathematicians not only enriches student learning but also complicates the work of teaching, increases the complexity of teacher thinking, and, perhaps, contributes to the incompleteness of a given lesson's anticipated learning outcomes. Entering the classroom without the expectation of this uncertainty increases the likelihood that early-career teachers will abandon their ambitions in favor of narrow, prescribed (but predictable) curricula.

CONCLUSION

In this essay, I have argued that experiencing and appreciating the aesthetic dimension of mathematics is not an upshot of mathematical inquiry but, rather, is a catalyst for it. Mathematicians both *think* through and *feel* their way through problems and solutions. Therefore, if students are to engage in authentic mathematical inquiry, teachers must encourage students to explore both the rational and the aesthetic dimensions of mathematics. Additionally, teachers should recognize that rationality and affect—logic and beauty—are present in all domains of mathematical inquiry (including arithmetic). Thus, any standards-based mathematical curriculum—independent of how closely aligned it is with a high-stakes assessment—presents prime opportunities for aesthetic experiences. It is the responsibility of the teacher to make room for such opportunities, and it is the responsibility of teacher education to cultivate teachers who have this disposition.

What does it mean to *know* mathematics? Dewey and Eisner would both argue that there are multiple forms of knowing: One form is rational, logical cognition; another, equally valid form, is aesthetic intuition. Analogously, mathematical knowledge can take the form of a generalizable, abstract theory or the form of a singular, evocative experience. Cantor's axioms of set theory, for example, can be memorized and understood, but they can also be used as the catalyst for creativity and inspiration.

I hope that I have provided the reader of this essay with an experience that demonstrates that mathematics has the potential to not only deepen our knowledge of logic but also to deepen our capacity for feeling. Engaging with the ideas of Cantor, Kruchenykh, Malevich, Bach, Gödel, Escher, and Magritte should be treasured experiences for the generalizable knowledge we can take away from these encounters and for the way that these encounters make us feel. For, "[i]f the arts are about anything, they are about emotion.... Becoming aware of our capacity to feel is a way of discovering our humanity. Art helps us ... to discover our own interior landscape. Not an unimportant achievement" (Eisner, 2008, p. 11). I encourage teachers and teacher educators to continue to explore the ways in which mathematics—like all art—can reveal and create the interior landscape of our thinking and feeling.

REFERENCES

Ainsworth, S. (2006). DeFT: A conceptual framework for considering learning with multiple representations. *Learning and Instruction, 16*(3), 183–198.

An, S. A., Capraro, M. M., & Tillman, D. A. (2013). Elementary teachers integrate music activities into regular mathematics lessons: Effects on students' mathematical abilities. *Journal of Learning through the Arts, 9*(1), 1–19.

Barrow, L. H. (2006). A brief history of inquiry: From Dewey to standards. *Journal of Science Teacher Education, 17*(3), 265–278.

Bates, A. B., Latham, N., & Kim, J. A. (2011). Linking preservice teachers' mathematics self-efficacy and mathematics teaching efficacy to their mathematical performance. *School Science and Mathematics, 111*(7), 325–333.

Bekdemir, M. (2010). The pre-service teachers' mathematics anxiety related to depth of negative experiences in mathematics classroom while they were students. *Educational Studies in Mathematics, 75*(3), 311–328.

Bengtson, E., & Connors, S. P. (2014). Puppets and puppeteers: External mandates and the instructional practice of two first-year teachers. *International Journal of Educational Leadership Preparation, 9*(2), 128–152.

Beyer, C. J., & Davis, E. A. (2009). Using educative curriculum materials to support preservice elementary teachers' curricular planning: A comparison between two different forms of support. *Curriculum Inquiry, 39*(5), 679–703.

Bhola, D. S., Impara, J. C., & Buckendahl, C. W. (2003). Aligning tests with states' content standards: Methods and issues. *Educational Measurement: Issues and Practices, 22*(3), 21–29.

Brenner, M. E., Mayer, R. E., Moseley, B., Brar, T., Duran, R., Reed, B. S., & Webb, D. (1997). Learning by understanding: The role of multiple representations in learning algebra. *American Educational Research Journal, 34*(4), 663–689.

Brown, C. P., & Weber, N. B. (2016). Struggling to overcome the state's prescription for practice: A study of a sample of early educators' professional development and action research projects in a high-stakes teaching context. *Journal of Teacher Education, 67*(3), 183–202.

Bulgar, S. (2003). Children's sense-making of division of fractions. *Journal of Mathematical Behavior, 22*(3), 319–334.

Burkhauser, M. A., & Lesaux, N. K. (2017). Exercising a bounded autonomy: Novice and experienced teachers' adaptations to curriculum materials in an age of accountability. *Journal of Curriculum Studies, 49*(3), 291–312.

Bursal, M., & Paznokas, L. (2006). Mathematics anxiety and preservice elementary teachers' confidence to teach mathematics and science. *School Science and Mathematics, 106*(4), 173–180.

Clements, D. H., & Sarama, J. (2004). Learning trajectories in mathematics education. *Mathematical Thinking and Learning, 6*(2), 81–89.

Committee on Science and Mathematics Teacher Preparation & National Research Council. (2000). *Educating teachers of science, mathematics, and technology: New practices for the new millennium*. Washington, DC: National Academy Press.

Crespo, S. M., & Sinclair, N. (2008). What makes a problem mathematically interesting? Inviting prospective teachers to pose better problems. *Journal of Mathematics Teacher Education, 11*(5), 395–415.

Cuban, L. (2007). Hugging the middle: Teaching in an era of testing and accountability, 1980–2005. *Education Policy Analysis Archives, 15*(1), 1–29.

Dauben, J. W. (1990). *Georg Cantor: His mathematics and philosophy of the infinite*. Princeton, NJ: Princeton University Press.

Dewey, J. (1933). *How we think: A restatement of the relation of reflective thinking to the educative process*. Lexington, MA: Heath.

Dewey, J. (1934). *Art as experience*. New York, NY: Capricorn Books.

Dewey, J. (1938). *Experience and education*. New York, NY: Touchstone.

Dixon, M., & Senior, K. (2011). Appearing pedagogy: From embodied learning and teaching to embodied pedagogy. *Pedagogy, Culture & Society, 19*(3), 473–484.

Dreher, A., & Kuntze, S. (2015). Teachers' professional knowledge and noticing: The case of multiple representations in the mathematics classroom. *Educational Studies in Mathematics, 88*(1), 89–114.

Dreyfus, T., & Eisenberg, T. (1986). On the aesthetics of mathematical thought. *For the Learning of Mathematics, 6*(1), 2–10.

Eberle, R. S. (2014). The role of children's mathematical aesthetics: The case of tessellations. *Journal of Mathematical Behavior, 35*, 129–143.

Ede, A. (2006). Scripted curriculum: Is it a prescription for success? *Childhood Education, 83*(1), 29–32.

Eisner, E. W. (2002). *The arts and the creation of mind*. New Haven, CT: Yale University Press.

Eisner, E. W. (2008). Art and knowledge. In G. J. Knowles & A. L. Cole (Eds.), *Handbook of the arts in qualitative research* (pp. 3–12). Thousand Oaks, CA: SAGE.

Escher, M. C. (2016). *Drawing hands* [Lithograph]. In L. Gamwell, *Mathematics + art: A cultural history* (p. 333). Princeton, NJ: Princeton University Press. (Original work 1948).

Floden, R. E., & Clark, C. M. (1988). Preparing teachers for uncertainty. *Teachers College Record, 89*(4), 505–524.

Foucault, M. (1983). *This is not a pipe*. Berkeley, CA: University of California Press.

Frank, K. A., Penuel, W. R., Sun, M., Kim, C., & Singleton, C. (2013). The organization as a filter of institutional diffusion. *Teachers College Record, 115*(1), 306–339.

Gamwell, L. (2016). *Mathematics + art: A cultural history*. Princeton, NJ: Princeton University Press.

Garcia, J. A., & Lewis, T. E. (2014). Getting a grip on the classroom: From psychological to phenomenological curriculum development in teacher education programs. *Curriculum Inquiry, 44*(2), 141–168.

Graham, K. J., & Fennell, F. S. (2001). Principles and standards for school mathematics and teacher education: Preparing and empowering teachers. *School Science and Mathematics, 101*(6), 319–327.

Gresham, G. (2007). A study of mathematics anxiety in pre-service teachers. *Early Childhood Education Journal, 35*(2), 181–188.

Gresham, G. (2017). Preservice to inservice: Does mathematics anxiety change with teaching experience? *Journal of Teacher Education*. doi:10.1177/0022487117702580

Griffiths, M. (2010). Mathematics suggested by a logo: Both rich and beautiful? *Teaching Mathematics and Its Applications: An International Journal of the IMA, 29*(4), 216–229.

Große, C. S., & Renkl, A. (2006). Effects of multiple solution methods in mathematical learning. *Learning and Instruction, 16*(2), 122–138.

Grossman, P., & Thompson, C. (2008). Learning from curriculum materials: Scaffolds for new teachers? *Teaching and Teacher Education, 24*(8), 2014–2026.

Hadzigeorgiou, Y., & Schulz, R. M. (2017). What really makes secondary school students "want" to study physics? *Education Sciences, 7*(4), 84.

Herbel-Eisenmann, B., & Breyfogle, M. L. (2005). Questioning our patterns of questioning. *Mathematics Teaching in the Middle School, 10*(9), 484–489.

Hofstadter, D. R. (1999). *Gödel, Escher, Bach: An eternal golden braid*. New York, NY: Basic Books.

Holt-Reynolds, D. (1992). Personal history-based beliefs as relevant prior knowledge in coursework: Can we practice what we teach? *American Educational Research Journal, 29*(2), 325–349.

Hourigan, M., Leavy, A. M., & Carroll, C. (2016). "Come in with an open mind": Changing attitudes towards mathematics in primary teacher education. *Educational Research, 58*(3), 319–346.

Humphreys, C., & Parker, R. (2015). *Making number talks matter*. Portland, ME: Sternhouse.

Kazemi, E., Gibbons, L. K., Lomax, K., & Franke, M. L. (2016). Listening to and learning from student thinking. *Teaching Children Mathematics, 23*(3), 182–190.

Kennedy, M. M. (2005). *Inside teaching: How classroom life undermines reform*. Cambridge, MA: Harvard University Press.

Koichu, B., Katz, E., & Berman, A. (2017). Stimulating student aesthetic response to mathematical problems by means of manipulating the extent of surprise. *Journal of Mathematical Behavior, 46*, 42–57.

Labaree, D. F. (2011). Consuming the public school. *Educational Theory, 61*(4), 381–394.

Land, T. J., Tyminski, A. M., & Drake, C. (2015). Examining pre-service elementary mathematics teachers' reading of educative curriculum materials. *Teaching and Teacher Education, 51*, 16–26.

Lester, F. K. (Ed.) (2007). *Second handbook of research on mathematics teaching and learning: A project of the National Council of Teachers of Mathematics*. Charlotte, NC: Information Age.

Magritte, R. (2016). *La trahison des images* [Oil on canvas]. In L. Gamwell, *Mathematics + art: A cultural history* (p. 327). Princeton, NJ: Princeton University Press. (Original work 1929).

Malevich, K. (2003). *The non-objective world: The manifesto of suprematism*. Mineola, NY: Dover.

Mandelbrot, B. (1982). *The fractal geometry of nature*. San Francisco, CA: W. H. Freeman.

Martone, A., & Sireci, S. G. (2009). Evaluating alignment between curriculum, assessment, and instruction. *Review of Educational Research, 79*(4), 1332–1361.

McCaffrey, D. F., Hamilton, L. S., Stecher, B. M., Klein, S. P., Bugliari, D., & Robyn, A. (2001). Interactions among instructional practices, curriculum, and student achievement: The case of standards-based high school mathematics. *Journal for Research in Mathematics Education, 32*(5), 493–517.

McDuffie, A. R., Choppin, J., Drake, C., Davis, J. D., & Brown, J. (2017). Middle school teachers' differing perceptions and use of curriculum materials and the common core. *Journal of Mathematics Teacher Education*. doi:10.1007/s10857-017-9368-0

McPherson, A., & Saltmarsh, S. (2017). Bodies and affect in non-traditional learning spaces. *Educational Philosophy and Theory, 49*(8), 832–841.

Moos, D. C., & Pitton, D. (2014). Student teacher challenges: Using the cognitive load theory as an explanatory lens. *Teaching Education, 25*(2), 127–141.

Mulcahy, D. (2012). Affective assemblages: Body matters in the pedagogic practices of contemporary school classrooms. *Pedagogy, Culture & Society, 20*(1), 9–27.

Nicol, C. C., & Crespo, S. M. (2006). Learning to teach with mathematics textbooks: How preservice teachers interpret and use curriculum materials. *Educational Studies in Mathematics, 62*(3), 331–355.

Ogawa, R. T., Sandholtz, J. H., Martinez-Flores, M., & Scribner, S. P. (2003). The substantive and symbolic consequences of a district's standards-based curriculum. *American Educational Research Journal, 40*(1), 147–176.

Parrish, S. D. (2010). *Number talks: Helping children build mental math and computation strategies*. Sausalito, CA: Math Solutions.

Penuel, W. R., Fishman, B. J., Yamaguchi, R., & Gallagher, L. P. (2007). What makes professional development effective? Strategies that foster curriculum implementation. *American Educational Research Journal, 44*(4), 921–958.

Peterson, I. (2001). *Fragments of infinity: A kaleidoscope of math and art*. Hoboken, NJ: John Wiley & Sons.

Porter, R. E., Fusarelli, L. D., & Fusarelli, B. C. (2015). Implementing the Common Core: How educators interpret curriculum reform. *Educational Policy, 29*(1), 111–139.

Purpura, D. J., Baroody, A. J., & Lonigan, C. J. (2013). The transition from informal to formal mathematical knowledge: Mediation by numeral knowledge. *Journal of Educational Psychology, 105*(2), 453–464.

Quigley, C. F., & Herro, D. (2016). "Finding the joy in the unknown": Implementation of STEAM teaching practices in middle school science and math classrooms. *Journal of Science Education and Technology, 25*(3), 410–426.

Reeve, J. (2009). Why teachers adopt a controlling motivating style toward students and how they can become more autonomy supportive. *Educational Psychologist, 44*(3), 159–175.

Remillard, J. T., & Bryans, M. B. (2004). Teachers' orientations toward mathematics curriculum materials: Implications for teacher learning. *Journal for Research in Mathematics Education, 35*(5), 352–388.

Remillard, J. T., & Kim, O. K. (2017). Knowledge of curriculum embedded mathematics: Exploring a critical domain of teaching. *Educational Studies in Mathematics, 96*(1), 65–81.

Richardson, G. M., & Liang, L. L. (2008). The use of inquiry in the development of preservice teacher efficacy in mathematics and science. *Journal of Elementary Science Education, 20*(1), 1–16.

Riordan, J. E., & Noyce, P. E. (2001). The impact of two standards-based mathematics curricula on student achievement in Massachusetts. *Journal for Research in Mathematics Education, 32*(4), 368–398.

Ryan, A. M., Ensminger, D., Heineke, A. J., Kennedy, A., Prasse, D. P., & Smetana, L. K. (2014). Teaching, learning, and leading with schools and communities: One urban university re-envisions teacher preparation for the next generation. *Issues in Teacher Education, 22*(2), 139–153.

Saariaho, E., Pyhältö, K., Toom, A., Pietarinen, J., & Soini, T. (2016). Student teachers' self- and co-regulation of learning during teacher education. *Learning: Research and Practice, 2*(1), 44–63.

Satyam, V. R. (2016). The importance of surprise in mathematical beauty. *Journal of Humanistic Mathematics, 6*(1), 196–210.

Schiller, K. S., & Muller, C. (2003). Raising the bar and equity? Effects of state high school graduation requirements and accountability policies on students' mathematics course taking. *Educational Evaluation and Policy Analysis, 25*(3), 299–318.

Schiro, M. S. (2013). *Curriculum theory: Conflicting visions and enduring concerns* (2nd ed.). Los Angeles, CA: Sage.

Schoenfeld, A. H. (1988). When good teaching leads to bad results: The disasters of "well taught" mathematics courses. *Educational Psychologist, 23*(2), 145–166.

Schoenfeld, A. H. (2002). Making mathematics work for all children: Issues of standards, testing, and equity. *Educational Researcher, 31*(1), 13–25.

Schoenfeld, A. H. (2006). What doesn't work: The challenge and failure of the What Works Clearinghouse to conduct meaningful reviews of studies of mathematics curricula. *Educational Researcher, 35*(2), 13–21.

Sherin, M. G., & Drake, C. (2009). Curriculum strategy framework: Investigating patterns in teachers' use of a reform-based elementary mathematics curriculum. *Journal of Curriculum Studies, 41*(4), 467–500.

Silver, E., & Metzger, W. (1989). Aesthetic influences on expert mathematical problem solving. In D. McLeod & V. Adams (Eds.), *Affect and mathematical problem solving* (pp. 59–74). New York, NY: Springer.

Sinclair, N. (2004). The roles of the aesthetic in mathematical inquiry. *Mathematical Thinking and Learning, 6*(3), 261–284.

Sinclair, N. (2009). Aesthetics as a liberating force in mathematics education? *ZDM, 41*(1–2), 45–60.

Sleep, L., & Eskelson, S. L. (2012). MKT and curriculum materials are only part of the story: Insights from a lesson on fractions. *Journal of Curriculum Studies, 44*(4), 537–558.

Smith J. P., III. (1996). Efficacy and teaching mathematics by telling: A challenge for reform. *Journal for Research in Mathematics Education, 27*(4), 387–402.

Stein, M. K., Engle, R. A., Smith, M. S., & Hughes, E. K. (2008). Orchestrating productive mathematical discussions: Five practices for helping teachers move beyond show and tell. *Mathematical Thinking and Learning, 10*(4), 313–340.

Stuckey, M., Hofstein, A., Mamlok-Naaman, R., & Eilks, I. (2013). The meaning of "relevance" in science education and its implications for the science curriculum. *Studies in Science Education, 49*(1), 1–34.

Timberlake, M. T., Thomas, A. B., & Barrett, B. (2017). The allure of simplicity: Scripted curricula and equity. *Teaching and Teacher Education, 67*, 46–52.

Tirosh, D. (2000). Enhancing prospective teachers' knowledge of children's conceptions: The case of division of fractions. *Journal for Research in Mathematics Education, 31*(1), 5–25.

Toraman, C., & Demir, E. (2016). The effect of constructivism on attitudes towards lessons: A meta-analysis study. *Eurasian Journal of Educational Research, 62*, 115–142.

Trafton, P. R., Reys, B. J., & Wasman, D. G. (2001). Standards-based mathematics curriculum materials: A phrase in search of a definition. *Phi Delta Kappan, 83*(3), 259–264.

Webel, C., & Conner, K. A. (2017). Using simulated teaching experiences to perturb preservice teachers' mathematics questioning practices. *Mathematics Teacher Educator, 6*(1), 9–26.

Windschitl, M. (2003). Inquiry projects in science teacher education: What can investigative experiences reveal about teacher thinking and eventual classroom practice? *Science Education, 87*(1), 112–143.

Wittgenstein, L. (2009). *Philosophical investigations.* Oxford, England: Wiley-Blackwell.

Wood, M. B., Jilk, L. M., & Paine, L. W. (2012). Moving beyond sinking or swimming: Reconceptualizing the needs of beginning mathematics teachers. *Teachers College Record, 114*(8), 1–44.

Zeichner, K. M. (2010). Rethinking the connections between campus courses and field experiences in college- and university-based teacher education. *Journal of Teacher Education, 61*(1–2), 89–99.

Zembylas, M. (2005). Beyond teacher cognition and teacher beliefs: The value of the ethnography of emotions in teaching. *International Journal of Qualitative Studies in Education, 18*(4), 465–487.

Zembylas, M. (2007). Risks and pleasures: a Deleuzo-Guattarian pedagogy of desire in education. *British Educational Research Journal, 33*(3), 331–347.

OUTTAKE

RECRUITING QUEERS

The Complexities of Finding Participants in an Often Invisible Population

Lesley N. Siegel

A year ago, I set out to study the experiences of lesbian- and gay-identified faculty working in schools and departments of education. As a lesbian- and queer-identifying faculty member, I am interested in learning about the ways in which other lesbian-, gay-, and/or queer-identified faculty working in teacher preparation make their sexual identity visible to their students. To this end, I designed a qualitative study that pulled from the tradition of phenomenology in order to contextualize the experiences of a group of people with shared experiences (Creswell, 2007; Padilla-Diaz, 2015).

After many months negotiating with my university's institutional review board (IRB), I had well-defined inclusion and exclusion criteria for participation, strict guidelines for maintaining confidentiality, and permission to use persons in my professional network as "gatekeepers," persons who have insider status with the potential study participants (Creswell, 2007). When I set out to do this work, I functioned under the assumption that working through a shared friend or colleague (the gatekeeper) would inspire confidence in individuals to participate. In addition, this shared association would give reason for the participants to place trust in me as the researcher. Furthermore, because being gay in higher education is highly personal and certainly not without consequence, I assumed that because I also lived the experience of being queer in the academy, it would encourage potential participants to put their trust in me as a researcher and volunteer. I was wrong.

The challenges of recruiting gay and lesbian persons to participate in research are ongoing for many researchers across disciplines because the population is not only difficult to define but also relies on self-identification (McCormack, 2014; Meyer & Wilson 2009). The difficulties of recruiting participants for this study have far exceeded the complexities I anticipated. My hope was, and remains so, to recruit study participants from sociopolitical and geographically diverse regions of the country, various types of institutions of higher education, and faculty in different positions (e.g., pretenured faculty, tenured faculty, adjunct faculty). Most important, I want to hear voices that extend beyond the voices I already know.

My recruitment model is as follows: I ask colleagues and friends if they know of someone who might fit the inclusion criteria for participation in my study: identify as gay, lesbian, or queer faculty; work in teacher preparation; and, must be willing to professionally identify as "out" (as determined by the participants). If indeed my colleague does know someone who fits the criteria, I pass along a description of the study with my contact information to be delivered to the potential participants. Then I wait for the potential participants to contact me and agree to the interview process. I have done an exceptional amount of waiting the past nine months.

Sexual orientation can be an invisibility identity; unlike more visible marginalized identities, there is no demographic box to count us, no census records us. Conversely, some persons shy away from the thought of visibly identifying as gay (or being "out") as the prospect of being visible can be fraught with consequences. Even with assurances of confidentiality, perhaps it is the step of contacting an unknown researcher to identify as gay that prevents persons from raising a hand to participate.

Alternatively, it is possible that the gatekeeper model is a barrier to participant recruitment. In this study, the gatekeeper is more than a liaison between researcher and participants; the gatekeeper is trusted with the marginalized sexual identity of the potential participants. The gatekeeper must also protect the identity of the potential participants by only supplying the potential participants with information on the study. With this information, potential participants may choose to reach out and, by doing so, choose to make visible their gay or lesbian identities to an unknown researcher. This protection provided by the gatekeeper is absolutely necessary; however, it creates a unidirectional flow of information. I can only wait to see if participants will take the information and reach out. This leaves me at the juncture of trying to determine whether it is logistics, the vulnerable nature of a marginalized and often invisible population, or a combination of both that is making recruiting participants so difficult.

The institutional, geopolitical, and personal variables that either support or oppress queer faculty vary tremendously across institutions of higher education. While exploring these variables is at the heart of my study, these very variables could make individuals feel too vulnerable to speak about their experiences as faculty with an unknown person. I knew this going in to the study and I anticipated difficulties, especially given that I am not an established academic, but I assumed my positionality and the trust of a gatekeeper would help pave the way. My optimism has been shaken, but my belief in this work, and the encouragement I have received from colleagues and (few) participants, motivates me to press on.

REFERENCES

Creswell, J. W. (2007). *Qualitative inquiry and research design: Choosing among five approaches*. Thousand Oaks, CA: SAGE.

McCormack, M. (2014). Innovative sampling and participant recruitment in sexuality research. *Journal of Social and Personal Relationships, 31*(4), 475–481.

Meyer, I. H., & Wilson, P. A. (2009). Sampling lesbian, gay, and bisexual populations. *Journal of Counseling Psychology, 56*(1), 23.

Padilla-Diaz, M. (2015). Phenomenology in educational qualitative research: Philosophy as science or philosophical science? *International Journal of Educational Excellence, 1*(2), 101–110.

OUTTAKE

REACHING NEW POSSIBILITIES ON LESSON STUDY COLLABORATION

Dittika Gupta, Mollie Appelgate, Lara Dick, Melissa Soto, and Shawn Broderick

As a group of five early-career Mathematics Teacher Educators (MTEs), we are fortunate to collaborate with each other to focus on our teaching and research. Early in our collaboration, as we planned a lesson to gather data from our preservice teachers (PSTs) on their mathematical noticing, we realized that not only could we study our PSTs' learning, we could also research ourselves, our lesson and instruction. In this outtake, we discuss our "aha" moment during collaboration and how that has taken our teaching and research to a whole new dimension.

JOURNEY

Our journey began when we established a research group to explore PSTs' ability to make whole class instructional decisions based on analysis of written student work using the professional noticing of children's mathematical thinking constructs (Jacobs, Lamb, & Philipp, 2010). We designed a lesson to engage our PSTs with these ideas (Gupta, Soto, Dick,

Broderick, & Appelgate, 2018). We regularly met via Google Hangout to discuss the lesson and reflect on our teaching of it. One day it was a like a light bulb went off—"Oh my gosh!" In the process of constructively critiquing the lesson and our teaching of it, we were essentially engaging in a lesson study across five different institutions in five different states. It was truly an "aha!" moment for us. We were excited and wanted to formalize this research process.

EXTENDING THE COLLABORATION

Our "aha" moment led us to officially conduct lesson study research at the university level. The purpose of lesson study is to examine teaching and student learning through reflection with a goal of improving instruction. The lesson study cycle is comprised of four steps: (a) study the curriculum and formulate goals, (b) plan, (c) conduct research on the lesson, and (d) reflect (Lewis & Hurd, 2011). Though Cerbin and Kopp (2006) and Kamen et al. (2011) adapted the lesson study cycle to investigate how to improve their teaching in mathematics methods courses, literature on lesson study across states or institutions has been very slim. Hence, we were motivated to explore this realm of lesson study further.

As a group, we decided to teach five iterations of the same lesson at our respective institutions. Teaching the lesson at different times allowed us to view the video, individually reflect on the instruction, debrief with the instructor, and discuss how we would adapt the lesson for the next iteration. Our discussions and reflections about each other's instruction led to many teachable moments for us as individuals. To document our thoughts on the lesson study process, each MTE kept an online journal. The journal entry below contains MTE 2's takeaways after viewing and discussing MTE 1's lesson implementation.

> MTE 1 deviated from the lesson to talk about the [design of the story] problem with her students (problems including wordiness that could challenge English language learners, and context) and that was like Wow! Gosh! You definitely can never anticipate what your [PSTs] would say. They were talking about giving a direct problem without the context and then in another breath talking about how math needs to be linked to the real world more. I was flabbergasted. It's good this happened. Gave us more insight. (MTE 2, online journal, 3/17/2016)

By engaging in the lesson study process, we shared and critiqued our teaching constructively, which highlighted common struggles. For example, MTE 3 reflected on common struggles as teachers: "We debriefed MTE 4's lesson, and it was fascinating because of a few things: We all struggle with time, particularly making sure there is time for discussion about the whole class next steps ..." (MTE 3, online journal, 3/17/2016). We also recognized common struggles our PSTs had and how we could adjust the lesson to better support them. For example, MTE 5 reflected, "We discussed a lot about how to end our lesson with a good discussion and closure. We need to have the PSTs consider more as they propose their next tasks as a whole class" (MTE 5, online journal, 3/8/2016).

The process of developing and analyzing our lesson iterations became an important part of our professional growth.

NEW POSSIBILITIES

Even though we began analyzing each other's teaching individually and discussing it, we wanted to further explore this realm of collaboration and lesson study at the university level. For our next semester's iteration, we observed one of the taught lessons via Google Hangout in order to be present in the moment of teaching, provide real-time feedback, and extend the notion that collaboration is not dependent on place or time zone. Lesson study served as a tool to develop both our teaching practice and our scholarship and created new possibilities for us to research our PSTs' thinking.

REFERENCES

Cerbin, W., & Kopp, B. (2006). Lesson study as a model for building pedagogical knowledge and improving teaching. *International Journal of Teaching and Learning in Higher Education*, *18*(3), 250–257.

Gupta, D., Soto, M., Dick, L., Broderick, S., & Appelgate, M. (2018). Noticing and deciding the next steps for teaching: A cross-university study with elementary pre-service teachers. In G. J. Stylianides & K. Hino (Eds.), *Research advances in the mathematical education of pre-service elementary teachers: An international perspective* (pp. 261–275). New York, NY: Springer.

Jacobs, V. R., Lamb, L. L. C., & Philipp, R. A. (2010). Professional noticing of children's mathematical thinking. *Journal for Research in Mathematics Education*, *41*, 169–202.

Kamen, M., Junk, D. L., Marble, S., Cooper, S., Eddy, C. M., Wilkerson, T. L., & Sawyer, C. (2011). Walking the talk: Lessons learned by university mathematics methods instructors implementing lesson study for their own professional development. In L. C. Hart, A. Alston, & A. Murata (Eds.), *Lesson study research and practice in mathematics education* (pp. 165–174). Dordrecht, Netherlands: Springer.

Lewis, C. C., & Hurd, J. (2011). *Lesson study step by step: How teacher learning communities improve instruction*. Portsmouth, NH: Heinemann.

OUTTAKE

A CULTURALLY CANDID RESPONSE

Tale of Two Professors' Reflections

Melanie Fields and Laura Isbell

As two assistant professors at the same state university, we began our collaboration by working, observing, and supervising preservice teachers. We were within the same department; however, we taught different educational certification levels. One taught elementary educator certification, while the other taught secondary educator certification. Additionally, we were both supervisors working with preservice teachers. In the role of supervisor, we observed, monitored, and evaluated preservice teachers in the teacher preparation program.

We currently teach at an institute where students come from various backgrounds, cultures, ages, and experiences. To meet our students' diverse needs, the teacher preparation program offers preservice teachers opportunities to experience residency in a variety of school districts, both urban and rural. Upon entering the teacher preparation program, we noticed preservice teachers were having preconceived notions or generalizations about what their experiences would be like in the field and how they viewed themselves as classroom teachers. We had several conversations about their teaching practices and more specifically about culturally relevant teaching, which ultimately led to the emergence of the current project.

A STUDY EMERGED

We began the collaboration by following up with graduates from the teacher preparation program; many reported that what they had learned during their residency was positive and beneficial. However, one graduate was brutally honest and explained that she felt we neglected teaching her how to effectively instruct underprivileged, non-white students. This instance narrowed our focus to one particular student's experiences, responses, and reflections in the teacher preparation program.

This particular student, "Piper," was placed in a privileged, affluent, almost all Caucasian school for her student teaching assignment. She stated that "her goal was to always go back and teach her people." Piper did not feel the teacher preparation program and student teacher assignment did anything that would ultimately help her instruct her students adequately. She claimed that her students (primarily Hispanic) required only direct instruction rather than the use of other instructional practices such as activity-based lessons or project-based learning (PBL), which were highly encouraged in her preparation program.

CANDID POINT OF VIEW

In the following conversation, Piper offered a candid point of view about how the teacher preparation program prepared her for classroom teaching. The secondary educator sparked a conversation by asking Piper about her experiences in the program.

Piper: I hated PBL. Because that's like, I mean, it's not about direct teaching, and that's what I am. I mean, that's not me always 100% but the most part, that's me.

Piper: Because I feel, in the program, they're looking more at schools like what if you end up being in Monaco or Paris (pseudonyms for privileged, predominately White districts)?

Interviewer: What do you mean?

Piper: Because those kids were very focused. In general, you're not going to have a lot of trouble with them. Whereas, for example, here, a ton of them were immigrants, so they struggle.

Interviewer:		English language learners?
	Piper:	Yes. They have a lot of personal problems. Parent involvement was almost none.
Interviewer:		So you feel like the program teaches to the perfect world and not the less perfect world, your reality.
	Piper:	Yeah. They did not teach me how to teach my people but more like the people in those rich districts.

Throughout the interview, the teacher, Piper, was consistent in the above views regarding the use of the preparation she received. In summary, she believed that the program prepared teachers for affluent, suburban districts. Unfortunately, the program did not prepare her to teach students who were mostly Hispanic immigrants and who came from homes with much lower socioeconomic backgrounds.

HUMBLING REFLECTION

Wow, this was a very humbling experience for us! To hear candid feedback and reflection about how our preparation of teachers was dramatically different than what the teachers hoped for really shifted our mind-set. Initially, we were a bit offended by the comments, but then we paused and took time to reflect honestly. This particular situation led us to question the rigor and reality of our program. We derived that we needed to be more reflective on culturally responsive teaching and on implementing the best teaching practices for all learners in diverse classrooms.

As the nation's schools become more diverse, educators and researchers must closely examine culturally responsive teaching practices to ensure all students receive a culturally relevant education in a positive learning environment. Furthermore, teacher educators must learn the importance of culture by self-reflecting and evaluating their own teaching practices. Learning about students' backgrounds and cultures potentially encourages teachers to emphasize and infuse their students' desires into the classroom, thus building upon student experiences. We can become more culturally responsive in our teaching practices if we pay attention to students' needs, because it allows our lens to be constantly changing to suit the needs of the students we have each semester. We were definitely changed by this one particular moment from one candid teacher, and it shifted our mind-set to create a more culturally diverse classroom.

OUTTAKE

IRB IS NOT REQUIRED

A Reflection on Oral History, Disability, and Playing by the Rules When the Rules Get in the Way

Cristy Sellers Smith

In spring 2014 I entered the Georgia archives, searching for evidence of the history of special education in and around Atlanta. After hours of examining board minutes, policy documents, superintendent correspondence, and recognitions and awards given during state board meetings, I left the archive starkly aware that the archived history had failed to include the stories and experiences of students. The absence left the history void of the students for whom special education was created. Three years later I began my dissertation research, an oral history of students in special education in metro-Atlanta, 1975–2005. In the same way that African American history or women's history is incomplete without the voices and contributions of those groups of people, so is the history of special education without the input and voices of students with disabilities in need of special education services. Although my research expands the historical record by including students with disabilities in the telling of their history, my experience with the university Institutional Review Board (IRB) underscores the assumption of inability that people with disabilities face and demonstrates how IRB approval of oral history research is an unnecessary barrier to reconstructing the history of marginalized people. In this reflective research outtake, I share my experience with IRB and discuss the impact on my research.

IRB IS NOT REQUIRED ... OR IS IT?

It seemed so unscholarly, but I clicked the POST button on Facebook, broadcasting my hopes of finding individuals with disabilities who had attended school and needed special education support at school between 1975 and 2005 in the metro-Atlanta area for my oral history research. Despite my skepticism, I knew it would cast a broad net as I searched for research participants. I tagged acquaintances that had expressed interest in my research, had identified as having a disability, or who I suspected may have known someone interested in what I was hoping to accomplish. Several of the individuals I tagged were professors and doctoral students associated with my university. Within minutes of my post, a member of the research community questioned whether IRB approval had been obtained. Having learned in my graduate history coursework that oral history was exempt from IRB, and being familiar with essays by oral historians Donald Ritchie (2003) and Linda Shopes (2018), both of whom served as past presidents of the Oral History Association, I had not submitted a formal IRB application. I commented, but even before my comments were public, an astute methodologist came to the defense of oral history and stifled the interrogation. The commenter, who was likely well-meaning and intending only to ask a clarifying question, had rattled me and published an argument against my work for the world to see.

The methodologist who had interjected to stop the onslaught of questions, contacted me privately to discuss the interaction. She shared that the local IRB policy at my institution required that I obtain an oral history designation for my work, a requirement I had not seen when reviewing the university's research guidelines. After investigating further, I found, however, that she was correct. The process sounded straightforward, and to ensure that my research was properly designated, I completed the necessary paperwork. Within a week, I received word that my "subjects" were "vulnerable" and therefore a complete application for IRB approval would be required. Clearly, the assumption of inability was conflated with the legal designation of having a disability. Their label, not their story or its contribution to what we know about schooling and special education, had proved most compelling to the university IRB.

When Compliance Rules

It took six more submissions and several academic cheerleaders to keep me going; I wanted to quit. Each response was filled with questions about participants, assent form requirements, consent form revisions, and "suggestions for clarity" that generated no substantive change to what I was submitting. Between my second and third submissions, weeks passed with no response. I contacted the senior IRB compliance officer via e-mail without response. I left messages that were not returned. I finally reached out to a higher-ranking IRB program administrator and learned that the software "had a glitch" and they had not received my prior submission. They immediately assigned it to a reviewer for feedback.

For two submissions, the corrections and my response moved quickly. The reviewer seemed to understand the work, and I anticipated that I would soon be finished. However, on the next round, I was assigned a different reviewer. New changes rolled in that had not been cited in prior responses, and one reviewer asked that I adjust an adjustment that was made at a prior reviewer's request. The compliance process was ruling my research. No longer were they concerned about human subjects (had they ever been?), but instead we were playing a game: IRB tennis. How many times would I return the serve?

IRB'S ASSUMPTION AND INTERFERENCE

There has long been a struggle between oral historians and IRBs, but in a situation where you find yourself a graduate student of oral history in need of a degree, standing on principle becomes a little less interesting and rules seem easier to follow. I needed to graduate, so despite how badly I wanted to push against the IRB, I sacrificed my work quality, hoping to create a pathway where I could accomplish my goals. Instead of collecting narratives, I spent 6 months submitting and resubmitting for approval. Arguably, instead of protecting participants, IRB diminished the value of my research and voice of the people I had aimed to remove from the margins by delaying my research and minimizing the time table for collecting student narratives. Because my experience with the IRB illustrates the very definition of a structural barrier (a roadblock faced by people with disabilities every day), it is only appropriate that I use the experience to further illustrate the role of policy and bureaucracy in orchestrating the concept of disability and how institutions instituting these policies create barriers to oral history and other important humanistic research.

The IRB was established by the federal government to protect the rights and interests of human subjects participating in scientific research and was authorized by Title II of the National Research Act of 1974 (P.L. 93-348) and codified in Title 45 (Public Welfare), Part 46 (Protection of Human Subjects) of the Code of Federal Regulations, commonly referred to as 45 CFR 46 or the Common Rule (United States Federal Policy, 2017). The National Research Act of 1974 defines research as systematic investigation that includes evaluation and assessment that contributes to generalizable information (Shopes, 2018). However, the common rule also exempts oral history from regulatory oversight but allows local IRBs to determine if research is classified as oral history. This situation has led to a number of contentious interactions, much like my own experience, where the definition of oral history and the extension of the IRB to include oral history come into play. Some have suggested this "mission creep" is the result of recent human-subject violations in biomedical research and the resulting fear of litigation. In light of these concerns, many institutions, including Georgia State University, extended the common rule to all research involving human research (White, 2007). The back-and-forth with the IRB, as well as the disorganization of the IRB process at Georgia State, led to more time being focused on their "administrivia" instead of my research. Additionally, having to advertise for "subjects" or "participants" arguably diminishes rapport with interested individuals who see the opportunity as a study rather than a meaningful interaction with a historian interested in their independent perspective regarding a phenomenon, experience, or period of time.

Georgia State University's IRB ultimately deemed my research as requiring review based on the "vulnerable" nature of the population I had proposed to "study." Yet, other than a mention that I would be talking with individuals who received special education services between 1975 and 2005, there were no "participants" defined. No mention of cognitive or physical ability was included in the application, yet they were defined as vulnerable and assumed to need more assistance and be less able than other citizens. This deficit model of thinking clarifies how the definition of disability as a social, cultural, and political phenomenon contrasts to the medical model that focuses more on areas of weakness instead of the worth, value, and ability of people. Additionally, the assumption of inability assumed by the Georgia State University IRB is a prevalent one, leading the United Nations Committee on the Rights of Persons with Disabilities (2006) to develop a preamble of agreements that defines disability as resulting from "the interaction between persons with impairments and attitudinal and environmental barriers that hinders their full and effective participation in society on an equal basis with others," and also recognizes that persons with disabilities "should have the opportunity to be actively involved in decision-making processes about policies and programmes, including those directly concerning them." Given the incompatibility of the behavior of Georgia State University's local IRB with the convictions of the UN's committee to focus on the rights of disabled persons, I suggest that IRB members at any university be required to demonstrate an understanding of the basic social justice concepts of equity and compassion for people. At no point should the function of the IRB come before the basic human rights and interests they were established to protect.

Finally, a valuable insight into the interaction between oral historians and narrators that Antoinette Errante (2000) discussed is the perception of what an interview should look like and the concern for the meaningfulness of the narrator's contribution. Narrators, she claims, will point out when you are not performing the interview in accordance with their perception of what it should be (pp. 19–20). Much like my own preferences, Errante (2000) expressed the desire for an open-ended interview that allows the narrator to lead the discussion. The IRB also seems to have an image of an interview, albeit different from the one most oral historians describe. The IRB requires pre-determined questions for approval and expects that researchers will adhere to only this list. Undoubtedly, given the definition of research in the common rule, the purpose of this is for generalization. However, one could argue that the objectivity gained by talking directly with those who have experienced the timeframe or past events being studied is lost when questions must be predetermined and created without consideration for the individuals serving as narrators of the past. I felt strongly that the questions I developed for the purposes of the IRB application were watered down, general, and demographic-focused instead of serving as meaningful inquiries into the nature of the narrator's experiences, but these questions were required for approval of my research. Rigid and predetermined questions, instead of a free-flowing conversation that allows for storytelling and spontaneous memory recall, create a stale (laboratory-like) environment. Particularly in my first interview, I followed the script precisely. It was not until I deviated near the end that my first narrator and I began to have a comfortable dialogue. The questions I asked were often repetitive because I was simply following a script; many of them she had already answered. I do not think it is a coincidence that the first narrative is the shortest, least specific, and contains the least number of in-depth sporadic memories. The question-and-answer, interview-like protocol made it difficult to engage deeply with the memories of her experiences in school.

The use of IRBs to govern oral history research, although heavily researched already, requires additional scrutiny and further commentary and should continue to be a topic of future research. On January 19, 2017, the common rule was updated by the federal government and explicitly states that oral history is no longer subject to IRB approval. This rule was effective in January 2018. Oral historians are instructed to follow the ethical guidelines of the Oral History Association and continue to utilize precautionary measures such as informed consent (United States Federal Policy, 2017). Although a collective sigh has been heard across the historical profession, I remain skeptical that local institutions will relinquish their control over student and faculty research. Like most federal policy, states and institutions continue to have the right to interpret the common rule for local institutional policy. Until the time that oral historians can freely interview individuals to produce invaluable historical records, the attention to this topic should remain steady and focused on the impact of the IRB on historical and humanistic research.

REFERENCES

Errante, A. (2000). But sometimes you're not part of the story: Oral histories and ways of remembering and telling. *Educational Researcher, 29*(2), 16–27.

Ritchie, D. A. (2003). *Doing oral history: A practical guide*. Oxford, England: Oxford University Press.

Shopes, L. (2018, 2007). Oral history, human subjects, and institutional review boards. *Oral History Association*. Retrieved from http://www.oralhistory.org/about/do-oral-history/oral-history-and-irb-review/

Convention on the Rights of Persons with Disabilities [CRPD]. (2006). Retrieved from https://www.un.org/development/desa/disabilities/convention-on-the-rights-of-persons-with-disabilities/preamble.html

Federal Policy for the Protection of Human Subjects ('Common Rule'). (2017). Retrieved from https://www.federalregister.gov/documents/2017/01/19/2017-01058/federal-policy-for-the-protection-of-human-subjects#p-1354

White, R. F. (2007). Institutional review board mission creep: The common rule, social science, and the nanny state. *The Independent Review, 11*(4), 547–564.

OUTTAKE

COMPUTATIONAL PROBLEM-POSING WITH URBAN LATINX YOUTH

Make Science Teaching Great Again

Rouhollah Aghasaleh, Patrick Enderle,
Anton Puvirajah, Andrew Boehnlein, Jennifer Rickard,
Jacob Bornstein, and Renesha Hendrix

Computational thinking, an "analytic approach to problem solving, designing systems, and understanding human behaviors"(Sengupta, Kinnebrew, Basu, Biswas, & Clark, 2013, p. 352), is regarded as a fundamental requirement of all science, technology, engineering, and mathematics (STEM) disciplines. Access to computer science education is limited for non-Asian minorities, students of low socioeconomic status (SES), and girls (Goode, 2007; Wilson, Sudol, Stephenson, & Stehlik, 2010). Thus, this becomes a profound social justice issue that privileges certain students more than others and creates segregation in computer science education that extends to the workplace.

To address this inequity, we are conducting a 3-year-long project that focuses on developing a reciprocal model for teaching and learning computational competencies. The project's goal is to develop a model based on principles of culturally relevant pedagogy (Ladson-Billings, 2014) and to implement it in an extant after-school program for middle school Latinx students in an urban school district in the Southeastern United States. The reciprocal nature of the model involves after-school teachers (university preservice teachers) and the Latinx students learning from and teaching each other. The teachers learn to develop and implement culturally relevant computational experiences through seminar classes and field experiences in the after-school setting, and the Latinx students learn computational competencies.

PRESERVICE TEACHERS TEACH, LEARN, AND REFLECT

In what follows, three preservice teachers (Jennifer, Andrew, and Max) reflect on their experience of working with urban Latinx middle school students learning programming with Scratch, a block-based computer programming platform. The teachers highlight how two distinct educational constructs (computational competency and culturally relevant pedagogy) are synthesized in their thinking and practice. Our culturally relevant pedagogy approach in the project encouraged students to bring their lived experiences, concerns, and interests to the classroom through a Freirian problem-posing approach (Freire, 1996/1968) informed by feminist standpoint epistemology (Harding, 1992). Situated in a Southeastern state, in the heat of the 2016 presidential election and its aftermath, many students chose to focus on the rise of Donald Trump as a sociopolitical phenomenon as a topic for their computer projects.

Freirian Problem-Posing Is Culturally Relevant (Andrew)

Starting with a brainstorming activity, students assembled in groups and bounced ideas off each other about different problems they saw in the world. What surprised us the most about this experience was the extent to which the students made national and global issues more personal. For instance, the groups wanted to focus on Donald Trump. We as instructors wanted them to focus more on issues instead of people, so we recommended that the students focus on some of the issues Trump represented instead of the person himself. However, when we asked many of the students why they picked Trump, their reasons were often personal, such as "he's a bully," "he doesn't like women," or "he's racist." While those reasons could be abstracted to broader issues (e.g., combative politics, misogyny, and racism), the students chose to internalize those character flaws in Trump rather than think of them as broad issues.

Loops of Donald Trump (Jennifer)

A few weeks after the 2016 presidential election, students worked on their Loop projects. Loops are operations that make an action happen repeatedly. Students used sounds, recorded music, and voiceovers to create songs related to their topics. One group with the topic of Donald Trump titled their sound Loop project "F*ck Trump." The students were apprehensive about sharing their controversial title. They said, "You're going to be mad!" I saw the title, and I let them know that their feelings were valid. The students gave me some reasons: "He's tearing apart our communities; he's a woman abuser; and he's racist." After writing these down, the students used Scratch to record a group member speaking this list of issues into a microphone. Using coding from Scratch, the students played the dialogue on a loop including background music and created a background using their own design.

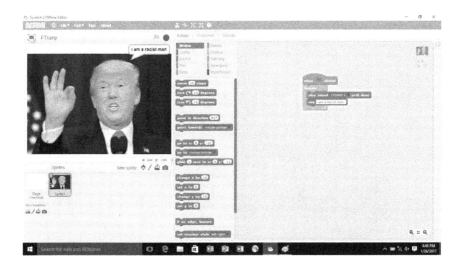

Figure 1. Scratch Program

Discussing the election of Donald Trump was important because many students felt fear. Several incidents had happened in the school district that made them uncomfortable at school. For instance, two teachers were removed from a nearby high school for making anti-immigration comments following the election; many students experienced their friends and families facing deportation due to the increased Immigration and Customs Enforcement raids. The after-school program was a safe space where we could provide a constructive and creative environment for students to explore these topics. Having students explore their oppressions while working on computational thinking projects was away that we practiced critical pedagogy in the after-school program.

Trump Versus El Chapo (Max)

One group created an interesting project that depicted a scenario pitting U.S. president-elect Donald Trump against Mexican cartel leader Joaquín Guzmán, known as El Chapo. Students expressed a strong preference for just about anyone over Donald Trump, and he was often portrayed as an archvillain. The Trump versus El Chapo project illustrated this, as the students presented an evil Trump and an almost heroic El Chapo. We were fascinated by the students' responses when we asked them why they felt El Chapo should be seen as a positive figure. One student claimed that El Chapo "does a lot for poor people." This philanthropic view of a drug lord reminds me of the many different opinions about Pablo Escobar, a figure described as a sociopath and terrorist to a philanthropist and ethical policeman of the underground drug world, depending on who is speaking.

Figure 2. Pseudocode.

Culturally Relevant Coding for Personal Expression and Social Justice

The innovation and creativity that students showed through their projects helped us see the power of culturally relevant pedagogy and Freirian problem posing. Freirian problem posing enabled the students to voice the concerns and issues central in their thinking about their communities. As seen in the stories above, pseudocoding and the creation of Scratch programs provided students a different platform upon which to express their ideas. As we continue to rethink schools as places that welcome contributions from all students, coding and pseudocoding can provide another avenue for students to express their ideas, and one that does not have to solely reside in a science class.

ACKNOWLEDGMENT AND DISCLAIMER

This project has been funded with support from the National Science Foundation (Award Number 1433440). This article reflects the views of only the authors and not those of the National Science Foundation or other federal or Georgia State authorities.

REFERENCES

Freire, P. (1996). *Pedagogy of the oppressed* (Rev. ed). New York, NY: Continuum. (Original work published 1968)

Goode, J. (2007). If you build teachers, will students come? The role of teachers in broadening computer science learning for urban youth. *Journal of Educational Computing Research, 36*(1), 65–88.

Harding, S. (1992). Rethinking standpoint epistemology: What is "strong objectivity?" *The Centennial Review, 36*(3), 437–470.

Ladson-Billings, G. (2014). Culturally relevant pedagogy 2.0: aka the remix. *Harvard Educational Review, 84*(1), 74–84.

Sengupta, P., Kinnebrew, J. S., Basu, S., Biswas, G., & Clark, D. (2013). Integrating computational thinking with K–12 science education using agent-based computation: A theoretical framework. *Education and Information Technologies, 18*(2), 351–380.

Wilson, C., Sudol, L. A., Stephenson, C., & Stehlik, M. (2010). *Running on empty: The failure to teach K–12 computer science in the digital age*. New York, NY: The Association for Computing Machinery and the Computer Science Teachers Association.

OUTTAKE

FITTING IT ALL IN

Time Challenges in Lesson Pacing

Melissa Soto, Shawn Broderick, Lara Dick, Mollie Appelgate, and Dittika Gupta

Planning a common lesson to achieve specified goals is challenging for a group of five mathematics teacher educators from different institutions across the United States. Deciding the exact sequence of tasks, determining how much support to provide our students, and considering levels of understanding for students, all while scheduling meetings across three different time zones, gets complicated. One of the biggest, unanticipated challenges we faced, however, was the amount of time it took to implement the lesson and ensure all topics were adequately discussed.

We began our research project in June 2015, as we gathered to investigate what elementary preservice teachers (PSTs) notice when they analyze children's written mathematical solutions strategies (Jacobs, Lamb, & Philipp, 2010). We drew upon Jacobs et al.'s "Professional Noticing of Children's Mathematical Thinking," in which teachers first attend to students' mathematical strategies, interpret their mathematical understanding, and then decide on the next steps to guide instruction.

Specifically, our interest was in examining how multiple student work samples could assist PSTs in making instructional decisions for a whole class rather than an individual student. To achieve this goal, we planned a lesson in which PSTs analyzed a case study that described a third-grade teacher's lesson on multiplication (National Council of Teachers of Mathematics, 2014) and then in small groups decided what problem, number choices, and questions they would pose to the case study class to engage them in a new instructional goal. In fall 2015, four of the five instructors piloted the lesson with their students; for each iteration, we ran out of time before we could get to the "meat" of the lesson, which was discussing those instructional next steps. We made changes as we went along, but we continued to struggle with the lesson timing and pacing and could not fit the final component in as we should.

We wanted to ensure that we addressed our goals and that our PSTs engaged in the final piece of the noticing framework, so we engaged in a formal lesson study with this particular lesson, in which we made systematic changes and discussed our challenges in teaching. Even though we all followed the original lesson plan template, we each had our individual teaching styles and incorporated aspects that were important for us in the lessons, which included: discussing issues of equity in mathematics, connecting to the *Common Core State Standards for Mathematics* (National Governors Association Center for Best Practices & Council of Chief State School Officers, 2010), and integrating technology into the lesson. Knowing that we wanted flexibility in incorporating these individual touches into our lessons, we began negotiating which components of the main lesson that we could adjust or remove to ensure enough time at the end for rich discussions about the whole class next steps.

In spring 2016, we decided to reteach the lesson to our new semester PSTs. Once we decided on the changes from the fall, the mathematics educators video- and audio-recorded themselves teaching the new version of the lesson and reported on the success or limitations of the changes made. With each taught lesson, changes and revisions were made to accommodate pacing.

The first change in the spring lesson was streamlining the analysis of the student work samples. We initially began by having PSTs analyze all six student work samples in small groups but generate informational posters of only one child's strategy. Then the PSTs completed two gallery walks: First, they reviewed how their fellow classmates interpreted their assigned child's work sample (first gallery walk), and then they viewed each group's ideas for the individual child's next step decision (second gallery walk). We found this process was ineffective: The PSTs became disengaged in the second gallery walk because they had already analyzed all six student work samples. We decided to save time and engage PSTs by having only groups analyze one child's work sample, share their conclusions and next steps on a poster, and complete only one gallery walk. In this way, they analyzed the other posters' conclusions more carefully and examined the children's work samples closely as they traveled from one poster to the other, because they had to use the information to create the class's next task.

During the second round of implementation, even with the changes made, we were still experiencing some challenges with our pacing. We were getting to the final, important component of the lesson of discussing next steps for the whole class, but the discussion is still cursory. We never thought that this would be our biggest challenge when starting this research project; however, we are continuing to make changes and improve our practice at the same time.

We have often heard our PSTs indicate that they do not have time to implement certain teaching methods or activities in their classrooms. We typically respond by telling them they need to make the time. This research project is a reminder to us as mathematics educators and instructors that we, too, need to make the time to allow our students to engage in the goals of the lesson in their entirety for success. And while we know we need to make the time, it is often as difficult for us as it is for our PSTs.

REFERENCES

Jacobs, V. R., Lamb, L. L. C., & Philipp, R. A. (2010). Professional noticing of children's mathematical thinking. *Journal for Research in Mathematics Education, 41*(2), 169–202.

National Council of Teachers of Mathematics. (2014). The case of Mr. Harris and the band concert. In *Principles to Action Professional Learning Toolkit*. Retrieved July 30, 2015 from http://www.nctm.org/Conferences-and-Professional-Development/Principles-to-Actions-Toolkit/The-Case-of-Mr_-Harris-and-the-Band-Concert/

National Governors Association Center for Best Practices & Council of Chief State School Officers. (2010). *Common core state standards for mathematics*. Washington, DC: Authors.

BOOK REVIEW

TEACHING IN A GLOBALLY-CONNECTED WORLD: PREPARING LEARNERS FOR THE FUTURE

edited by Ervin F. Sparapani and Pamela L. Ross McClain

Kim Stevens Barker

Preparing children for jobs that do not yet exist and technologies that have yet to be invented is a quote, attributed to Richard Riley, secretary of education under President Clinton, that remains a frequently cited clarion call for educators. Riley named the then-distant year of 2010 as the year of reckoning (Gunderson, Jones, & Scanland, 2004), but a decade later, the challenge of preparing students for uncertain job duties and skills remains a talking point from professional education literature to local school faculty trainings. In *Teaching in a Globally-Connected World: Preparing Learners for the Future*, Sparapani and McClain (2016) present a collection of essays that seek to add to the literature about the challenge of preparing K–12 students to succeed in future contexts by thoroughly examining the issues through a lens that takes into account the global society.

The editors argue in the introduction to the book that 21st-century learners must be equipped with a global competence in order to navigate a globally connected world. Targeting K–12 teachers and other leaders in education, Sparapani and McClain explore the realities of global influences on education through 17 articles arranged in 3 sections addressing: (a) a global society, (b) visionary leadership and empowerment, and (c) teaching toward the future.

To illustrate the growing challenges of a global society, Sparapani and McClain first present essays that address historical and current social, political, economic, and religious facets of globalization as a framework for preparing students. Considering 21st-century phenomena described in the section that seem on the surface to be problematic and at times paradoxical (i.e., the significance and insignificance of race and ethnicity, political sovereignty not centered in ruling states, and definitions of knowledge influenced by world religions), readers find new vocabulary for naming 21st-century challenges and solutions. For example, in an essay on economic globalization, the authors argue for the need to teach skills supportive of *cognitive leapfrogging,* that is, skillful responses to rapidly changing, or *hyperdynamic,* environments as well as a perspective of *diversimilarity,* in order to value both differences and similarities among people in the workforce.

After establishing the need for education to support learners who will operate in a global society, Sparapani and McClain introduce the second section of the book as a "new blueprint" for effective school environments for the 21st-century. Written by authors whose credentials are described as "forward-thinking educational architects," these essays address the need for enlightened and empowered leadership in the development and delivery of the curriculum, principal- and district-level leadership, professional learning communities, teacher leaders, and parent and student activism. The notion of building power and capacity for all stakeholders at each level of the educational system is synthesized with McClain and Shepard's essay applying Friedman's (2005) concept of "glocalization" to teaching global citizenship for K–12 students (p. 111).

Teacher leaders are identified as the authors of the essays in the third section of the book, and their contributions provide real-world examples of teaching that are at once interdisciplinary, rigorous, and creative. Detailed vignettes in the domains of literacy, mathematics, science, social studies, arts, foreign language, and technology have something to offer not only K–12 teachers and administrators but also the teacher educators who are preparing the nation's future teachers. A persistent focus on creative approaches to resources and opportunities is exemplified in the vignettes from primarily middle and high school classrooms, achieving a perspective labeled "mentalpreneurial" in an essay by Orori-Dankwa, Sesti, Krupp, and Titus-Glover (p. 122).

Sparapani and McClain have assembled a collection of essays that makes a comprehensive case for teaching toward a globally influenced future in *Teaching in a Globally-Connected World: Preparing Learners for the Future*. The first section of the book accomplishes a concise but up-to-date and convincing overview of the impact of globalization on the United States, which I found helpful in preparing future teachers. Teacher leaders in section 3 demonstrate ways they are implementing the curriculum in a variety of domains with the future-oriented vision that essayists in the middle section of the book describe. For teachers who are overworked and most concerned about what and how they are going to teach their students tomorrow, the teaching vignettes offer practical instructional ideas for teaching students skills for lifelong learning to meet the challenges of the globally connected world.

Teaching in a Globally-Connected World: Preparing Learners for the Future contains essays that thoroughly address the theme despite a number of distracting (if amusing) typographical errors (i.e., "To give an example from the United States, several people [sic] from Mexico have moved into the United States in search of better conditions of work and quality of life" p. 31 and "… is far more likely to produce high-levels of student engagement within the classroom, and students will immolate desired behaviors" p. 90). However, the authors of the essays themselves remain largely anonymous. Prefaces to the second and third sections identify the writers as teacher leaders, middle and high school teachers, and in one essay as graduate students, but the reader is left to wonder who the writers are, where they come from, and how they came to write on this subject. Including the credentials of the contributing authors would add to the strength of the overall argument and be a step toward the authors' stated desire to empower teacher leaders who are preparing students for a future of uncertain opportunities.

I gleaned some useful information and practical pedagogical examples from reading this book, although the work did little overall to add to my already strong commitment to preparing lifelong learners—both teachers and children. I was left to ponder the fact that the frenzied cry for educators to prepare students of the United States for a future of unknown advancements and challenges is, in fact, a centuries-old concern. Long before Riley uttered his famous quote in 2004, Massachusetts courts enacted the "Old Deluder Satan Act" in 1647 to set up town schools to ensure that students of the future would not lose their knowledge of the scriptures (Urban & Wagoner, 2008). The future has been and remains uncertain and a continuing concern for those who intend to prepare children for it. The teaching vignettes described in this book have the best potential for adding value to the work of K–12 educators, but the remainder may simply be preaching to the choir.

REFERENCES

Friedman, T. L. (2005). *The world is flat: A brief history of the twenty-first century*. New York, NY: Farrar, Straus and Giroux.

Gunderson, S., Jones, R., & Scanland, K. (2004). *The jobs revolution: Changing how America works* (2nd ed.). : Pennsylvania State University, PA: Copywriters Inc.

Sparapani, E. F., & McClain, P. L. R. (Eds.). (2016). *Teaching in a globally-connected world: Preparing learners for the future*. Lanham, MD: Hamilton Books.

Urban, W. J., & Wagoner Jr., J. L. (2009. *American education: A history* (4th ed.). New York, NY: Routledge.

BOOK REVIEW

A. B.A.L.A.N.C.E: AN INTERACTIVE WORKBOOK FOR THE "KID" IN ALL OF US

by Reggie Gwinn

Katherine Perrotta

In this fast-paced digital age where children are bombarded with 24/7 news content, Twitter feeds, Snapchats, and Facebook posts, balancing one's health and interactions with others is of great importance. Reggie Gwinn, a doctoral student at the University of Denver, delivers interactive tips and strategies aimed at promoting self-awareness and well-being in *A. B.A.L.A.N.C.E.* The subtitle on the inside title page is *An Interactive Workbook for the "Kid" in All of Us. A. B.A.L.A.N.C.E.*, an acronym for the main tenets of each chapter, is not a typical academic or self-help book. Gwinn provides inviting pictures, anecdotes, and activities that engage readers in reflecting on how their feelings, abilities, and actions impact themselves and the people in their lives.

A. B.A.L.A.N.C.E. is organized into 10 chapters—including an Introduction and Conclusion—that highlight commonsense advice aimed at achieving and maintaining physical and emotional well-being. Gwinn argues that maintaining *A. B.A.L.A.N.C.E.*, based upon Maslow's hierarchy of needs, is essential for being "happy" and fostering "awareness and understanding" (p. 11) in one's life. In order to achieve *A. B.A.L.A.N.C.E.*, Gwinn outlines eight criteria that are explored in each chapter. These criteria include "Acceptance" of one's self (Chapter 1); "Belonging" to a community (Chapter 2); "Actualization" of one's interests and passions (Chapter 3); "Life Needs," which include food, water, and shelter (Chapter 4); "Active" exercise (Chapter 5); "No Fear" concerning issues of safety (Chapter 6); "Confidence" in one's abilities (Chapter 7); and "Everyone" with regard to how people can help others and themselves (Chapter 8). Gwinn contends that when children are conscious of these eight criteria, they are equipped with the tools that can foster happiness, well-being, and intrinsic motivation to achieve their goals.

There are several strengths of this book. First, Gwinn argues that concepts of self-help have been primarily based on what teachers, parents, and school administrators deem "what's best for students." As a result, the *A. B.A.L.A.N.C.E.* approach is designed in a student-centered manner for children to take ownership in becoming self-aware of their needs and actions, which can foster "positive change and impact even in the midst of power and privilege" (title page). Gwinn uses his own life and family as examples of applying the eight elements of *A. B.A.L.A.N.C.E.* throughout the book. He does not take a preachy tone while explaining the elements of *A. B.A.L.A.N.C.E.*, which makes him relatable and accessible to his readers.

Second, the activities in the book are steeped in reflexivity and a nondenominational spirituality of what makes individuals unique, capable, and deserving of living the best life possible. For instance, Gwinn's analogy of the color of light and the different colors of the spectrum serves as an uplifting reminder that one's unique talents and abilities lead to self-acceptance and allow "the light of the world to exist" (p. 21). To further illustrate the beauty of the unique talents and abilities of people, Gwinn (2017) notes that "it seems like the purpose of life is all about helping others" (pp. 100–101), and follows up with an activity where readers can highlight the various people in their community who help them and how they can help others. Overall, the strength of this book is the emphasis on how self-care not only promotes individual well-being but also civic-mindedness with regard to how one's actions impact his or her community.

There are several areas in which Gwinn's arguments can be strengthened, particularly with regard to how *A. B.A.L.A.N.C.E.* can contribute to existing scholarship on holistic education. First, the inclusion of research about child development and psychology, such as Vygotsky's social development theory and Garner's multiple intelligences, as well as scholarship about care theory (Noddings, 2002) and moral/character education (Nucci & Narvaez, 2008), would further situate this book in the existing literature about the importance of self-awareness and well-being in educational and other social contexts. Moreover, Gwinn (2017) notes that he wrote this book because "self-help is a novice concept broached towards children" (title page). However, there are numerous examples of academic research, self-help books, and school curricula aimed at fostering children's physical, mental, and emotional health and mindfulness (see Ashdown & Bernard, 2011; Cohen, 2006; Covey, 2014; Schonert-Reichl, 2017; Schonert-Reichl & Lawlor, 2010). Expansion on how and why Gwinn's *A. B.A.L.A.N.C.E.* approach is either unique or contributory to existing scholarship would strengthen his authority as a scholar and practitioner of mindfulness and holistic education.

Second, although Gwinn (2017) contends that the book is intended for children of all ages, inclusion of differentiated methods of implementing *A. B.A.L.A.N.C.E.* for various grade levels would be beneficial to parents, teachers, and other stakeholders who may consider using this book with individual children or groups. For example, the chapter on confidence addresses taking risks, but the examples provided are low stakes with regard to feeling comfortable with singing in public or giving people compliments. Risks will be different for elementary children as opposed to preteens and adolescents in middle and high schools. Gwinn could strengthen this argument by highlighting different examples of risks, such as bullying or drug use, and how the elements of *A. B.A.L.A.N.C.E.* relate to one another with regard to making safe decisions that contribute to a child's confidence and safety at an age-appropriate level (p. 93).

Third, issues of diversity are not addressed in this book. For example, Gwinn (2017) states that the reader should engage in physical activity for at least 60 minutes a day (p. 70), which is recommended by the Centers for Disease Control and Prevention (CDC, 2013). Although daily exercise is very important, especially with rising childhood obesity rates (Hales, Carroll, Fryar, Ogden, & Flegal, 2017), Gwinn overlooks major socioeconomic issues that may preclude children who shoulder family obligations, do not have recess in school or access to playgrounds and expansive greenspaces, or have special needs from engaging in an hour of physical activity. Gwinn could strengthen this argument by providing readers with suggestions that are aligned with CDC recommendations and the other elements of *A. B.A.L.A.N.C.E.* to make choices that promote healthy habits while negotiating real-world challenges within and out of their control.

A. B.A.L.A.N.C.E. is an engaging book that is sure to bring a smile to any reader's face. Reggie Gwinn's (2017) work is an innovative resource that teachers, parents, and other educational stakeholders can use to foster healthy habits and self-awareness techniques in children and the kid in all of us. Since Gwinn is a doctoral student, I wonder if this book is related to his dissertation research. If so, I look forward to learning how this scholarship may contribute to existing literature on how and why promoting *A. B.A.L.A.N.C.E.* can be beneficial to students' academic achievement and personal well-being in this technologically driven world.

REFERENCES

Ashdown, D. M., & Bernard, M. E. (2011). Can explicit instruction in social and emotional learning skills benefit the social-emotional development, well-being, and academic achievement of young children? *Early Childhood Education Journal, 39*(6), 397–405.

Centers for Disease Control and Prevention. (2013). *Comprehensive school physical activity programs: A guide for schools.* Atlanta, GA: U.S. Department of Health and Human Services.

Cohen, J. (2006). Social, emotional, ethical, and academic education: Creating a climate for learning, participation in democracy, and well-being. *Harvard Educational Review, 76*(2), 201–237.

Covey, S. (2014). *The 7 habits of highly effective teens: The ultimate teenage success guide.* New York, NY: Simon & Schuster. (Original work published 1998)

Gwinn, R. (2017). *A.B.A.L.A.N.C.E: An interactive workbook for the kid in all of us.* Aurora, CO: A. B.A.L.A.N.C.E. Publications.

Hales, C. M., Carroll, M. D., Fryar, C. D., Ogden, C. L., & Flegal, K. (2017). Prevalence of obesity among adults and youth: United States, 2015–2016. *NCHS Data Brief 219*, 1–8. Retrieved from https://www.cdc.gov/nchs/data/databriefs/db219.pdf

Noddings, N. (2002). *Educating moral people: A caring alternative to character education.* New York, NY: Teachers College Press.

Nucci, L. P., & Narvaez, D. (2008). *Handbook on moral and character education.* New York, NY: Routledge.

Schonert-Reichl, K. A. (2017). Social and emotional learning and teachers. *The Future of Children, 27*(1), 137–155.

Schonert-Reichl, K. A., & Lawlor, M. S. (2010). The effects of a mindfulness-based education program on pre- and early adolescents' well-being and social and emotional competence. *Mindfulness, 1*(3), 137–151.

BOOK REVIEW

ACROSS THE DOMAINS: EXAMINING THE BEST PRACTICES IN MENTORING PUBLIC SCHOOL EDUCATORS THROUGHOUT THE PROFESSIONAL JOURNEY

by Andrea M. Kent and Andre M. Green

Aubrey Brammar Southall

Andrea M. Kent and Andre M. Green's edited book, *Across the Domains: Examining the Best Practices in Mentoring Public School Educators Throughout the Professional Journey*, provides a review of mentoring research well-grounded in literature. The text is intended for university faculty, but it would work well with preservice teachers, in-service teachers, school administrators, and grant writers. "Teaching is hard" (Allison & Martin, 2018, p. 170) and "mentoring ... serves as a transformative catalyst for beginning educators" (McMahan, Fredrickson, & Dunlap, 2018, p. 13) are themes carried throughout the entire text. The various authors' use of critical reflection and active engagement in the field of mentoring offers practical applications for the reader. The chapter questions provide the reader with university classroom and professional development application. The editors' goals for focusing on what "really matters" (p. vii) in mentoring is evident throughout the text.

The book presents 12 chapters. Each chapter explores different facets of mentoring programs. The chapters are thoroughly researched and organized with each providing background information on a specific mentoring program. The contextual evidence provided throughout the chapters provides the readers with a variety of mentoring models. The discussion questions at the end of each chapter allow readers to review important ideas from that chapter. The authors include an array of mentoring examples throughout the text through case studies. The nature of the book would work well with graduate students interested in creating or getting involved with mentoring programs.

As the title suggests, the book examines "best practices" in mentoring. The editors' choice of topics gives the readers a comprehensive look at career mentoring throughout their educational journey. The book chapters range from first-year teacher programs to teacher leader programs. Authors of chapters also discuss mentoring outside of public school classrooms, such as in clinical settings and religious schools. The chapters feature mentoring programs from various parts of the United States—most notably the Southeast—and Brazil. Research from the various chapters often supports claims made in other parts of the text. For example, the claim that "there is not a 'one size fits all' mentoring model" (McMahan et al., 2018, p. 3) is evident throughout the chapters.

The relationship aspect of mentoring is a component to all mentoring program models listed. Throughout the chapters, relationships with qualified mentors are the foundation of many successful mentoring programs. Two examples include: "Mentors who are trained and attentive to the needs of the teachers they support are essential to the transformational learning experience" (Horn, 2018, p. 42) and "growing evidence indicates that trusting relationships between mentors and teachers are crucial for effective mentoring" (Efron, Winter, & Bressman, 2018, p. 69).

Mentoring for retention purposes is expressed throughout numerous chapters as well. Many incentives for mentoring programs are grounded in retention as "losing a teacher is expensive" (Horn, 2018, p. 35) and the need to maintain quality candidates is crucial to student success. Furthermore, several chapters look at mentoring outside of the first year to retain teachers in new roles, such as teacher leaders and literacy specialists. "Mentoring pyramids" (Brannan & Kent, 2018) showed evidence of impacting teachers, graduate students, and university faculty.

Many chapters emphasize the need for mentoring to help teachers "develop a deep cultural understanding of and sensitivity to the school and community" (Efron et al., p. 90). Ladson-Billings (2016) states culturally competent and critical consciousness should be traits of all teachers. Chapters detail experiences of successful mentoring programs in areas where first-year teachers are interacting with students of different cultural backgrounds.

Several chapters are dedicated to informal mentoring programs. Electronic mentoring is highlighted as a form of mentoring in both the formal and informal space. "E-mentoring" (Morton & Nguyen, 2018) and "MathTwitterBlogosphere" (Parrish, 2018) are two examples of electronic mentoring described in the text. Electronic mentoring is portrayed as a way to overcome traditional mentoring obstacles such as money and time. Additionally, informal mentoring programs such as coworker interactions are described. Allison and Martin (2018) state "there is little room to distinguish between a mentor and a good team member" (p. 169). The rise of informal mentoring practices and the need for research on these practices are indicated in the text.

While the title of the book indicates the chapters will focus on public schools, three chapters are dedicated to other arenas of mentoring. One chapter is situated in an Orthodox Jewish school. Another chapter is positioned in a clinical literacy lab. Important ideas set in the context of these different mentoring locations also can be beneficial to public school teachers. Additionally, one chapter is dedicated to the small schools movement, but mentoring appears to be an afterthought in this chapter.

Across the Domains: Examining the Best Practices in Mentoring Public School Educators Throughout the Professional Journey would benefit preservice teachers, in-service teachers, school administrators, teacher educators, and grant writers. Although other books address some of the topics discussed in this text, this book provides a critical look at a variety of mentoring programs. Current practitioners may see it as a resource of talking points to use with school administrators, new teachers, and teacher leaders. The text would work well in undergraduate and graduate teacher education courses.

REFERENCES

Allison, E. R., & Martin, L. (2018). It's just what we do: A teacher's story of trust, support, and friendship. In A. M. Kent & A. M. Green (Eds.), *Across the domains: Examining the best practices for mentoring public school educators throughout the professional journey* (pp. 155–172). Charlotte, NC: Information Age Publishing.

Brannan, L. R. & Kent, A. M. (2018). The mentoring pyramid: A case study of mentorship. In A. M. Kent & A. M. Green (Eds.), *Across the domains: Examining the best practices for mentoring public school educators throughout the professional journey* (pp. 173–188). Charlotte, NC: Information Age Publishing.

Efron, S. E., Winter, J. S., & Bressman, S. (2018). Mentoring across cultures: Relationships that inspire professional growth. In A. M. Kent & A. M. Green (Eds.), *Across the domains: Examining the best practices for mentoring public school educators throughout the professional journey* (pp. 69–96). Charlotte, NC: Information Age Publishing.

Horn, P. J. (2018). A quality teacher induction program to improve teaching and learning. In A. M. Kent & A. M. Green (Eds.), *Across the domains: Examining the best practices for mentoring public school educators throughout the professional journey* (pp. 33–68). Charlotte, NC: Information Age Publishing.

Kent, A. M., & Green, A. M. (Eds.). (2018). *Across the domains: Examining the best practices for mentoring public school educators throughout the professional journey*. Charlotte, NC: Information Age Publishing.

Ladson-Billings, G. (2016). Who can teach our children? Restating the case for culturally relevant teaching. *Michigan Reading Journal, 48*(2), 35–37.

McMahan, S. R., Fredrickson, R. R., & Dunlap, K. (2018). Faculty mentoring through the preservice to in-service teacher pipeline. In A. M. Kent & A. M. Green (Eds.), *Across the domains: Examining the best practices for mentoring public school educators throughout the professional journey* (pp. 1–18). Charlotte, NC: Information Age Publishing.

Morton, B.C., & Nguyen, K.T. (2018). e-Mentoring: Guiding across barriers through technology. In A. M. Kent & A. M. Green (Eds.), *Across the domains: Examining the best practices for mentoring public school educators throughout the professional journey* (pp. 97–112). Charlotte, NC: Information Age Publishing

Parrish, C. W. (2018). Informal mentoring within an online community: The MathTwitterBlogosphere. In A. M. Kent & A. M. Green (Eds.), *Across the domains: Examining the best practices for mentoring public school educators throughout the professional journey* (pp. 113–132). Charlotte, NC: Information Age Publishing.

BOOK REVIEW

WHITE FATIGUE

by Joseph Flynn

Shelley Harris

In Joseph Flynn Jr.'s first book, *White Fatigue,* he attempts to define *white fatigue* and does so relentlessly. Flynn employs intertwining genres of writing that encompass personal vignettes as well as scholarly research. This book is about race and social justice, specifically "helping White folks develop habits of mind that promote social justice for all groups" (p. 2). Although suitable for everyone, the book specifically targets those in the education profession who can teach the critical discourse most needed for today's education profession.

    Flynn is an educator, activist, and family man at heart. Early in his life, he found a purpose: to learn as much as he could about other people and their experiences. Using what he has personally experienced, as well as the stories of others, has been the motivation of his writings. Whether he writes a scholarly article, presents at a national conference, or has a fireside chat among colleagues, Flynn listens and uses what he hears to deliberately break the barriers between race, ethnicity, and privilege. He is not afraid to bring up "hard topics" and knows the only way we can build a better tomorrow is to engage in dialogue.

    White Fatigue is a nonfiction piece that exposes Flynn's personal experiences with race, building a fellowship of like-minded individuals to participate in those deep and truthful conversations we so desperately need in these challenging times. This topic encapsulates many of the struggles with education, as well as with politics and other professions. Everyone is touched with some form of marginalization, and this book stresses the need to confront the truth and converse freely about humanity's similarities and differences in a respectful way.

The book jacket itself is half black and half white. Nevertheless, do not let its color mislead you. The concept expands across race and ethnicities, pressing the need for solidarity among all brothers and sisters. However, written from an African American's perspective, each chapter is relatable to anyone who has been put down, has felt different, did not realize they were different until someone told them, or simply wants to understand different perspectives.

Flynn challenges readers to first look into themselves and realize that everyone has racist tendencies. This recognition is groundbreaking because many feel uncomfortable with this introspection or deny their feelings. He argues that the first step in moving past our deficiencies is to realize we have common ground: humanity. Many terms used throughout the book that people use freely in their everyday vernacular are *ally, advocate, racism, multiculturalism,* among others, as well as movements such as *Black Lives Matter*. Flynn combines research, personal experiences, and common sense to define these terms accurately and provides reasons for their use. Education is paramount when learning about other cultures. Language changes on a daily basis. It is crucial that we all speak with the same intent.

I eagerly accepted the opportunity to read and evaluate this book. Following Flynn in the conference circuit, I am very familiar with his work. Each time I have a chance to listen to his ideas on race and how it affects every side of the equation, I learn something new. This book was no different. Flynn utilizes a critical lens to examine Americans as a people: where we have been, where we are now, and where we need to go. Our current and future leaders have a right to stand up for equal rights and treatment. As a reader, recognizing my privilege hit me hard, but it forced me to open my eyes to the world both near and far and inspired me to do something about it. Flynn's *White Fatigue* does not gloss over the facts or the hard truths. It is in your face, and that is the only way change will take place. I highly recommend reading this book as it will challenge readers' understandings of race.

ACKNOWLEDGMENT

The publisher of this book is Peter Lang Publishing, Inc., New York. It is part of an eight volume series on social justice across contexts in education. It can be purchased online at https://www.amazon.com/White-Fatigue-Rethinking-ResistanceEducation/dp/1433150263/ref=sr_1_4?ie=UTF8&qid=1520234028&sr=8-4&keywords=white+fatigue

BOOK REVIEW

REEL EDUCATION: DOCUMENTARIES, BIOPICS, AND REALITY TELEVISION

by Jacqueline Bach

Bradley Conrad

Since the inception of the common school, various narratives about students, teachers, administrators, and schools have permeated the national discourse on education in the United States. Although those narratives have shifted slightly over the years, they tend to have in common an underlying negativity that paints an image of ineffectual educators, passive and detached students, and an educational system that is not very effective in educating youth. With the launch of *Sputnik* in 1957 and the release of the *A Nation at Risk* report in 1983, the intensity of that underlying negativity increased, creating a schism between the lived realities of many of those who attend or work in schools everyday and those on the outside. This disconnect between reality and the dominant narrative about schooling is the impetus behind Jacqueline Bach's *Reel Education: Documentaries, Biopics, and Reality Television*.

Bach lays out the premise that although reality cannot actually be accessed in any form, a postmodernist mantra, filmmakers have not ceased in trying to portray what really happens in schools. As such, throughout the book she seeks to examine what causes those who make films or television shows about education to perpetually miss the mark. Utilizing a media studies lens, she examines what is real about education in school films, focusing on documentaries, biopics, and reality television portrayal of educators, students, and schools. She closely examines specific portrayals from each of those genres to not only deconstruct the narratives they put forth about educators, students, and schools but also to examine the archetypes/stereotypes they create about those entities often influenced by the contemporary political and social context surrounding public education. Concurrently, Bach examines how educators might bring the three film genres into the postsecondary classroom when working with students, most specifically but not exclusively those studying education.

Bach carefully examines the elements, or codes, from each genre to help the reader understand the inherent limitations and audience expectations associated with each mode. By understanding the conventions, narrative structures, and purposes of each genre, she is able to illustrate for the reader why films continue to portray teachers, administrators, and students in a way that does not match up with reality. In the process, she points out the numerous archetypes/stereotypes created in these genres that lend themselves to the popular narratives that surround education (e.g., we need outsiders to come in and teach the hardest-to-reach students). One example Bach provides is from the movie *The Class*, an award winning French biopic about the relationship between a White teacher and his ethnically diverse group of students. In this film, based on the autobiographical work by teacher Francois Begaudeau (who plays himself in the movie but is instead named Marin), the White teacher struggles to connect with his students because of a cultural disconnect—highlighting the teacher as hero archetype found in films such as *Dangerous Minds*. Unlike Michelle Pfeifer's character in *Dangerous Minds*, Marin perpetuates the stereotype of the disinterested teacher who is disconnected from his students. As Bach writes, "What troubles me with *The Class* is that Marin is not what I consider a good teacher, no matter how much he seems to care about his students' futures, and many of his actions and comments are not professional" (p. 93). The teacher as savior archetype and the disinterested teacher stereotype simultaneously portrayed in the film only serve to perpetuate the notions that all poor kids of color need a savior and there are many burned out, unmotivated, disconnected teachers in K–12 classrooms.

On the other side of the narrative, she deconstructs the narrative elements, archetypes, and codes from specific works in each genre for university professors to consider, before providing concrete examples of how teachers might incorporate these entities into their own classrooms.

Bach is the Elena and Albert LeBlanc Associate Professor of English Education and Curriculum Theory at Louisiana State University. She has published several works on how film influences teaching, and she utilizes film in her classroom to help students deconstruct narratives and myths that surround the teaching profession. In addition, she has published several articles that focus on how young adult literature inspires discourse for teachers and students around various social issues, how pop culture can inform teaching, and how to develop/teach secondary English Language Arts teachers. She is a former English teacher and coeditor for the "Engaging Texts" section of the *Journal of Curriculum Theorizing*. *Reel Education* appears to be a culmination of her work as a K-12 teacher, university professor, and scholar examining how film affects the educational enterprise. More specifically, she draws upon that expertise to carefully delineate how documentaries, biopics, and reality television shows have helped contribute to a metanarrative that public schools are failing, students in urban schools are unmotivated and/or resistant, and educators who have been mired in the system are ill-equipped or unwilling to do what it takes to help students succeed.

The book is divided into three sections, each representing a genre explored in the book—documentaries, biopics, and reality television shows. Within each section are three chapters. The first provides an explanation and analysis of the genre along with a contextualization of seminal works within the larger social and political conversation about education. The second focuses on a particular example from the genre where the author weaves a synopsis of the work with analysis of the codes, conventions, and narratives of the film, examining how these films attempt to portray reality as well as how and why they fall short in achieving that end. The third considers the implications of each genre on the educational enterprise before providing concrete examples for how one might incorporate each genre into the classroom (across disciplines but focused on education).

Through close analysis of the various stereotypes perpetuated in documentaries, biopics, and, to a lesser extent, reality television, Bach masterfully illustrates why the dominant narrative on education is not a positive one, tying that analysis to the social, cultural, and political context in which these films appear. These stereotypes/archetypes include the kind, loving teacher vs. the heartless bureaucratic system, the resistant, angry urban student of color, the urban teacher-hero outsider (usually White), the teacher as performer, the naïve teacher with good intentions who ultimately breaks through in ways others couldn't, and the teacher as lone wolf. Bach not only deconstructs these and other archetypes, she connects them to the larger context, illustrating the importance of not only students of education but of all citizens to watch films about education with a critical eye. Moreover, she illustrates how these pieces were influenced by or served to influence public policy on education, which has been overwhelmingly anti–public school, prostandardization, and proaccountability, all three of which are shown to lead to teacher attrition, administrator attrition, inhibited student learning, and a narrowing of the curriculum.

While the chapters illustrating how one might incorporate elements from each genre into the classroom are concrete and easy to adapt, the reality television chapter falls a bit short only if because to date there is one example available (*Teach: Tony Danza*), which she closely critiques earlier in the book. Though she makes a strong case for using elements of reality television shows to help construct more engaging lessons, unlike the teaching illustrations of documentaries and biopics, outside of *Teach: Tony Danza*, the author cannot utilize any reality television show for the purposes of critical examination of teaching, learning, and educational policy. As such, the author does put forth the unique notion of reality pedagogy, which is a set of strategies for using and examining reality television. This concept appears to be most salient to noneducation concentrations such as media studies, sociology, or political science, though that may well be the case due to a lack of reality shows about teaching and learning.

As a whole, this book adds much to the literature around mass media and public perceptions of students, teachers, administrators, and schools. Moreover, the book provides a deep dive into several salient works that have manifested over the past 30 years, "highlight(ing) the larger conversation about education that was occurring during a particular era" (p. 11). Anyone in the field of education who is interested in how the popular narrative espoused in television and movies shapes or is shaped by public policy would be well served to read this book. Educators interested in bringing critical examination of how students, teachers, and educators are portrayed would also be well served to read this book. There is much to be discovered about the relationship between film and television and its attempt to portray what really happens in schools. In the end, Bach does an excellent job nuancing why film and television continue to miss the mark on portraying the reality of what happens in schools. Those findings alone make this book worth reading.

REFERENCE

Bach, J. (2016). *Reel education: Documentaries, biopics, and reality television.* New York, NY: Peter Lang.

BOOK REVIEW

CRITICAL DEMOCRATIC EDUCATION AND LGBTQ-INCLUSIVE CURRICULUM: OPPORTUNITIES AND CONSTRAINTS

by Steven Camicia

Lauren Yarnell Bradshaw

Steven Camicia's *Critical Democratic Education and LGBTQ-Inclusive Curriculum: Opportunities and Constraints* challenges schools, curriculum, and communities to become more inclusive and critically democratic for students. He gives specific emphasis for the promotion of inclusivity and recognition for Lesbian, Gay, Bi-sexual, Transsexual, and Queer (LBGTQ) identifying students who have been historically disenfranchised and ostracized by the educational system. Camicia guides his readers through complex philosophical and theoretical paradigms in order to create a space where educators and policymakers may "recognize" (p. 66) the need of inclusive education in the pursuit of a critically democratic society. He examines the roles that culture, politics, and communities play in the development of the internal and external exclusionary measures that favor the dominant heteronormative values.

Camicia argues that the utilization of critical democratic practices, queer theory, and intersectionality enables educators and policymakers to create LGBTQ-inclusive communities and transformative curriculums. As "curriculum works toward constructing and maintaining a dominant culture's perspective" (p. 5), the exclusion of LGBTQ peoples from historical narratives creates curriculum that functions to reinforce dominant forms of sexual and gender identity. The inclusion and exclusion within the state mandated curriculum informs what "can and can't be said about social injustices, transphobia, sexism, and homophobia" (p. 5) in the schoolhouse. Democratic communities are defined by the participation of all people; the exclusion of LGBTQ persons by internal and external means causes all students stuffer, LBGTQ and non-LGBTQ alike. By allowing "students embodying dominant identities" opportunities "to see the value in having more information and choices," they are better prepared to participate and be active democratic citizens (p. 9). Queer theory, which seeks to challenge "fixed" definitions, is critical to Camicia's argument to discredit assumptions of "normal" and "neutral" standards in schools (p. 15). The creation of "critical democratic social studies curriculum" would change the "focus from deficient individuals to deficient norms" and could provide a space for continuous discourse in the promotion of social justice (p. 16). Queer theory aligns with critical democracy to create a "third" space where students and teachers can explore discussions on "norms, identities, and social inequalities" in order to continuously push toward a more inclusive and just classroom community (p. 44). Within this third space, the intersections of a person's race, age, ethnicity, sexual identity, and class may be explored thus creating discourse and recognition of social inequities. This intersectionality creates a transformative democratic and inclusive curriculum.

Utilizing Utah and California as case studies, Camicia explores the impact of internal and external exclusions of LGBTQ peoples from the official and hidden school curriculums. Utah law dictates that any act by a teacher that is seen as a promotion of homosexuality is illegal. Camicia provides examples of previous lawsuits to illustrate the intense fear that Utah teachers endure surrounding LGBTQ issues. Camicia describes his struggle to locate teachers who actively sought out ways to make their classroom LGBTQ friendly, he finally decided to interview three teachers recommended by colleagues who were willing to speak on how they addressed LGBTQ issues. Teachers remarked how they used what Camicia defined as a third space to discuss issues of inequality that extended to LGBTQ people in their social studies lessons. In what would appear to be in direct contrast to Utah, California is in the process of revising their state social studies standards to include the contributions of LGBTQ peoples in the numerous historic, civic, artistic, and literary movements. From Langston Hughes to Harvey Milk, LGBTQ peoples transform the California state curriculum to represent the communities and peoples that the schools serve. Yet, Camicia finds in his interviews with educators that the revised standards do not reflect the viewpoints of the diverse people who live in the vast state of California. When traveling from urban to rural areas, there is a stark contrast in the view and ability of educators to teach and support this revised curriculum. Much of the work California is able to do currently is due to legislation known as the Fair, Accurate, Inclusive, and Respectful (FAIR) Education Act that prohibits any negative reflection or people due to their "race, sex, color, creed, handicap, national origin or ancestry," and "sexual orientation" (p. 52). While Utah's state legislation seeks to remove any promotion of LGBTQ peoples in schools, California's law seeks to prohibit any hindrance to LGBTQ peoples in schools. Camicia is quick to note that neither system is perfect, noting the internal and external constraints felt by teachers in both states.

Creating equitable, ethical, democratic, and inclusive schools are not new goals for educators and policymakers; Nel Noddings and John Dewey have both written extensively on the necessity of democratic and socially just schools (Noddings 2013; Dewey 1916). Yet, Camicia builds on the works of these philosophical foremothers and forefathers to push for the inclusion of LGBTQ persons. A clear strength of the work is showcasing California's thoughtful and transformative social studies curriculum. The thorough and approachable means in which the curriculum seeks inclusion of LGBTQ peoples will astound many readers and inform the gaps that exist within their own education. Utah and California both provide excellent case studies for the reader to examine the ways in which LGBTQ youth are included and excluded within state curriculums. While Camicia states that his findings are not generalizable, it would have been beneficial to add additional states to his research that offer additional data for the reader. As educators, we must struggle to become more critically democratic in our pedagogy and curriculum. Camicia's work guides us in the development of our own discourses while encouraging us to challenge the heteronormative restrictions in our classrooms and schools.

REFERENCES

Dewey, J. (1916). *Democracy and education: An introduction to the philosophy of education.* New York, NY: The Free Press.

Noddings, N. (2013). *Education and democracy in the 21st century.* New York, NY: Teacher's College Press.

ABOUT THE AUTHORS

Aghasaleh, Rouhollah

Rouhollah Aghasaleh is a postdoctoral researcher at the department of Middle and Secondary Education, Georgia State University.

Appelgate, Mollie

Mollie Appelgate is an Assistant Professor at Iowa State University. Her research focuses mathematics teacher learning and STEM education.

Barker, Kim Stevens

Kim Stevens Barker, PhD, is an Assistant Professor in the Department of Teaching and Leading at Augusta University.

Bhatnagar, Ruchi

Ruchi Bhatnagar, PhD, is a Clinical Assistant Professor and Assessment Coordinator at Georgia State University.

Boehnlein, Andrew

Andrew teaches 10th and 11th Grade Language Arts at North Springs High School in Atlanta, GA.

Bornstein, Jacob

Max Bornstein is a high school physics and environmental science teacher and former graduate student at Georgia State University.

Bradshaw, Lauren Yarnell

Lauren Yarnell Bradshaw is an Assistant Professor at the University of North Georgia. She has published on topics related to educational biography, the history of education in the American South, and social studies curriculum.

Broderick, Shawn

Shawn Broderick is an Assistant Professor at Keene State College. His research focuses on elementary/secondary preservice teachers' mathematical thinking.

Brugar, Kristy A.

Kristy A. Brugar is an Assistant Professor of Social Studies Education at the University of Oklahoma. Her research interests include elementary social studies education and interdisciplinary instruction.

Capps, Matthew

Matthew Capps is a Professor of Educational Leadership and Dean of the West College of Education at Midwestern State University.

Chalfin, Gregory

Greg Chalfin is a third-year EdD student at the University of Northern Colorado.

Chawla, Louise

Louise Chawla is Professor Emerita of Environmental Design at the University of Colorado. Her research and publishing covers children and nature, children in cities, and the development of active care for the natural world.

About the Authors

Cloninger, Kevin

Kevin Cloninger is a researcher, an educator, and a coach, and currently serves as Executive Director of the Anthropedia Foundation, a nonprofit dedicated to promoting health and decreasing rates of lifestyle and stress-related illness through scientific research and education. He is Past President of AATC.

Conn, Daniel R.

Daniel R. Conn spent ten years of K–12 classroom experience in rural Colorado and is an assistant professor at Minot State University.

Conrad, Bradley

Bradley Conrad is an Associate Professor of Education at Capital University in Columbus, Ohio.

Curry, Daphney L.

Dr. Curry is an Assistant Professor in the West College of Education at Midwestern State University.

Dick, Lara

Lara Dick is an Assistant Professor at Bucknell University. Her research focuses on professional noticing and mathematical knowledge for teaching.

Enderle, Patrick

Patrick Enderle is Assistant Professor of science education at Georgia State University, focusing on teaching and learning through scientific practices.

Fields, Melanie

Melanie Fields is an Assistant Professor in the department of Curriculum and Instruction at Texas A&M University-Commerce.

Gupta, Dittika

Dittika Gupta is Assistant Professor at Midwestern State University. Her research focuses on teacher preparation, lesson study, fractional understanding and children's mathematical thinking.

ABOUT the AUTHORS

Harris, Shelley

Shelley Harris is Associate Professor and Assistant Dean in the College of Education and Human Development at Texas A&M, San Antonio.

Hendrix, Renesha

Renesha L. Hendrix is a doctoral student in the Department of Computer Science at Georgia State University. Her concentration is Computer Science Education.

Hinton, Harvey

Harvey Hinton, III is an Assistant Professor of Urban Education at North Carolina Central University.

Isbell, Laura

Laura Isbell is an Assistant Professor in the department of the Curriculum and Instruction at Texas A&M University-Commerce.

Johnson, Chrystal S.

Chrystal S. Johnson is an Associate Professor of Social Studies Education and Past President of the African American Educators for Social Studies.

Lindt, Suzanne F.

Suzanne F. Lindt is an Associate Professor in the West College of Education at Midwestern State University in Wichita Falls, Texas.

Many, Joyce E.

Joyce Many, Ph.D. is an Associate Dean in the College of Education and Human Development at Georgia State University.

Masko, Amy L.

Amy L. Masko is a Professor of English Education at Grand Valley State University in Michigan, whose research lies in urban education.

McIntyre, Christina Janise

Christina Janise McIntyre is an Associate Professor in Curriculum and Learning Department of the West College of Education and is the program coordinator for Curriculum and Instruction. She earned a Ph.D. from the University of Oklahoma. Her research interests include preservice teacher education and professional development.

Miller, Stacia C.

Stacia C. Miller is an Associate Professor of Kinesiology in the West College of Education at Midwestern State University in Wichita Falls, Texas.

Parkison, Paul

Paul Parkison holds an EdD in Curriculum and Instruction, with current interests in public pedagogy and research emphasis on the teacher as nomadic border-crosser and community member. He is Chair and Associate Professor in the Department of Childhood Education, Literacy, & TESOL, College of Education and Human Services, University of North Florida.

Pecore, John

John L. Pecore is an associate professor in the Department of Teacher Education and Educational Leadership in the College of Education and Professional Studies at the University of West Florida.

Perrotta, Katherine

Katherine Perrotta is a Part-time Assistant Professor of History at Kennesaw State University. She is the recipient of the 2017 John Laska Distinguished Dissertation Award in Teaching from the American Association for Teaching and Curriculum.

Petretti, Dante P.

Dante P. Petretti, EdD. has spent 25 years as an English Teacher, Department Chairperson, Vice Principal, and Principal for the Paterson Public Schools in New Jersey. Dr. Petretti also serves as an adjunct professor at New Jersey City University. He earned his doctorate in Curriculum and Teaching from Teachers College, Columbia University in 2015.

ABOUT the AUTHORS

Puvirajah, Anton

Anton Puvirajah is an Assistant Professor at the University of Western Ontario. He researches informal STEM teaching and learning.

Reeves, Emily

Dr. Reeves is an assistant professor in the West College of Education at Midwestern State University.

Rickard, Jennifer

Jennifer Rickard currently teaches 9th Grade ESOL World Literature at Clarkston High School in DeKalb County, Georgia.

Schneider, Melissa Peterson

Melissa has been a Colorado public educator for twenty years. She is a PhD student at the University of Denver.

Siegel, Lesley N.

Lesley N. Siegel, PhD, is an assistant professor at Arcadia University in the School of Education.

Smith, Cristy Sellers

Cristy Sellers Smith, PhD, is an Assistant Professor in the School of Learning and Teaching at Pacific University in Forest Grove, Oregon. Her research interests include oral history, teaching students with moderate, severe, and profound disabilities, and the history of special education.

Soto, Melissa

Melissa Soto is an Assistant Professor at San Diego State University. Her research focuses on children's mathematical thinking and technology.

Southall, Aubrey Brammar

Aubrey Brammar Southall, PhD,. is Assistant Professor at Aurora University. She instructs secondary methods courses and is the Chair of Secondary Education.

Tanguay, Carla Lynn

Carla Tanguay, PhD, is Associate to the Dean for Clinical Practice and Elementary Education Coordinator at Georgia State University.

Woodrow, Kelli

Kelli Woodrow is a Professor of Culturally and Linguistically Diverse Education at Regis University and has a PhD in Educational Foundations from University of Colorado.

Zajdel, Joseph

Joseph Zajdel is a former assistant professor and works independently with doctoral students on quantitative and qualitative dissertations.

Zimmerman, Aaron Samuel

Aaron Zimmerman is an Assistant Professor of Curriculum and Instruction in the College of Education at Texas Tech University.

CPSIA information can be obtained
at www.ICGtesting.com
Printed in the USA
BVHW07s0537180918
527791BV00002B/5/P